BEYOND BOGGY CREEK

IN SEARCH OF THE SOUTHERN SASQUATCH

LYLE BLACKBURN

Anomalist Books
San Antonio * Charlottesville

An Original Publication of ANOMALIST BOOKS
Beyond Boggy Creek: In Search of the Southern Sasquatch
Copyright © 2017 by Lyle Blackburn
ISBN: 978-1-938398-70-4

Cover artwork by Claudio Bergamin

Illustrations by artists as credited

Photos courtesy of individual photographers as credited

Book design by Seale Studios

For more information about the author, visit: www.lyleblackburn.com

For information about the publisher, go to AnomalistBooks.com, or write to: Anomalist Books, 5150 Broadway #108, San Antonio, TX 78209

In memory of J.E. "Smokey" Crabtree

CONTENTS

CONTENTS

PREFACE

This book contains actual accounts by real people based on personal interviews, newspaper archives, and other documented sources.

With the increasing number of research groups and individuals who collect and report sightings of ape-like creatures, it would be impossible to present each and every account for an area as large as the southern United States. As such, it is important to note that the accounts presented here were selected on the basis of credibility, location, dates, and the amount of information available. Any omissions—outside of those deemed uncredible or unsubstantiated—are based purely on the constraints of this book and the efficiency with which to tell an engaging story. For additional reports in these areas, please consult the various Bigfoot research organizations and dedicated individuals who publish on the World Wide Web. It is a mystery shared by all.

INTRODUCTION

It was sometime in the mid-1970s. My parents decided to attend a double-feature at a local drive-in theater. I was young at the time, and judging from past experience, they knew I would fall asleep in the backseat mid-way through the first film, thus allowing my parents to enjoy a night of entertainment without spending money on a sitter.

The films my parents liked bored me anyway, so I didn't mind getting cozy in the backseat with a blanket, a pillow, and perhaps a few comic books to save me from the melodrama of Robert Redford or some such 1970s movie star. However, that particular night held more promise since the bill included a horror movie. And not just any horror movie, but one based on allegedly true events that happened close by in Arkansas.

Being an avid fan of horror films and movie monsters, I sat through the previews until the feature finally flickered to life on the huge outdoor screen. My parents were a bit apprehensive about the subject matter, but the movie was rated G, so what's the worst thing that could happen? A few nightmares? Perhaps a life-time obsession?

As the opening sequence began to paint a serene, cinematic picture of a southern Arkansas bayou, I found myself curiously captivated. It was somewhat familiar territory since I had camped in Arkansas plenty of times, but the swamp setting was something new to me. The lush, watery landscape seemed more remote and dangerous. It was a place of mystery unlike I had ever seen.

The sequence continued as it showed local wildlife swimming and flying about the bayou, only occasionally hinting at anything spooky through the use of ominous soundtrack notes. I was beginning to think I'd been duped into watching a nature documentary. But that changed when the metallic shell of the drive-in speaker rattled with the bone-chilling cry of an unseen creature deep in the woods. I quickly crawled over the seat and nestled in between my parents. Forget sleeping in the backseat, this was something I had to see!

The feature was *The Legend of Boggy Creek*, a low-budget indie film that effectively dramatized stories of a Sasquatch-like creature said to exist near the small town of Fouke in southwest Arkansas. The movie had become so successful after its release in 1972, it went on to play for many years in theaters, drive-ins, and later on television. I was but one of thousands—perhaps millions—who saw the movie during its run. Little did I know the impact it would make on my life.

As you may be aware, the circumstances surrounding the movie inspired me to write my first book, *The Beast of Boggy Creek* (which is by no means required to understand and enjoy this pseudo-sequel you're reading now). When I first began researching the subject, it was little more than a personal crusade to find out the "true story" behind *The Legend of Boggy Creek* and the creature known as the Fouke Monster on which it was based. I had been involved in Bigfoot research for several years at that point and was aware the movie had inspired many of my fellow colleagues in that particular pursuit. However, I had no idea how many other people remembered this cinematic gem.

It wasn't until Anomalist Books published my book, *The Beast of Boggy Creek*, in 2012 that I came to understand the tremendous impact the movie had on the general populous. As I began to appear at book signings and was invited to speak at various conferences and conventions around the country, countless people began approaching me to relay their own fond memories of the film. They would invariably say something along the lines of "that movie scared the hell out of me when I was a kid." The statement would often be followed by a brief story about where they saw it or what they did afterwards, such as dress up as the Fouke Monster for Halloween or, better yet, take a trip to Fouke to look for the creature. But not all were funny childhood memories. People also told me of their own startling encounters with a creature around Fouke and in other locations.

INTRODUCTION

The more I considered people's interest in the subject and the additional stories, the more I began to realize the importance of providing a larger picture of similar cases and incidents that have been reported throughout the South. While Boggy Creek may arguably be ground zero for the Southern Sasquatch, this innocuous waterway is only the tip of a much broader mystery; one that spills into the surrounding states and beyond.

That being said, an investigation of this scope is not an easy one. Whereas to thoroughly document a cryptid case in a small area—such as that of the Fouke Monster or the Bishopville Lizard Man (the subject of my second book)—already requires exhaustive research, the Southern Sasquatch case is one that involves many more people and covers a far greater area through many types of rugged terrain. But the importance of establishing an overall, accurate history of man-ape encounters in the South is essential to the examination of beings such as the Fouke Monster on the whole. Given the number of southern states that have documented sightings, footprints, and other evidence, it's logical to conclude that the alleged creatures know no boundaries. The same ones that haunt the banks of Boggy Creek could just as easily follow its muddy waters up the nearby the Sulphur River into Texas. It could likewise travel from the Sulphur to the Red River, taking it down into Louisiana, then by wood and swamp to Mississippi and Alabama. And what about the Skunk Ape reported in Florida and the Bigfoot of Georgia, the Carolinas, Tennessee, and Oklahoma? How do these creature reports compare with each other? How many types of suspected habitat are there? Is there one or are there many possible species?

These are just some of the questions we must consider as we go beyond Boggy Creek to the wilds of the southern U.S. where indeed a host of hairy, man-like creatures have been reported for centuries. I've traveled the woods and waterways, battled mosquitoes and chiggers, delved into countless news articles, and talked directly to eyewitnesses and other researchers in order to document one of the South's most enduring mysteries. So sit back and relax as I guide you along a shadowy trail in search of the Southern Sasquatch.

1. Shadows in the Southern Woods

A chorus of bullfrogs echoed through the bottoms as Paul Matlock and his cousin lowered their jon boat into the murky waters of the Sabine River. It was still dark, but they wanted to get an early start on their morning hog hunt. The nuisance animals were starting to proliferate along the Texas-Louisiana border so it was a good way to keep in practice between deer seasons. If they timed it right, they'd be settling into their tree stands just before sunrise.

As they boarded the boat something unseen splashed in the water. The lower Sabine was full of life both in and around the river, making it one of the best places to hunt in the region. Matlock had a good feeling about this morning's hunt in particular, although in hindsight he would surely wonder why.

The boat's motor roared to life and the men began to navigate upstream. The place where they planned to hunt was best accessed by the water. Matlock found this particular site the day before while scouting near his normal hunting area. Upon seeing signs of hog rooting, he thought it would be an excellent place to try.

When they neared the spot, Matlock's cousin steered toward the west side of the river. He nudged the craft up to the muddy bank and paused long enough for Paul to grab his rifle and a bag of food scraps before stepping out. His cousin then backed up and continued upstream to his own hunting site.

As the motor's hum faded into the darkness Matlock used his flashlight to locate a tree stand he'd already placed there. Before ascending, he scattered a bag of apple slices and potatoes in a clearing about 20 yards away. He then climbed 25 feet up, donned a mosquito head net, and settled in for the wait. It was 5:00 a.m.

When the sun finally crept up over the horizon, he began to hear the distinctive sound of hogs. It was faint at first but gradually got louder as the animals worked their way towards Matlock. Finally, he spotted five of them 45 degrees to his left and about 50 yards away. They were approaching his bait area.

While waiting for a clear shot, Matlock caught a glimpse of something else moving between the trees 30 yards to the right of the hogs. He raised his rifle to get a better look through his scope. At first he could only see the side of a dark face peering out from behind a leafless tree, but after a few moments the thing stood up and moved to another tree. Now the hunter could see it was some sort of hairy creature standing upright on two legs. It didn't look like any animal he'd seen before, and it didn't appear to be another hunter... even one in a ghillie suit. In fact, it didn't look like a person at all. Matlock had been hunting those woods since he was a teenager and had never seen anything like it.

Despite a growing sense of alarm, Matlock turned the scope up to maximum power and trained it on the animal as it worked from one tree to another. Each time, the creature would crouch down on all fours and leap to the next tree where it would land at the base and stand up. It would then study the hogs intently before moving again. Its every movement was fluid and completely silent.

As the creature maneuvered closer to the hogs, Matlock studied its features. It appeared to be six-to-seven-feet tall with a thick coat of reddish-brown hair covering most of its body except for the hands, feet, and part of the face. The face itself looked human-like with dark brown eyes and small ears. The body was very heavily built and had breasts. Apparently it was a female. Whatever it was, Matlock was in shock.

The stalking continued for several more minutes until the five hogs were less than 30 yards from Matlock. Then, all at once, the thing crouched on all fours, curled its knuckles, and leapt towards its prey. As soon as it hit the ground, it let out a blood-curdling scream that pierced the morning air. The hogs panicked and scattered, but it was too late. Within two leaps the creature had descended upon them, slapping one hog so hard on its side it flew through the air and slammed into a nearby tree. When the squealing pig hit the ground, the creature leapt on it, first grabbing its neck with the right hand and then pummeling it with the huge fist of its left hand. Matlock could hear ribs cracking with every hit.

The remaining four hogs bolted into the woods. By the time their squeals faded, their brethren lay dead at the hands of the creature who then scooped it up under one arm as if it were no more than a pillow sack. The thing let out a series of whooping sounds, which were immediately answered by shorter whoops from an unseen animal deeper in the woods.

Matlock watched in fear and disbelief. It was only when the creature began to walk off that he felt any sense of relief. But it was short-lived. Without warning the creature dropped the hog to the ground and turned its head in the direction of his tree stand. At first it looked past the hunter with its eyes scanning at ground level. Then it tilted its head upwards and followed the tree trunk until its eyes focused on him. Matlock managed to keep the gun trained on it, but by then he knew he did not have enough firepower. If he missed or the shot didn't take the thing down, he would surely suffer the same fate as the hapless hog.

The beast studied the hunter intently for a few moments, moving its head slightly as it did. Then suddenly, as if it were satisfied, the creature bent down to retrieve the hog, tucked it under its arm, and casually walked off.

Matlock watched through his trembling scope until he could no longer see the animal, then slowly lowered the rifle and exhaled. He sat there for approximately 30 more minutes trying to calm himself down. Ultimately, he decided if the creature would have wanted to hurt him, it could have. It had not been the least bit afraid of five 150-pound-plus hogs with razor-sharp tusks, so what did it have to fear from him unless, of course, it was aware of the power of guns? But how could it? Questions railed through his mind like a locomotive.

Matlock finally crawled down from the tree and made his way back to the rendezvous point at the river's edge. In a short time his cousin motored up and stopped the engine. As the boat floated to rest on the bank, he could see that his fellow hunter was pale and shaken.

"What happened?" his cousin asked. "I heard some whooping sounds down this way."

Matlock nodded. For a moment he hesitated, but finally... reluctantly... told him what he'd witnessed, fully expecting laughter when he was done.

But there was no ridicule. His cousin merely looked him in the eye and said: "It's real. I've seen it too."

When Matlock's cousin explained that he had previously seen a reddish-brown creature of the same description, and also a larger one with white hair, Matlock felt a twisted sense of relief. While on one hand there were apparently huge, unknown creatures stalking his local woods, at least he wasn't crazy. His cousin admitted he had also been reluctant to tell anyone because of the same reservations. But now that they had both seen the creature, they could speak freely.

As they talked, the two men walked back to the site where the hog had been killed. Perhaps they could find footprints or other evidence. When they arrived, they found the hog's blood on the tree and ground, but unfortunately no discernable prints of the creature could be seen. A solid layer of leaves just didn't provide the conditions necessary for such remnants.

Still shaken, but at least able to deal with the reality of the encounter, Matlock followed his cousin back to the boat. He wasn't sure if he'd been lucky to see one of these creatures, or profoundly unlucky, but he was sure that hunting on the southern Sabine River would never be the same again.

LEGENDARY ARCHETYPE

While Matlock's story may have you double-checking the non-fiction classification of this book, rest assured it belongs here. Although dramatic, it was reported by a *real* person—Paul Matlock—who stands behind what he claims to have seen that day back in March 2003. Upon listening to the details and questioning him at length, I could find no justifiable reason to dismiss his testimony. It was something that seemed to have had a profound effect on him.

"Let's put it this way... I will never go in the woods again without feeling on edge," Matlock told me as he finished the account. "It's not something you forget."

The location where the incident took place is a strip of land tucked away on the Texas-side of the Sabine River near Logansport, Louisiana. I'm familiar with that area of Panola County and can attest to the sheer thickness of the woods and the availability of water and other resources that would be necessary to support large animals. In fact, Matlock said he'd once seen a bear in those woods, which, ironically, are not supposed to "exist" in that part of Texas either.

"The place where that is can only be accessed by the river," Matlock explained. "It's government land, but you won't find it on any of the state Wildlife Management Area maps. I think there might be a family of these things living up there," he concluded. It was his best theory given what he and his cousin had both witnessed.

It may be hard for some to imagine, but judging from a long history of evidence and reports like the one submitted by this witness, something shocking may be stalking the woods of the southern United States—something bipedal, ape-like, and covered in hair. A legendary creature that perhaps few will ever see.

Reports of these ape-like creatures can be traced backwards and forwards from the date of Matlock's encounter like a spidery web spanning the entire southern region. From Oklahoma and Arkansas down to Texas, over to Florida and all the southern states in between, anecdotal accounts and purported evidence fuel the premise that a breed of Southern Sasquatch has been successfully hiding in the shadowy foothills, piney woods, and murky swamplands of these areas. It is a belief held not only by the eyewitnesses, but by Bigfoot researchers and cryptozoologists alike, many of whom have been embracing it for many years.

To the general public, however, it's another matter. Until recently, when asked about their knowledge of Bigfoot, the average person would probably state that "he" is said to live in the Pacific Northwest region of North America. That is, they would surmise that "Bigfoot" is a singular creature generally reported in northern California, Oregon, and Washington state, and perhaps British Columbia if they were savvy with geography. Only a handful of these people would have knowledge regarding encounters with similar creatures—whether called Bigfoot, Sasquatch, Skunk Apes, or simply "monsters"—outside of that range. However, if you begin to sift through newspapers, books, television shows, and the internet, or simply ask the right people—those who live, work, and hunt in the rural areas of the South—it becomes apparent that sightings of large, man-like apes and "wildmen" are by no means confined to the traditional Pacific Northwest domain, and are in fact, prevalent in other places including the South.

A wave of recent internet articles and television shows such as *MonsterQuest, Finding Bigfoot,* and *Monsters & Mysteries in America* have helped disseminate the idea that "Bigfoot" is not singular creature and that these type of creatures have been reported all over the U.S. Yet, only the most enthusiastic of Bigfoot researchers, let alone average people, may realize just how much of a rich history and how *many* of these startling encounters have been reported in the southern states over the years.

There is, however, one exception to the general rule: The Legend of Boggy Creek. It's the South's most famous Bigfoot case and one that is often known beyond Bigfoot circles due to the success of the movie by the same name. If the general populous were to cite knowledge of Southern Sasquatch, this would likely be the source.

For those unfamiliar with the movie, *The Legend of Boggy Creek* was a docu-drama horror film inspired by alleged sightings of a Bigfoot-like creature near the small town of Fouke, Arkansas. Known as the "Fouke Monster," the creature first became publically known in 1971 when reports by local citizens made headlines in regional newspapers. The Fouke Monster gained a more considerable level of fame when its story went viral due to the movie, which ultimately reached an international audience and made $25 million dollars in profit.

The Legend of Boggy Creek was directed by first-time Arkansas filmmaker Charles B. Pierce who was initially drawn to the sensational reports printed in the newspapers. The reports ranged from dramatic incidents in which the creature allegedly attacked a family, to brief sightings on rural roads, to accounts of it traversing up and down a small waterway near Fouke known as Boggy Creek. These 1971 reports brought forth other eyewitness accounts, which established the creature's long history in the area, having been seen by locals and confronted by hunters for at least 50 years prior. When combined with the success of the movie, these accounts became instrumental in placing the Southern Sasquatch on the map and have served to create an archetype for these type of beings that endures today.

According to the numerous witnesses who claimed to have sighted the creature in and around Fouke, it stands approximately seven feet tall and is covered in thick, shaggy hair three-to-four inches in length. It's estimated to weigh anywhere from 300-to-500 pounds with its coloration ranging from dark black to brown to a reddish tone like dead pine needles. The face is generally devoid of hair, although oftentimes the creature is said to have longer hair on the head which falls down over its eyes. Its skin is typically described as being dark brown with a face that has a broad, flat nose and a strikingly human appearance, albeit ape-like in most respects. It effectively walks and runs on two legs though it has been seen moving on all fours much like known primates.

The description here fits with many historical and modern-day sightings of similar creatures all over the South. It's also within the parameters of Sasquatch descriptions found elsewhere in North America, although if the details are examined closely, the southern variety appears to be somewhat smaller and ape-like when compared to the forest giants of the Northwest. It's also, evidently, meaner.

As noted in several of the prominent reports (and likewise reflected in the movie), the Fouke creature appears to be aggressive at times and has even been known to attack humans. In the case of the Ford family, who made headlines in the *Texarkana Gazette* on May 3, 1971, Bobby Ford tangled with the creature as he and his brother, Don, and friend, Charles Taylor, confronted it one night outside their home.[1] The creature had been stalking around the house for nearly a week when the men decided to introduce it to a shotgun. After firing from the porch, the men moved cautiously to the woodline to scan for blood or other evidence that would indicate the animal had been hit. When they didn't find anything, Bobby Ford got spooked and promptly headed back towards the house in the dark. At that point he was reportedly "attacked" by the large, hairy creature when it lunged from the side of the house. After a narrow escape, Bobby was rushed to the emergency room at the Texarkana Hospital where he was treated for cuts, bruises, and outright shock.

Both before and after the seminal Ford attack, the creature had reportedly stalked other rural homes in the vicinity and had startled hunters who likewise responded with firepower. In 1965, 14-year-old Lynn Crabtree was squirrel hunting one evening when he was surprised by a hair-covered thing walking on two legs.[2] When the thing advanced toward him, Crabtree fired several shots before bolting for home, frightened to the core.

The Fouke Monster's unsettling nature and outward aggression has reverberated through Southern Sasquatch lore, combining with hair-raising reports from Florida and other states to ultimately solidify these creatures' reputation as that of unpredictable and dangerous. In some regards the reputation is just, although in most instances the creatures have been seen in fleeting glimpses like their counterparts in the northern states.

Whether the Southern Sasquatch's demeanor is an ornery result of being covered in hair and living in hot, humid environments or it's simply misrepresented, there's no doubt that people believe to have seen such creatures, not only on the banks of Boggy Creek, but along the many miles of connecting waterways and woodlands that branch out from that location all over the southern U.S. Boggy Creek may be the most famous of the Southern Sasquatch cases, but as we will learn, there are many other cases just as intriguing, and sometimes no less frightening than that of the Fouke Monster.

NAME GAME

In December 1970, an Oklahoma farmer by the name of Palmer was greeted with an unsettling surprise as he walked towards his chicken coop. To his horror, he could see the coop's door had been literally ripped from its hinges and thrown to the ground nearby. In a cautious search he found no sign of the intruder—who must have come during the night—only a number of strange handprints on the door that were like no others he had ever seen.

According to an article in *The Spokesman-Review*, Palmer immediately called the state game ranger for help.[3] When the ranger arrived to inspect the damage, he was just as puzzled as the farmer. The handprints, which measured approximately seven inches long by five inches wide, looked vaguely human, but then again not. It was certainly unlike any ordinary animal print. This stood to reason since there were no visible claw marks, and even more so, since the door appeared to have been torn away by something with opposable thumbs.

The ranger promptly sent the door to the Oklahoma City Zoo hoping zoology experts there could identify the culprit. However, they too were baffled. According to Zoo Director Lawrence Curtis, the prints appeared "to be like those of a primate," yet very unusual. "It resembles a gorilla," he told reporters, "but it's more like a man."[4]

Speculation began to run wild as to what kind of creature could have been prowling on the farmer's property, which was located near the town of El Reno. Director Curtis could only conclude that it was "some kind of strange-looking man." Other mammologists who had examined the prints felt it was definitely some type of primate. Reporters suggested it might be something akin the legendary Bigfoot, "a towering primate reported in Washington and British Columbia." (Remember, this is 1971.) As a result, the creature was dubbed the "Abominable Chicken Man" or more notably, the "El Reno Chicken Man."

As articles about El Reno's mysterious Chicken Man began to circulate via the Associated Press, a local man came forward suggesting it could be a free-roaming chimpanzee.[5] Howard Dreeson, who owned a sawmill in Calumet, Oklahoma, 13 miles west of El Reno, said he'd seen a "dark brown animal in that area several times," which was nothing more than an ordinary chimp. He had even tried to bait it with some bananas and oranges so he could apprehend it with a net.

When asked if the prints could possibly be that of a chimpanzee, Zoo Director Curtis confirmed it might be possible. But that brought up the obvious question: how did chimp get loose in the woodlands of Oklahoma? One explanation was that a psychologist living in the nearby city of Norman, who retained chimps for his studies, had inadvertently let one escape. Another explanation proposed that it wasn't a chimp at all, but a desperate human escapee from the federal reformatory located near the outskirts of El Reno. Whatever it was, it probably wasn't from a nearby zoo or circus, as there were no circuses in the area and the zoo could definitely account for all of its primate residents.

Needless to say, no chimpanzees were ever apprehended to confirm the chimp theory, so the case remains open in the universal Bigfoot file. One reason for this is obviously based on the fact that it was most likely some sort of primate, therefore, possibly an unknown one. Another reason is based on the geographic location of the incident. Palmer's farm was located just south of the North Canadian River, along which many Bigfoot sightings have been reported over the years. In fact, not only did a slough connect Palmer's farm to the river, but a sighting is alleged to have occurred in that precise area just prior to the chicken house incident. It was never reported to the news, however.

In this case, two men were coon hunting one night along the North Canadian River when they saw something they would never forget.[6] It was about 2:00 a.m. The hunters were parked near the old Foreman Road bridge where they sat in their car drinking coffee and trying to shake off the wintery chill. The moon was full, so visibility was good. When one of them spotted a skunk, he decided to get out of the car and take a shot. As he raised his gun, a large shadow behind a fallen tree caught his eye. At first he thought it was just that… a shadow. But then two red eyes opened and looked right at him.

The startled hunter quickly motioned for his partner to get out and take a look. As he did, the creature blinked its eyes and then slid down the riverbank towards the water. Both hunters were awestruck as they watched "a tall, upright animal run in a zig-zag pattern from sand bar to sand bar towards the west."[7]

This report, which was investigated by several of my colleagues, suggests that perhaps something other than an ordinary chimpanzee might be roaming the riverbanks of the North Canadian near the old farm. Was it a Bigfoot? Of course we can never be sure given the sparse physical evidence. But regardless of the case's solvability, it's another prime example of how Southern Sasquatch creatures are often bestowed with imaginative names.

Like the Fouke Monster, the El Reno Chicken Man has come to represent a menagerie of ape-like cryptids known throughout the South. Some of these are famous—like the Fouke Monster and the more generally classified, Skunk Ape—while some, like the Chicken Man, are only remembered in a more narrow, regional sense. The Caddo Critter, Sabine Thing, Belt Road Booger, Geneva Giant, Knobby, Holopaw Gorilla, Arp Ape, Noxie Monster, and Cold Point Creature, are just a few of the other creative nomenclatures attached to such accounts when they grab local headlines. Even in cases that are strictly passed around by word of mouth, the "old-timers" always apply a catchy name to the "monster." Bochito Beast, Red River Screamer, Hinton Howler, Duke Demon, Walaruckus, Wateree Walking Bear, and the list goes on. These entities may have never graced the pages of a newspaper, yet they fill the ranks of Southern Sasquatch suspects going back for more than a century.

The names undoubtedly give these alleged creatures an interesting local flavor, but by the same token they may also obscure them from the general scope of Bigfoot studies. Whereas a report of a hairy hominid in the Pacific Northwest is automatically going to be cataloged in the Bigfoot file, an article with the headline "Bardin Booger Legend Lingers," may or may not be scrutinized by someone doing general Bigfoot research. This makes it more of a challenge to track down all related reports, but it's a challenge that is both rewarding and full of Southern flair.

Of course the tendency to name these creatures is not exclusive to the southern states. Ohio has its Grassman, Missouri has its Momo, Spottsville has its Monster, and so on. However, it seems that an extreme number of the fuzzy cases that blur the lines between Bigfoot and other possible types of undocumented apes proliferate in the Deep South. Even generalized terms belie the fact that the creatures may indeed be part of a more global species of creature collectively known as Bigfoot or Sasquatch. Universal names like Wooly Booger, Brush Ape, Devil Monkey, Skunk Ape, Swamp Devil, and Wood Ape imply some sort of ape-like entity, but don't necessarily align the creature with the traditional persona of Bigfoot.

The unique naming naturally raises questions as to what these creatures, if they exist, might really be. In conversation, people often ask me if I think the Fouke Monster is actually a Bigfoot. The "Monster" moniker may certainly suggest something different than a Sasquatch, but given the basic description of a seven-foot-tall hairy, bipedal ape, it would be safe to assume it's at least related to other such creatures seen throughout the country. Perhaps an offshoot that has adapted to life in the sweltering swamplands of southern Arkansas.

The legendary Skunk Ape of Florida is another offshoot that often enters the conversation. Since it's described as being more "ape-like" with a shorter stature and a more primate-like foot, how does it compare to the traditional Bigfoot profile? Could the Fouke Monster and its southern ilk be more closely related to these creatures? Or are there many factions of undocumented apes stalking the southern woods, only related to Bigfoot by their elusive nature and legendary status? Or... are they simply figments of our collective imagination borne from wives tales and campfire stories? By venturing deep into the history of the Southern Sasquatch and taking a look at modern accounts, these are the questions we will attempt to answer.

DEEPER SOUTH

Before ultimately heading out in search of these elusive man-apes, we should take a moment to consider the geography and scope of the exploration. When speaking in terms of Bigfoot in "the South," it's often assumed that the southern United States couldn't possibly hide a species of unknown ape simply because the terrain does not provide enough contiguous woodland cover. Sure, the South may not offer vast uncharted wilderness areas on par with the Pacific Northwest, but it does contain an estimated 40 percent of the entire timberland found in the U.S.[8] In fact, the South is known to have some of the most "dynamic, diverse, complex, and productive forestlands in the nation" totaling a staggering 212 million acres.[9] Add in thousands of miles of river systems and wetlands, and that's plenty of rich resources and potential homeland to host animals of all shapes and sizes.

Fragmentation of the southern forestlands and bayous is certainly taking place, but the network of interconnecting waterways serves as a "wildlife highway," so to speak, allowing even large animals to move virtually undetected through the bottoms. This keeps open the possibility that Bigfoot creatures could do the same, but at the same time it creates a complex search grid that does not fit neatly into a single, remote forest area where the creatures' presence seems more likely. In keeping with this, the reports of ape-like creatures in the South are not exclusive to certain states or even geographical regions. They are literally sprinkled throughout the miles and miles of mountains, forests, and swamplands that make up the entire southern United States. This makes the task of thorough exploration challenging and therefore one where we must define some boundaries if this book is going to maintain a reasonable scope.

"The South," as defined by the U.S. Federal government, is made up of 16 states including Alabama, Arkansas, Delaware, Florida, Georgia, Kentucky, Louisiana, Maryland, Mississippi, North Carolina, Oklahoma, South Carolina, Tennessee, Texas, Virginia, and West Virginia.[10] It is often believed that these states were demarcated by their relation to the Mason-Dixon line, but in truth the Mason-Dixon was created as a result of a property dispute between English landowners and not intended to be a dividing line between North-South.[11] So although this line is commonly cited when separating the cultures of North and South, and most of the southern states do fall below the line, these 16 states are actually categorized by other factors, including agricultural growing season, staple crops, plantation systems, and in times past, the presence of slave labor.

When looking at these 16 states in relation to a U.S. map, it's interesting—and perhaps surprising to some—that several are positioned so far north upon the U.S. landscape. The states of Delaware, Maryland, West Virginia, and even the northern parts of Virginia and Kentucky sit well above the latitude of lower Missouri, a state which is not technically included in the South (although it's often associated with it). This makes sense from a standpoint of culture and politics, but not in simple terms of which states are positioned north and south on a map.

In view of this potentially confusing delineation, it's perhaps more logical to define the domain of the Southern Sasquatch in relation to U.S. Forestry regions. After all, any such creatures would have little regard for our borders and political lines since they would conceivably roam free based on biological needs and preferred environment. The U.S. Forest Service "Southern" region (Region 8) includes the forests and grasslands of Alabama, Arkansas, Georgia, Florida, Kentucky, Louisiana, Mississippi, North Carolina, Oklahoma, South Carolina, Tennessee, Texas and Virginia. These 13 states are all part of the traditional South yet do not include the three aforementioned states that lie farther north. As such, the area of Region 8 serves well to establish a more or less reasonable scope for this investigation; one that is defined by landscape attributes rather than human culture.

Within Region 8, we find examples of a great number of environments including mountains, forests, and lowland swamps, all of which have a notable history of man-ape sightings. These areas defy state-recognized boundaries as they consume the landscape in a dizzying array of geographic and ecological niches. Among other notable Southern Sasquatch stomping grounds, the region includes the Ouachita Mountains of Oklahoma and Arkansas, the Piney Woods of Texas, the bayous of Louisiana and Mississippi, the foothills of the Appalachians in Alabama, Georgia, North Carolina and Tennessee, and the costal marshlands of Florida and South Carolina. These and other key areas may hold the secrets to what is surely one of the most fascinating southern mysteries of all.

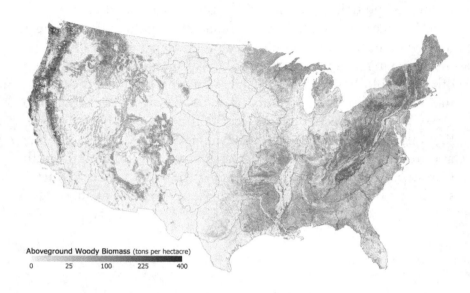

Forested areas of the United States

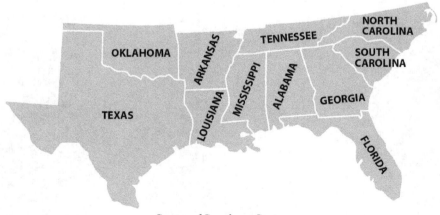

Scope of Southern States

2. THEY ALWAYS FOLLOW THE CREEKS

A few weeks prior to the release of *The Beast of Boggy Creek*, I received a promising email from a young woman named Heather Owen who claimed to have had a close encounter in Fouke. She first reported the incident to the Miller County Sheriff's Office, then to Frank McFerrin at the Miller County Historical Museum. McFerrin, who knew of my interest and my upcoming book, suggested she contact me. I was glad she did.

According to Owen, she had gone to a friend's house on the evening of September 28, 2011, to study for college courses. At around 10:00 p.m. Owen began to hear a dog barking very intensely somewhere outside the home. When Owen pointed it out, her friend told her it was their family pet, probably making a fuss to come inside. However, Owen was struck by the particular nature of the barking. "It sounded like the dog was very much distraught and was trying to alert the owner of some kind of danger," she told me. "But I dismissed the disturbance since my friend didn't seem alarmed."

The intense barking continued approximately 45 minutes more until it finally stopped. By midnight the girls were tired, so Owen packed up, said goodbye, and headed out into the night. It was clear and pleasant with a sliver of waxing moon overhead. It was also unusually quiet.

Owen got in her vehicle and started it up. She then rolled down the windows, opened the sunroof, and begin to navigate the narrow county roads. As she topped a hill, she spotted a figure standing beside a hay bale in the open field to her left. It appeared to be a human-like form although unusually tall and bulky. "My lights were on bright and there was no mistaking it for what it was," she stated. "It was standing up on two feet facing towards me."

As Owen continued at a slow speed, the figure suddenly slouched forward and ran across the road with huge strides. It was so sudden and quick that Owen slammed on her brakes for fear of hitting it. When it reached the opposite side of the road, it leapt over a drainage ditch and disappeared into to the darkness beyond. The creature was muscular and covered in dark hair. In the moments before it ran, it turned sideways giving Owen a profile view. She could see that "its shoulders looked massive and its thighs were big."

Owen was so terrified by the event she immediately rolled up the windows, locked the doors, and closed the sunroof. She then drove a short way down the dark road and called her friend to ask if there had been reports of anything strange in the area lately. After a short conversation, she hung up and called her mother. By now she was shaking and driving as fast as she could toward the main road. She breathed intensely as she told her mother of the incident.

The following day, Heather and her mother came back to the area to look for evidence of the creature's passage but could only find an area of matted grass where it had presumably run. Owen was reluctant to tell people of the encounter for fear of ridicule but finally decided it should be reported to the police after viewing a show about Bigfoot on television.

After hearing about the encounter, I contacted Owen by phone to arrange a personal meeting. A short time later, two fellow researchers, Jerry Hestand and Chris Buntenbah, and I made the drive to Fouke and met her one afternoon at the location of the sighting. It was located on a county road where homes and trailers are spread out upon large properties and farms surrounded by patches of thick woods. Owen recapped the details as I attempted to retrace the alleged creature's steps.

Since she had first seen it standing beside a hay bale, we measured the height of one such bale near the road. It wasn't the exact bale, since that one had long since been moved, but she was fairly certain it was the same in size. Judging from the height of the sample bale and Owen's approximation that the top of the hay came

*Owen and the author on the road where she encountered the alleged creature
(Photo by Chris Buntenbah)*

to the creature's chest, we concluded that the creature likely stood
between seven and eight feet tall.

I also examined the area on the opposite side of the road where
she said it ran. There was not only a small ditch there but a barbed
wire fence partially covered in brush and leaning away from the
road at about 45 degrees. It would have been extremely difficult for
anything other than a large animal with sufficient night vision to
jump the fence in the darkness, thus reducing the likelihood that it
could have been a person in a costume.

Having met with Owen, my fellow researchers and I felt she was
telling the truth. We were also able to meet the friend whose house
she had visited prior to the sighting and whom she called after the
sighting. Their stories matched up, and it seemed very unlikely that
both girls would have been able to come off as credible if a strange
event had not truly occurred.

During our investigation we noticed that the closest home had a garden within the creature's path of travel. It was brimming with berries and other edible delicacies, making it possible that the creature had ventured close to Fouke in pursuit of food. So we decided to knock on the door to see if anyone had seen or heard anything unusual. The resident was a bit shocked to hear of Owen's sighting, but only because it had happened so close to her home without her knowledge. She was comfortably familiar with the legendary beast of Boggy Creek, as she had been living in the home since before the famous movie was made. In fact, she and her husband owned the Boggy Creek Café during the monster's heyday back in the 1970s. She was very interested in our research, but unfortunately she had not seen anything fitting the description of the Fouke Monster recently or at any time. We also spoke to a gentlemen across the road, but like the woman, he had not seen anything out of the ordinary.

Aside from the food source, the location had another, even more notable feature. It was very close to the actual Boggy Creek. This is significant for obvious historical reasons, but also because of the correlation between water and sightings of this type. It's an important association to consider for several reasons.

First, if large creatures such as Bigfoot were to exist in the southlands, they would need plenty of water to offset the high heat conditions that prevail much of the year. Without a copious water supply, the creatures simply could not survive. Water not only provides hydration but ensures the proliferation of vegetation and animal-life critical to the diet of an incredibly large animal.

Waterways also create a "path of least resistance" through wooded areas and public land, so it would make sense for Bigfoot creatures to use these networks to move from one feeding area to another as they struggle to survive in the often harsh terrains of the South. With the ever-encroaching development imposed by humans, the areas of rivers, creeks, bogs, and bayous tend to remain untouched thus providing an environment where animals can live and move in relative peace.

And finally, water—specifically rainwater—is necessary to grow thick woodlands that would be critical in hiding such a conspicuous resident as Bigfoot. Not surprisingly, the majority of Bigfoot reports coming out of the South occur where the annual rainfall exceeds 40 inches per year. This is not to say that there aren't other credible reports that have occurred in places outside this zone, but even in these cases, they almost always correspond to a nearby body of water.

So it is either coincidence that people who "make up" stories about seeing huge, bipedal apes in the South most often choose a setting near water or high annual rainfall, or the proximity of water sparks outrageous misidentifications and hallucinations. Or, perhaps, the particular locations of the reported sightings provide circumstantial support to the theory that if a large, undocumented anthropoid does exist in the South, then it would naturally be seen near this sort of habitat more often than not.

"They always follow the creeks," states the narrator in *The Legend of Boggy Creek*. And it's eerie how true this seems to be as we examine Southern Sasquatch evidence so many years later.

UP THE RIVER

In November 2014, I received a surprising call just after Thanksgiving. My head was still soggy from too much turkey and leftovers, but I immediately perked up when the caller on the line told me there had been a Bigfoot sighting earlier in the week near the border of Texas and Arkansas near the Sulphur River.

It was my friend, Denny Roberts, who owns two convenience stores in the area. He said that a woman had come into the store where he was working on the morning of the 24th. She was distressed and outwardly shaken. As she purchased a soda, the woman asked if he was the same person who owned the Monster Mart in Fouke. Denny said "yes" and at that point she proceeded to confide in him an incident that had taken place just moments before.

The woman said she had been driving north from her home at around 10:00 a.m. when she realized she had forgotten something. As she completed a three-point turn on the narrow county road and began to head back south, she was startled by the sight of something in the middle of the road. At first she thought it was a kid dressed in a Halloween costume, but as she focused on the figure, she realized it was some sort of hairy animal, one that walked on two legs.

The creature had apparently come out of the thick patch of woods on her left and was crossing the road where her car had been moments before. Now that she had turned around, it paused as if caught in the act. The creature stood fully upright with an estimated height of five feet. It was covered in reddish-brown hair, except for the face which had dark leathery skin and particularly piercing eyes. She could see the wispy hair on its arms waving in the gentle morning breeze. It gazed at the woman for a few seconds before turning and running back into the woods.

Completely unnerved, the woman sped home, grabbed what she had forgotten, and drove back up the road until she reached the convenience store. She did not see the creature again but was still shaking so much she decided to stop and pick up a soda, hoping to calm her nerves. Trusting that Denny would understand because of his association with the Fouke legend, she told him of the encounter.

Denny felt the woman's story was solid, so he helped me arrange a meeting with her. She did not want any publicity, fearing her neighbors might think she'd gone crazy, so I promised to keep her name confidential.

A month later we met at Denny's store where she reiterated the story to me and my research partner Tom Shirley. As she spoke, we could sense the emotion in her voice. I watched the earnest expression in her eyes. It was apparent that feelings of fear and bewilderment still lingered. "It scared me to death," she told us. "I was shaking for days, and I'm still wondering if I really saw that."

Her description matched what Denny had originally told me, adding that the body hair was around four inches in length. She was puzzled, however, that its apparent height of five feet did not equal the towering Bigfoot stature she had heard about. I explained it's only logical that if these creatures *are* real, then naturally there would be younger ones who haven't reached full maturity, not to mention I had heard plenty of other witness reports where the creatures were of heights that varied from four to eight feet. Her description was not out of the ordinary and, in fact, quite common in the attributes of its reddish-brown hair and darker facial skin.

I asked her if there was any possibility that it could have been a person in a costume, perhaps trying to scare her? "At first I thought it was a kid in a costume, but the more I looked at it, I could see it wasn't," she explained. "And when it was running, it didn't look like a costume; it looked like a real animal."

Following the meeting, Tom and I visited the location where she said the creature entered the road. The thick woods standing to the east were indeed a likely place for an animal to emerge. There were a few houses in the vicinity, but it was a very rural setting with the houses far apart and mostly nestled into the trees. A large, open field sat on the opposite side of the road, presumably where the creature was headed. I wasn't sure why it would want to cross into

Location where the alleged creature was seen crossing the road
(Photo by Lyle Blackburn)

such an open area, but regardless, if a large animal were to move around there, this seemed like the mostly like place.

As Tom and I took a few photos and poked around in the woods just off the road, inevitably a resident drove up and questioned our intentions. The person was initially suspicious but after I explained who I was, it led to a phone conversation with the person who owned the wooded property. When I told him a woman had claimed to see an ape-like creature cross the road there, he was intrigued. He wasn't aware of any other reports or tales from his neighbors, but he did tell me that after a few houses, the woods basically ran unimpeded for miles in the direction of Fouke.

I also asked him if it was possible some kids in the area had dressed up in a Bigfoot costume in the days preceding Thanksgiving. He told me that there were no kids other than his own living along that stretch of road, and that it was highly unlikely. He also pointed out that kids would have been in school on Monday November 24 at 10:00 a.m.

Given all the information, it seemed as though the woman had a legitimate encounter, which is not only significant in regards to its probability but in its proximity to the Sulphur River. What she didn't realize was that there's a long history of sightings along the Sulphur River, a body of water that originates in Texas and eventually networks with Boggy Creek via Days Creek. In route, it passes just south of the road where she claimed to have seen the creature. In fact, if you were to keep driving, you would find yourself floating in the Sulphur since the road literally dead-ends into the riverbank!

SULPHUR WATERWEB

As we travel farther up the Sulphur River into Texas, it's not long before we come across other locations where people have reported strange, man-like beasts along the waterway. Near the modern site of Wright-Patman Lake, a Sulphur River flood control reservoir, a family claimed to have had a startling encounter in 1916. According to a retired geologist whose grandmother lived in a place called Knight's Bluff, she was returning from town one night with her family in their mule-drawn wagon when they began to hear a strange noise coming from the pasture near their home. It sounded like an eerie, high-pitched wail or howl. A few moments later, they saw a tall figure emerge from the treeline and walk into the moonlit field. His grandmother, who was 18 at the time, described it as being "tall or taller than a man and covered with long, dark hair." She also noted "it stood absolutely erect and walked slowly toward them like man… not slouching like an ape."[12]

As the creature approached the wagon, the father reached for his rifle and fired once in the animal's direction. It did not appear to be hit but nonetheless turned and ran back into the woods. Fearing for his family's safety, the father quickly drove the wagon back to the house and barricaded his family inside for the rest of the night.

More recently, in 1969, two men claimed to have encountered a strange creature near a levee that runs parallel to the South Sulphur River about 10 miles from Commerce, Texas. According to an article in the July 1979 issue of *Fate* magazine, Kenneth Wilson was first in the area around 11:00 p.m. hanging out with three friends.[13] As he sat in his car, his friends (one man and two women) were out walking along the levee. Wilson heard something moving in the bushes around him, then a short time later he heard his friends start screaming. They rushed back to the car in a panic, saying they had seen something down by the levee.

Frightened, Wilson drove the group to a nearby gas station where their friend Jerry Matlock worked (no relation to the aforementioned Paul Matlock). They asked to borrow his gun. Not wanting to part with the gun, Matlock accompanied them back to the area to investigate. When they arrived, they were greeted with a shocking sight as a huge, man-like creature covered in brown hair jumped over the levee and ran towards the car. "This thing was bigger than any man I've ever seen in my life," Matlock told the reporter. "You could have stretched a [3 foot] yardstick across its shoulders and its shoulders would've been wider than that."

Wilson also got a glimpse of the creature, saying that: "It was big and hairy, whatever it was." At that point he hit the gas and spun the car around. As they sped off, the man in the front passenger seat tried to fire at the beast with Matlock's gun. However, the gun didn't go off.

The next day Wilson and Matlock returned to the scene where they found footprints. "I put my arm down in one of the prints," Matlock said, "and that print was as long as from my elbow to the tip of my outstretched fingers."

Another sighting in proximity of the South Sulphur River occurred in August 1978. As documented in the same *Fate* article, High School Senior, Harvey Garrison, was driving along a country road at about 10:15 p.m. when he claimed to have seen a seven-foot-tall creature standing by the side of the road.

"I slammed on my brakes and came within a few feet of hitting the thing," he told investigators. "It turned slightly toward my car. Then in one step it was across the road!"[14] It disappeared into the blackness of the night.

Two days later, three more teenagers from the small community of South Sulphur west of Commerce were reportedly frightened by a similar beast while walking on the very same road at midnight. Upon hearing something moving in the trees, they walked over to investigate when a large animal jumped up and ran away. They described it as being larger than a gorilla and "well over seven feet tall."

Following the incident, one of the teenagers, Wayne Matlock (no apparent relationship to the two previous Matlocks!) saw the alleged beast a second time. On or around August 19, Matlock was walking home along another rural road at 5:00 p.m. when a creature fitting the same description ran out of the woods and headed for the river.

"It crossed the road several yards in front of me and headed off across a pasture toward the Middle Sulphur River," he told investigators. "The cattle in the pasture went running in all directions and cattle usually run together in the same direction unless they're really scared."

Matlock said he was so startled he ran the rest of the way home.

He and one of the other boys eventually returned to the site to look for evidence. They claimed to have found two footprints in a ditch at the side of the road. "Each one was over 12 inches long," he stated.

Matlock's father, Harold, went on record saying that he believed the boy's story. He theorized that "the creature could be migrating along the rivers from some other area, such as Boggy Creek in Arkansas."

Apparently it continued to follow the creeks. In October 1984, a witness claimed to have seen a startling creature along a small tributary of the Sulphur River called Anderson Creek. In a report on file with the North American Wood Ape Conservancy (NAWAC), the witness said she was walking along the creek in Bowie County one evening at dusk when she began to hear the sound of footsteps in the leaves as a rank smell entered her nostrils.[15] Looking towards the sound, she saw something standing by the edge of the water. It had rained earlier in the day, leaving a light fog hanging in the air, but there was still enough visibility to see that it was not human.

The thing, she recalled, was approximately seven feet tall with a body covered in black hair. It had long arms that hung down almost to its knees. In the foggy dusk it was hard to make out facial details, but she was certain it had no visible ears atop its head, which would indicate a bear. Frightened, the witness turned and ran as fast as she could back home, never looking back to see if the creature was following.

"I have never been as scared as I was in that moment," she reported. "I remember seeing it breathe. It was completely motionless except for the slight movement as it breathed in and out, and that is what frightened me so very bad, because I knew that it was real and I was not just seeing something among the trees."

Perhaps something unknown had been living in the Anderson Creek bottoms for years. According to local rumors, a farmer allegedly found strange tracks near his well in the 1940s.

27

Boggy Creek Beast by D.W. Frydendall

RED RIVER CONNECTION

The Sulphur River is but one of several main tributaries associated with the Red River of the South. The Red River is the second-largest basin in the southern Great Plains, flowing along the border between Oklahoma and Texas, and extending across several ecoregions as it moves into southwest Arkansas and on into Louisiana (where it eventually merges with the Mississippi). Since these rivers are part of the same drainage network and join together only a few miles south of Boggy Creek, one could reasonably expect a similar history of sightings along both. And indeed, that seems to be the case, further reinforcing that the Southern Sasquatch inhabit areas near waterways.

A 1965 article from *The Paris News* documents early sightings of a strange creature near the town of Direct, a short distance from the Red River.[16] According to the article, a woman claimed to have seen a creature referred to by locals as the "Manimal." She was out one evening near her house when she spotted the thing with her flashlight. Frightened, she hurried back to the house where she and her cousin watched it jump a fence on all fours then stand up on two legs. "It [was] about [six feet, two inches] as it stood up," she told reporters. (The fact that the woman could make such a precise height estimate makes this report suspicious and should be regarded as such.)

The woman later found tracks at the scene, which were examined by a game warden. Although they were described as being large, they were also said to have claw marks, leaving some doubt as whether the Manimal even falls into the Bigfoot classification. Either way, the article goes on to say that sightings by "oldsters" in the area date back at least 50 years.

According to David Holley of the Texoma Bigfoot Research and Investigations Group, old-timers in the nearby Red River County tell of a strange creature or "wildman," near Cuthand Creek during the 1960s and 70s.[17] Referred to as the "Cuthand Critter," it was allegedly seen by farmers and ranchers on several occasions. Holley also heard stories in the 1980s about a "large, hair covered creature who resembles a huge gorilla" seen walking across some pastures not far from Cuthand Creek.

A woman whose family is from Hooks, Texas, just south of the Red River, told me her late father was adamant about encountering a Bigfoot on the river in about 1965. Angie Smith said her father, Larry Jaggears, was hanging out on the bank one night with several friends when he had to relieve himself. He walked into some nearby brush and was proceeding to do his thing when he noticed a pair of red eyes looking at him. He could also smell a horrible odor. He called out, thinking it was one of his friends trying to scare him, but there was no response. He quickly zipped up and walked toward the eyes. As he did, the eyes moved from behind the brush. At that point he could see a large, bipedal creature standing at least eight feet tall. Jaggears turned and ran for the safety of his group. They investigated but found no further trace of the creature.

In April 1982, two boys claim to have seen a Bigfoot-like creature near Bagwell, a town 50 miles west of Hooks in Red River County. According to a report published by the North American Wood Ape Conservancy (formerly the Texas Bigfoot Research Conservancy),[18] the two boys were sent to fetch their uncle, who was working in a pasture. It was starting to get dark, so the boys hurriedly jumped a fence and started toward their uncle in the distance. When they got within 50 feet, however, they came to the stark realization that the figure standing there was not their uncle. It was, instead, a hairy, man-like creature between six and seven feet tall.

"It turned around to look at us, grunted and ran toward the woods," the boys said. "We screamed as it turned."

The animal jumped a fence and disappeared into the dusky twilight just as their uncle came out of a nearby barn to investigate the commotion. He did not believe their story… until one evening eight months later.

> It was a Saturday night and we were going into town to see a movie. Rain and sleet had been falling most of the day. We lived back off the main road and had to travel logging roads to the highway. About 1,000 yards from our driveway, my aunt suddenly screamed. We looked up in time to see it. It was crossing the road right in front of us. It jumped across a ditch on the side of the road and disappeared into the woods. In the headlights, the color of the animal was that of a brown bear. He was covered with hair. The hair was not very long. There were missing patches of hair on the arms and legs. Again he seemed to be about six and a half feet tall, kind of sloped up the back.[19]

The boys also said a man who lived near their uncle's house, deeper in the woods, reported seeing a similar creature. "One night he woke up when he heard something rummaging around in the trash barrels out back," the boy said. "He got his shotgun and went outside to shoot what he thought was going to be a raccoon. To his surprise, he was face to face with the creature. He said it grunted and ran away with great speed."

The Red River
(Photo by Lyle Blackburn)

Another interesting cluster of Bigfoot sightings can be found in Cooke County, Texas, near the site of an old bridge. The bridge, which spans the Red River, was built in 1893 to accommodate wagon passage to and from the town of Callisburg. The now historic bridge was recently relocated to Callisburg Park due to its age, but not before it could garner an esteemed reputation for being haunted by more than one sort of strange entity. According to an article published by the *Gainesville Daily Register* in 2004, "The 1893 bridge is one of the four oldest in the state. Local officials wanted to keep it because of its history, which includes ghost and Big Foot [sic] stories as well as its age."[20]

Some of the ghostly tales involving the bridge seem well rooted in urban legend and teenage pranks, but there have been a number of credible witnesses who attest to the presence of ape-like creatures. My colleague Jerry Hestand, who assisted a great deal in my documentation of the Boggy Creek incidents, has personally investigated some of these accounts. According to Hestand, there seems to be a pattern of Bigfoot sightings between Grayson County and Cooke County along the Red River. Also, north of the River in Love and Marshall Counties the same has been occurring for quite some time.

One of these encounters allegedly occurred in the winter of 1976.[21] At the time, a teenage boy was standing on the Texas-side of the Callisburg bridge watching ice float down the river when he heard what sounded like coon dogs chasing something on the Oklahoma side. As they came into view, he could see two hounds on the trail of some kind of huge, dark, hairy animal. The animal ran on two legs, but did not appear to be human.

The boy watched as the creature jumped over a dead tree log and plunged into the surrounding brush. The lead dog followed and began yelping a few seconds after it went out of sight. The second dog followed, but immediately turned around and ran back in the direction it had come. The first dog fell silent and never re-emerged.

Frightened, the boy jumped on his motorcycle and sped home. He later mustered enough courage to return to the location but never saw the strange beast again.

Hestand interviewed the boy in 2004 and found him to be credible. "The witness seemed sincere in his statements," Hestand stated. "There was no doubt in his mind as to what he saw. The witness claims the animal was about 150 yards or so away, and he saw it for only two or three seconds, but he was sure it was not human."

Two years later, the boy—now a teenager—and a friend found a large man-like footprint in a creek bed close to where he'd seen the unknown creature. According to the witness, the print was much larger than that of any grown man.

Just across the Red River in Love County, Oklahoma, we find Brown Springs, an area with an even more sinister reputation for strangeness. Situated in the bottoms south of Leeper Lake, Brown Springs was so named because of the natural spring that seeps into a muddy and lifeless lagoon at the edge of the river. According to a 1999 article in *The Oklahoman*, the area—which includes an old cemetery containing 26 scattered gravemarkers—has long been thought of as haunted.[22] A former Love County prosecutor and appeals court judge claimed to have experienced one such chilling event when he went to visit the area. As he entered the cemetery, he saw one of the old gravemarkers literally teeter and fall to the ground in front of him. "It made the hair on the back of my neck stand up," he told reporters. Another man, Butch Bridges, claimed to have taken a photo of one of the graves that revealed a startling image when he scanned it into his computer. "In the upper left corner of the photo is a shadowy image of a child's face," the article explains.

As spooky as teetering gravemarkers and ghostly face are, they seem to pale in comparison to the grim reality of other events recorded at Brown Springs. Since the 1970s several dead bodies have been found, apparently murdered and then dumped in the desolate area. In 1988, a woman's car was even found partially submerged in a pond south of Brown Springs Cemetery. She was lying dead on top of the vehicle.

These type of events tend to fuel the fires for ghostly hauntings

and urban tales, but the place does seem to cast an air of percep-
tible darkness even in daylight. I know, I've been there. In walking along the hilltop cemetery, dirt roads, and boggy bottoms of
Brown Springs, I couldn't help but notice a certain ominous and
unexplainable sense of gloom. It extended to the murky site of the
lagoon where the menacing shadow of a man-ape would not seem
out of place.

But what is the reality of man-apes in the area? Is it just part of
the greater urban legend or do Bigfoot creatures pass through as
they travel the Red River network? The area is certainly wooded
and off the beaten path, enough that it could possibly conceal a
large animal coming to and from the riverbank. Take the following
report into consideration:

In 2004, just a few miles north of Brown Springs, Dan Dunston
said he was hog hunting when he began to smell a skunky, musky
order. Assuming it was a large boar moving along the top of a nearby
ridge, he decided to abandon his stand and stalk the animal on foot.
As he ascended the slope, suddenly something flew by his head and
crashed into the brush behind him. A moment later, another object
whizzed by and hit the ground out of sight. Judging from the sound,
it seemed like rocks.

Dunston froze and began to scan the ridge intently. He could
only assume one of his hunting partners was playing a joke on him.
They had all entered the wildlife area together, but their stands
were in different positions along the ridge. He didn't see anyone,
however, so he resumed his climb up the slope. As he did, a large
piece of rock rolled down the hill and stopped at his feet. Just then
he caught a glimpse of something moving above him. Whatever it
was had the general shape of a man, yet it looked to be much taller
and wider than a typical man.

The hunter slowly raised his rifle and peered through the scope.
He could only see the head and upper chest in the thick under-
growth, but it was enough to confirm it was some sort of human-like
beast. It was covered in dark, shaggy fur that swayed gently in the
slight breeze.

Dunston stood transfixed for what seemed like minutes, trying to comprehend what he was seeing. He didn't "believe" in Bigfoot, but the entity standing before him challenged his logic and made him wonder whether he should be fascinated or terrified. It appeared to be merely watching him, so Dunston took the opportunity to slowly back down the hill and get out of the area. As he passed, he examined the rock that had landed previously at his feet. It appeared to be a large chunk of a tombstone—perhaps from the abandoned graveyard on the hill—probably weighing in excess of 50 pounds. Whatever had launched it had to have been strong.

When Dunston finally rejoined his fellow hunters, he decided not to mention what he had seen for fear of ridicule. It wasn't until several months later, after viewing a show on Bigfoot sightings in Oklahoma, that he decided to report his encounter to the Texas Bigfoot Research Center (TBRC), who had concentrated many of their efforts on the Oklahoma area. I recently communicated with Dunston, as I began to study reports in the area. He assured me of his story's validity, one that could only reinforce what I had already found. The more I researched, the more I could see an undeniable pattern of sightings dispersed along the Red River and the miles of lakes and creeks networking from it.

THE OTHER BOGGYS

Although it's legendary, the Boggy Creek of Fouke is not the only one of its kind. Several waterways in Texas, Oklahoma, and Florida, also boast the name "Boggy Creek." While most don't have an extensive association with Bigfoot, if at all, some do. Perhaps this is not coincidental since these creatures seem to have an affinity for murky tributaries.

The two best examples are Clear Boggy Creek and Muddy Boggy Creek in Oklahoma. Clear Boggy Creek (also known as Clear Boggy River) originates in the central part of the state and eventually converges with Muddy Boggy Creek before dumping into the Red River just east of Arkansas. The area along these creeks is reputed to be the stomping ground of a Bigfoot beast known as the Boggy Bottom Monster.

Reports of the Boggy Bottom Monster date back many decades with a particular cluster having occurred along Clear Boggy in Atoka County. A particularly chilling incident was reported by Jackie Marlow in 2006. According to a story by *NewsOK*, Marlow ended up being hospitalized after seeing a tall, reddish-brown creature approach her house.[23] On the morning of July 18, Marlow was sitting on her porch at about 8:00 a.m., smoking a cigarette, and gazing at the woods surrounding her two acre property in Caney, a short distance from Clear Boggy Creek. Suddenly her dogs began to bark as she saw a figure emerge from the trees. It was reddish-brown in color and walked on two legs. She stepped off the porch to get a better look. She had heard of the Boggy Bottom Monster but never thought much of the stories until that moment when she believed she might be witnessing it for herself.

"It had very long legs, and it had a head," she told reporters. "People asked, 'Does it have hair?' and I don't know. I just know that it was a big reddish-brown tall thing, and it scared the fire out of me."

The creature lingered for several minutes, causing her smallest dog to go silent and huddle with fear. The thing finally made a loud snort and vanished back into the woods.

Excited and somewhat frightened, Marlow ran back into the house and phoned several friends to tell them what she had seen. The more she talked and thought about the possibility of the Boggy Bottom Monster, the more she began to panic. When she began to have trouble breathing, she called an ambulance for help.

Paramedics arrived a short time later, followed by police officers who tried to determine just what Marlow had seen. They scoured the area on ATVs but found no trace of the creature or other evidence. (Marlow later reported that she found part of her chain-link fence "bent in a way that no human hand could have done.")

Ms. Marlow was eventually taken to the local Atoka hospital where she was treated and released. When asked if the animal could have been a bear, cow, or coyote, Marlow scoffed. "I don't know what it was, but it was a tall creature," she stated. "I'm not gonna tell you I saw Bigfoot, but it was a tall, huge thing that walked."

It's hard to say just what Marlow saw that day, but she was not the first person to see a strange animal in the vicinity. A few weeks prior, two teens said they saw a similar animal—possibly two—on the banks of Clear Boggy Creek. According to the same *NewsOK* article—along with television coverage and a subsequent report to the Texas Bigfoot Research Conservancy—Morgan (13) and Garrett (12) Whatley had ridden four-wheelers to the area where they parked and began to play around the creek. Morgan was the first to see it. In her own words:

> I was playing with my brother on the creek when we heard the brush moving. I looked up and it was just standing there. I yelled to my brother, "What is that?" When he looked it was gone. He didn't believe me when I said there was something tall, hairy and reddish-brown standing there looking at us until a couple minutes later the brush was moving again. We got really scared and decided to leave. As we were leaving on our 4-wheelers it ran right in front of us as we went home. It was tall maybe 7 to 8 feet tall reddish-brown hair, lots of hair, long legs and arms. I don't know what its face looked like.[24]

The siblings immediately raced home and told their parents. The Whatleys were skeptical of Bigfoot but couldn't ignore the sincerity evident on their children's faces. "I believe there's something out there," their mother, Tracy, told reporters. "My kids were pretty scared when they came home."

Following the later sighting by Jackie Marlow and the subsequent news coverage, the TBRC received a call from a landowner in the area who invited them to take a look around. Investigators Jerry Hestand and Mark Porter visited the property where they spoke to several people about the case. They were also able to interview the Whatley teens about their sighting and take a look at the location. Hestand found them to be intelligent and seemingly truthful. Morgan recalled that the subject she saw "stood upright on two legs and was completely covered with reddish-brown hair." She estimated that it was taller and more bulky than her father who is over six feet tall. As soon as she told her brother to look, the creature fled from sight. However, he could hear movement in the bushes, verifying that something was there. At that point they were frightened and retreated to their ATVs. Seconds later, the creature—or another like it—ran across the road giving Garrett his split second view.

After bidding the family goodbye, Hestand and Porter returned to the site of the incident where they staked out a position along the creek bank. At approximately 9:00 p.m., they were scanning the area with night vision monoculars and a powerful UV light when they heard "something or someone" walking in the woods, breaking dead limbs and twigs. The rustling continued for half an hour and was often accompanied by a huffing or snorting sound. They surmised that whatever it was seemed to be wary of the human presence, as it managed to stay just out of view. Eventually the night went silent and the investigators left empty handed.

Whether the witnesses in this cases actually saw an unknown animal is debatable, but there's no denying that the Red River and its tributaries are inexplicably linked by sightings of this kind. Perhaps this makes sense from a geographical perspective. As the Red River continues eastward, it passes by Fouke before eventually entering Louisiana where we will soon learn of other ape-like beasts that haunt these watery habitats.

3. MARAUDING MANIMALS

On a chilly afternoon in December 1981, Mike Wooley ascended the steps of his old, rickety deer-stand near the Sabine Parish Game Reserve in western Louisiana. The creak of its metal frame seemed out of place in the unusually quiet woods. Other than the hunter, nothing seemed to be moving that day.

Wooley disregarded the strange silence as he sat down and laid his rifle across his lap. He'd missed the opportunity to hunt earlier that morning, so he was eager to make the most of the evening.

After he'd finally settled in, it wasn't long before a young doe emerged from the dense brush in front of him and approached the base of his tree stand. She appeared to be out of breath and foaming slightly at the mouth. She immediately sat down in the grass, unaware the hunter was perched above.

Figuring the doe was being chased by a buck, Wooley turned his attention back to the woods ahead. Sure enough, he caught a glimpse of something moving toward him a few degrees to his right. He waited with anticipation, fully expecting to see a male deer walk out. But what emerged from the woods was far from a deer. It was a large, bipedal ape-like creature that stood at least seven feet tall with an extremely muscular build and hairy body.

Wooley immediately grappled with the possibility he was looking at a Bigfoot. He was familiar with the legendary creature, but the thought that it could actually exist seemed ridiculous. He closed his eyes and took a deep breath, hoping it was his imagination playing tricks. When he opened his eyes again, however, the creature was still there, looking directly at him.

The hunter considered his options. He called out to the figure, thinking perhaps it was some kind of prank or hoax. The land

39

where he was hunting was free game back then. Perhaps it was another hunter trying to scare him out of the area. But the figure's only response was to stare back.

Wooley raised his rifle and set the scope to 3x power. He didn't intend to shoot, but perhaps a gun pointed in its direction would put an end to the joke.

"I looked through the scope and I could see everything," he told me in one of several interviews. "Then I knew it was the real deal."

The hunter's action helped determined what he was dealing with but unfortunately had an adverse effect on the animal. As a result of the rifle being pointed at it—or merely due to Wooley's movement—the creature became agitated and began to growl in a loud, guttural voice. The sound rumbled through the woods.

A few seconds later, a shrill whistle echoed from about 75 yards away. The creature briefly turned its head in the direction of the noise, then looked back at the hunter with an even more aggressive glare.

"Now I could hear bipedal movement coming from the direction of the whistle, and at that point, I knew I was in trouble," he recalled.

Wooley told me a wave of sheer terror shot through his body as he started down from the tree stand. "I was young back then; 26 years old, 150 pounds... I could move," he said. "I was thinking 'if the thing wanted me, he was gonna have to run me down.'"

The hunter descended most of the steps, then jumped the rest of the way. Once he hit the ground, he began to run full speed for his truck, which was parked nearly a half mile away down a logging road. As his footsteps pounded on the packed dirt, he could hear a ruckus in the trees at the side of the road. The thing was pursuing him, tearing its way through the brush.

Wooley fumbled in his pocket for his keys. He had parked the truck so that it was facing out of the woods, but it was locked and he knew he would have to open the door quickly. The creature was still in pursuit, flanking him just off the road, grunting and crashing through the brush.

When Wooley finally reached the truck, he decided to ensure

the creature would not have the opportunity to grab him as he tried to unlock the door.

"When I got to the truck, I swung around and fired a shot in his direction," Wooley told me. "I didn't want to hit it; it was just a shot to buy me time to unlock the truck, get in, and go."

The shot almost hit the creature as the bullet splintered a small pine only a few feet from its head. It was a close call but enough to get Wooley safely into the truck. He hurriedly fired up the engine and hit the gas pedal. As he sped away, he looked in his rearview mirror. He could now see two of the creatures standing in the road where his car had been just moments before.

"There was two of them running me," Wooley explained. "The other one had come up the logging road behind me, but I didn't know anything about that one because I hadn't looked that far behind me. They came together on the road as I was driving off."

As the hunter drove, his hands shaking from fear and adrenaline, he wondered how close he had come to dying. Given the size, agility, and probable strength of the muscular creatures, it was not hard to imagine they could've run him down, if they had wanted to. If they were only trying to scare him out of their territory, then it had worked. In the face of such power and aggression, Wooley felt lucky to be alive.

BAD REPUTATION

Stories of man-apes acting aggressively toward humans have long been a part of Southern Sasquatch lore. Fueled in part by early newspaper accounts and movies, this reported behavior has earned the creatures a reputation for being ill-tempered and downright dangerous. In some cases, such as the one reported by Mike Wooley, the aggressive creatures stop short of harming anyone. But in other cases, people claim to have been hurt by them... or worse.

One reason for the Southern Bigfoot's bad reputation is undoubtedly the movies. In *The Legend of Boggy Creek*, the creature was often portrayed as a menace or shown to stalk around people's home. In one of the most memorable scenes, the Fouke Monster crashed its hand through the bathroom window of the Ford's rental house while Bobby was sitting on the toilet. Although this scene was added by director Charles Pierce for dramatic effect, the fact that Bobby did end up in a Texarkana hospital following a perceived attack on their home resonates within Bigfoot history to this day.

The 1976 film, *Creature From Black Lake*, also fueled early impressions that Southern Bigfoot were not to be messed with. In the movie, the "monster" drowns a man in the swamp, terrorizes a family, and even tries to kill the researchers who are desperately trying prove its existence. *Black Lake* was far more fictionalized than *The Legend of Boggy Creek*, but nevertheless, it was loosely based on reported man-ape sightings in eastern Louisiana, which were then dramatized for maximum effect.

Modern Bigfoot horrors carry on this tradition by offering creatures who won't hesitate to kill bickering, party-oriented teens if they set foot in the swamps along the border between Texas and Louisiana. (And who can really blame them?) A recent example, *Skookum: The Hunt For Bigfoot*, was actually inspired by Mike Wooley's

A swampy scene from Creature From Black Lake
(1976 Howco International)

account. It was filmed in the same location as *Creature From Black Lake* in and around Caddo Lake and Oil City, Louisiana.

Movies are obviously geared towards entertainment, but newspaper articles dating back many years also contain accounts where alleged Bigfoot turned on humans. According to 1965 article in the *Marshall News Messenger*, 13-year-old Johnny Maples was walking along a rural road in nearby Marion County on the afternoon of August 20 when he heard a noise in the bushes.[25] He thought it might be a friend who lived nearby, so he called out. When the "person" did not answer, he threw a few rocks into the bushes, figuring it was just a small animal. Suddenly, a "large hairy man or beast" emerged from the trees behind a fence, presumably having been hit by one of the rocks. Maples immediately panicked and started running down the road.

According to the boy, the beast jumped the fence and started after him. "I ran as hard and fast as I could, but he kept up with me and he wasn't running, either, just sort of walking along behind me," Maples told the reporter. Maples even ditched his shoes in order to run faster, all the while looking back to see the hairy beast in pursuit. "The last time I turned around the beast had gone off the road and disappeared into the woods. I could hear him moving around but I didn't see him again."

The teenager was eventually picked up farther down the road by a neighbor in a car and taken home where he told the story to his mother, who noted that her son was in a "state of shock." The Marion County Deputy Sheriff was called to the scene, but he could find no evidence, tracks, or otherwise.

Maples described the beast as a seven-foot-tall ape with long black hair all over its body except for the face, stomach, and palms of its hands, which, he noted, "hung down below his knees." His claim of such an alarming creature set off a monster hunt. In a 1965 United Press International article titled "Town Fed Up With Monster Hunters," Sheriff Luke Walker of Jefferson, Texas, told a reporter that Bigfoot hunters from three states had overrun his small town since the news of Maples' encounter had spread.[26]

A particularly harrowing report of murderous, ape-like creatures around the same time was recorded by the now defunct *Bigfoot Bulletin* in 1970.[27] The report was submitted by Nick E. Campbell, an Army trainee stationed at Fort Ord, California. Campbell relates that two of his fellow trainees from the Texas National Guard, Private David Lawson and Private Royal Jacobs, both from Longview, Texas, told him that: "In or about the year 1965, there was a rash of reports of a giant hairy creature roaming the thickets and back country between Jefferson and Longview, Texas, but nearest to Longview. A man and his little daughter reported it as being large, black and not a bear. Several head of cattle and a couple of people were supposedly killed by it. Private Jacobs was a member of a posse that hunted the creature when he was a teenager. He told me that he saw the body of one of the murdered people and that the victim had been torn apart. At the time he threw his gun back in the car and went home."

Jacobs, Campbell said, was a licensed minister and he would vouch for the truthfulness of both men. There must have been some other reports or information since the section is titled "Concerning the Longview, Texas, Reports." But as it stands, this is the only written information available regarding this rather outrageous claim. An investigation into the matter was conducted by Bigfoot researcher Charles DeVore. The trail led to Dwain Dennis, a journalist and Jefferson resident, who actually interviewed Johnny Maples at the time he claimed to have been chased by the "monster." Dennis had also looked into the 1965 killings reported in the *Bigfoot Bulletin* but found no evidence that a posse was formed to hunt the creatures down or that there were ever any killings in Marion County that could be blamed on Bigfoot.

In the fall of 1977, a man was reportedly attacked by an ape-like animal in Valusia County, Florida. According to an article from Orlando's *Sentinel Star*, a security guard by the name of Donnie Hall was checking out a noise at a plant nursery in Apopka around 2:00 a.m. when he was "grabbed from behind by an apelike animal twice his height, covered with long hair and smelling like a goat."[28] Hall managed to break loose, grab a shotgun, and fire at the creature, hitting it twice. The creature hunched over and let out a moan but still managed to turn and run away. Hall shined his flashlight on it, noting that its hair was brownish-red except around its face where it had some gray hairs.

Hall said he had also seen the creature two nights prior as it tried to break down the door of the nursery. After the attack, he reported it to the local sheriff's office. A deputy who investigated the scene found "footprints," but examiners from the Florida Game and Fresh Water Fish Department did not believe they were from a real animal.

A few years later, in 1979, a family's serene Easter Sunday turned into a nightmare when they allegedly encountered an aggressive, ape-like creature several miles south of Jefferson, Texas. According to a report on file with the North American Wood Ape Conservancy, a couple and their two young girls were enjoying the afternoon on a 460-acre tract of property near Woodlawn when they heard a "loud crunching" in the brush.[29] They could not see an animal but were spooked enough to return to their car. At that point, the husband decided to do some target shooting with his pistol near a deep ravine. According to the woman: "We shot several times when suddenly, a large animal lunged into the ravine in front of us only about 10 to 15 feet. He paused, looked at us and then in one leap, jumped out of [the] ravine. We froze for a moment then [my] husband grabbed our six year old and I took the hand of the nine year old. We ran towards the car."

They could hear the animal pursuing them as it crashed through the surrounding brush, but apparently stopped before it reached the car. She described the animal is being grayish in color, covered in five-to-six inch-long hair, under which they could still see skin. It had wide shoulders, long arms, and was "powerful looking." She added that: "Unlike the drawings of Bigfoot, he had a short neck and round head. Far more human looking than the blocky thick shapes of the drawings."

The frightened family promptly fled the scene in their car. Any notions of Bigfoot being a benevolent creature were left in the dust.

MAN MOUNTAIN

One of the earliest Southern Sasquatch attacks is said to have taken place in 1829 within the borders of Okefenokee Swamp located in south central Georgia. The Okefenokee, which encompasses a staggering 700 square miles of rugged wetlands and wilderness, was initially home to various factions of the Creek Indian Nation who were willing to brave the swamp's dangers in exchange for the rich sustenance it provided.[30] Panthers, bears, alligators, poisonous snakes, relentless insects, and quicksand were all part of daily life, but even those paled in comparison to the reputed "mortals of superhuman dimensions and incomparable ferocity" whom they said inhabited a virtually inaccessible island at the heart of the swamp. According to an article from the *Milledgeville Statesman* newspaper, the most terrifying of these shadowy mortals was a giant half-man, half-ape known as "Man Mountain."[31]

As white settlers began to move into the area—following several tragic battles and treaties between expanding conquerors and the native peoples—they heard tales of the legendary swamp giants but were quick to dismiss them as superstitious Indian folklore. That is, until the summer of 1829, when two men and a boy decided to trek deeper into the heart of Okefenokee.

Taking advantage of an unusually dry season, they traversed for two weeks penetrating the interior of the swamp until they came upon an "ominous" footprint so large it measured 18 inches in length and 9 inches in width with a toe-to-heel stride that easily stretched 6 feet. Thoughts of the Man Mountain immediately crossed their minds, resulting in their hasty retreat out of Okefenokee.

As the tale of their spooky discovery began to spread among friends and locals, a group of nine Florida hunters came forward requesting directions to the spot. Within a short time they made their way to the area where they discovered similar tracks, which they followed several more days into the dismal bog.

They finally set up camp on a ridge, hoping to refresh themselves before continuing further. As they were relaxing, however, a "wild beast" of some sort rushed out of the brush and advanced on them. Two of the men immediately fired upon it with their rifles causing it to howl with a "deafening roar." The echo of the gunshots apparently aroused the maker of the giant footprints. According to the report: "The next minute he was full in their view, advancing upon them with a terrible look and a ferocious mien."

The hunters gathered in a close group and began to fire upon the hulking Man Mountain. They were finally able to drop the creature with a hail of bullets, but not before it ruthlessly killed five of their number by literally twisting their heads from their necks.

As the creature lay exhausted and dying, the four survivors "had [the] opportunity to examine the dreadful being as he lay extended on the earth, sometimes wallowing and roaring." It measured 13 feet in length with its massive proportions complementing its towering height.

Fearing retaliation from any other "giants" living in the area, the men scooped up the remains of their comrades and fled from the swamp. Presumably they told others of the incident, since the story was later related to the newspaper by a Mr. John Ostcan, who resided on the borders of the swamp in Ware County. The article concludes by saying: "The story of this report, as related above, is matter of fact, and the truth of it is accredited."

The details are unquestionably fantastic, and although at no point does the article specifically say the being was covered in hair, it no doubt fits well within the category of Bigfoot stories considering the massive size and footprint measurements of the alleged creature. Okefenokee is without question a place where large creatures could have found sanctuary, especially in the early days of American settlement. I have personally canoed through the wilds of the swamp and even today it offers a vast woodland environment rich in food and protective cover. Bigfoot sightings have continued to emerge from Okefenokee and the surrounding Georgia-Florida area over the years (more of which we will explore later), making

Marshlands of the Okefenokee Swamp
(Photo by Lyle Blackburn)

the Man Mountain tale something to consider in terms of historical accounts.

A similarly violent Bigfoot attack was reported in the May 8, 1856, edition of the *Hornellsville Tribune*. The article, titled "The Wild Man Again," references the writings of a *Caddo Gazette* correspondent from "Parailifta, Arkansas" who told of an incident that supposedly occurred in Sevier County north of Texarkana.[32] (Presumably, Parailifta should have been *"Paraclifta,"* since Paraclifta was the county seat of Sevier County.)

As the story goes, a party of men were in pursuit of a "famous wild man," which had often been seen in the wooded areas between Arkansas and Louisiana. They were finally able to get close when their hunting dogs ran it onto the frozen ice of Brant Lake. As the "monster of the forest" crossed, the ice gave way, causing it to fall into the icy waters. Since the hunters could not cross the ice on horseback, one of them circled around the lake where he observed the thing "breaking ice with his arms" as it tried to escape the grasp of the frozen lake.

The hunter promptly concealed himself in the nearby brush and watched as the creature finally crawled from the ice and shook himself off. He described it as "… a stout, athletic man, about six feet four inches in height, completely covered with hair of a brownish cast about four to six inches long. He was well muscled, and ran up the bank with the fleetness of a deer."

The man could have killed it with his gun, but since the party was trying to take the man-beast alive, he approached it on horseback hoping to keep it at bay until the rest of the men arrived. The wild man, however, lashed out and "in an instant dragged the hunter to the ground and tore him in a most dreadful manner, scratching out one of his eyes… and biting large pieces out of his shoulder and various parts of his body. The monster then tore off the saddle and bridle from the horse and destroyed them, and holding the horse by the mane, broke a short piece of sapling, and mounting the animal, started at full speed across the plains." The party came to the aid of their friend, vowing to continue their pursuit of the elusive beast at a later time.

The story does have a few problems, such as the creature's skill on horseback and the fact that there's no Brant Lake in Arkansas (although this could have been another error like the misspelling of "*Paraclifta*"). But regardless, as with the Man Mountain tale, it's interesting to examine the story from the perspective of Bigfoot.

SIEGE AT HONOBIA

On a cold night in January 2000, Tim Humphreys grabbed his rifle and burst out onto the porch of his country home. Something big was fleeing toward the trees, glancing back at him with reflective, red eyes. Moments ago it had been scratching at the window, frightening his wife and children to a state of panic. As the creature made its getaway, Tim took aim and pulled the trigger. The blast echoed in the hills as the thing stumbled and kept running.

Tim Humphreys had finally had enough. He and his family had expected a reasonable amount of danger and hardship when they moved to the Kiamichi Mountains of Oklahoma, but hostile, ape-like creatures assailing their home was too much. If the creatures would not stop prowling around the property, trying to force their way into the house, or stealing food from the storage freezer, then they would face the wrath of his bullets.

These incidents, collectively known as the "Siege of Honobia," have already become legendary—if not controversial—within Bigfoot circles. Documentation of the case started with a message sent to the Bigfoot Field Researchers Organization (BFRO) in January 2000. According to notes posted on the BFRO website, a family living near the small town of Honobia, Oklahoma, had endured a series of strange occurrences and threatening behavior from one or more entities they believed fit the description of Bigfoot. The message read in part:

> Please have someone contact us. This is no hoax and my brother is afraid for his family. This creature is getting bolder every time it returns. This thing is huge, walks upright, smells like a musky urine, burned hair type odor. It has on more than one occasion tried to enter their home. Everyone thinks we are crazy when we mention it. Please, we don't know what to do but I do know that something needs to be done![33]

The brother, Mike Humphreys, explained to representatives of the BFRO that the incidents had been going on for nearly two years and he and his brother, Tim, believed multiple creatures were involved. At first, only one of the animals prowled around the home. It was seen on several occasions, but at the time family members dismissed the sightings even though they were sure it wasn't a bear. But as time went on, they saw more of these ape-like prowlers, each unique in features and hair color. They began to steal deer meat from a heavy freezer the family stored in an open-sided shed near the house, then tried to force their way into the home, wriggling door knobs, beating on doors, and scratching at the windows. The Humphreys said they could also hear "loud vocalizations, tree thrashing, chattering and whistling outside the house at night." It seemed that whenever one of the animals assaulted the home, screams could be heard in the nearby hills which surround the property.

In order to find out more details about this incredible story I tracked down Mike Humphreys, who agreed to answer my questions. I inquired about speaking to his brother as well, but Tim denied my request, saying that he's no longer willing to discuss it. His family had endured enough already and he simply wanted to move on. After hearing more of the story, I can certainly understand his position.

Mike told me that it all started in 1998 when he himself spotted a Bigfoot-like creature on Tim's property in Honobia. Mike owned property in nearby Talihina and often visited his brother's home. "I didn't tell anyone about it until after I knew for sure my brother had seen one," Mike told me. He didn't want to alarm his brother or sister-in-law, but it wasn't long before they had sightings themselves. At first these were scant glimpses, but the animals gradually became bolder and were seen with increasing frequency.

"I have no way of knowing how many sightings were had between all of us," Mike explained. "All I can tell you is there were a bunch of sightings."

The Humphreys were hunters and would often store venison along with other meats in the outdoor freezer. When the animals became aware of the food source, they began to steal it. The creatures were stealthy and primarily conducted their activities by night, but on occasion they could be seen skulking around the shed and other places on the property. As if that weren't enough, the creatures began to assail the house itself. With each occurrence, the creatures — who, according to Mike were "tall, hairy, stinky animals that walked both on all fours and upright" — became more aggressive. Perhaps they had become accustomed to the easy meals from the freezer and suspected there might be more inside the home. Or perhaps they felt the family was encroaching on their territory. Either way, the situation was becoming more alarming by the day.

"These things were screaming around, beating on his house,

coming up on the porch, peeking in the windows and scratching on them," Mike told me. "One of them even twisted the door knob off the back door."

By late 1999, the strange activity became so frequent Tim began to fear for his family's safety. Shortly before Mike sent his plea to the BFRO, the family was at home one evening when one of the animals attempted to get inside. Seeing the terrified look on his children's faces, Tim grabbed his rifle and headed outside. In the hazy darkness, he could see a hairy, ape-like animal running away from house. He quickly raised the gun and took a shot. The animal kept running, but he was sure he had hit it.

Mike arrived 20 minutes later and Tim told him of the incident. They could hear strange cries and chattering coming from the hillside, as if the creatures were agonizing over their injured family member. Fearful they may seek revenge, the brothers waited until daylight to investigate the area more thoroughly. The next morning they did find a blood trail leading into the woods, however, it led to a freshly killed deer. The Humphreys assumed the deer had been shot, but upon closer inspection found that it had not. It appeared to have been killed by some other means with one of its legs noticeably twisted and broken. It also appeared to have been carried, not dragged, to the spot.

Realizing they might be up against something they couldn't handle by themselves, Mike took it upon himself to contact the BFRO. I asked if they had considered calling the police, but Mike said it would have been a waste of time. They felt the sheriff would simply laugh them off as soon as the word "Bigfoot" was mentioned. The BFRO seemed like a more logical starting point if they were going to solicit outside help.

After receiving the distress message, representatives from the BFRO conducted an initial phone interview with Mike. Concluding the case was worth investigating, two of their investigators were asked to visit the property, Roger Roberts and Miles Lawler, along with Roberts' father who had years of hunting experience.

The three investigators arrived within 48 hours of Tim taking the shot at the creature. They immediately inspected the dead deer,

View of the mountainous region behind the "siege" location
(Photo by Lyle Blackburn)

but it was hard to glean much from the carcass since it was mostly eaten up by then. According to Roger Roberts in the BFRO report, the deer had most likely been devoured by Tim's 15 dogs, whom he witnessed gnawing on it. "It was too far gone to tell anything, just a skeleton from the hind quarters forward to the upper neck," he noted.

The investigators then interviewed all the family members, and even a few neighbors, to find out what was going on. The neighbors, like the family, related experiences with Bigfoot-like creatures in the area. Roberts is a professional private investigator, so he listened carefully and observed the facial characteristics of each person. In the end, the investigators concluded that: "The witnesses all appeared to be honest." And, in their opinion, there was probable "Bigfoot activity in the area."

Lawler remarked about the geography of the area, which can be surprising to people not familiar with eastern Oklahoma. "That area is extremely remote and heavily forested and mountainous," he stated. "I have been all around the country hiking (Pacific

Northwest, British Columbia, Alaska, Great Smokey Mountains, etc.) and I was really caught by surprise. It is a perfect spot with all the protected government land."

As the evening progressed, dark clouds began to gather overhead, eventually culminating in a storm. Despite the inconvenience, Roberts and Lawler drove around the area with a spotlight, attempting to get a glimpse of the creatures. However, in the daunting rain and darkness, they saw nothing.

At around 1:00 a.m. they returned to the house where they came upon a frantic scene. The Humphreys were all gathered on the porch, holding rifles and scanning the woods around them. They had just shot at one of the creatures as it moved across the road in front of the house. The hunt was on!

While Rogers' father slept in the car, Rogers, Lawler, and the Humphreys spent the next two hours standing vigil in the cold night air, waiting for any more creatures to venture close. At one point, the Humphreys spotted pinkish-red eyes moving in the darkness and fired on what they believed was one of the creatures. The BFRO investigators were not in a position to see what they were firing at, but Lawler believes he did see something a few minutes later. "It was there for just a second in the trees across the road (thick small saplings and brushy area) around 7 or 8 feet high," he recalled.

A short time later, the Humphrey brothers caught another glimpse and responded with gunfire. Again to no avail. Whatever it was did not make any identifiable noises such as screams or heavy movement in the brush. Roberts aimed his video camera at the fleeting shadows, but it was too dark to capture any useful footage. The rain also hampered the visibility and forced the group to hunker on the porch for most of the night. If there were creatures taunting them, the conditions were in the creatures' favor.

The following morning the men scoured the hillside for tracks or other evidence, but nothing could be found. Amid the heavy leaf litter and mud, they could hardly discern between boot prints of the residents and potential foot tracks. Once again, conditions were in favor of the shadowy intruders, leaving more mysteries than answers.

The haphazard shooting and tense situation ultimately left the BFRO investigators with a nervous feeling. They were certainly interested in potential evidence or proof, but it was apparent the Humphreys just wanted the beasts to be gone as opposed to implementing some elaborate system to obtain evidence. Roberts and Lawler felt confident that Tim and Mike could protect themselves in that case, and decided to leave before someone was shot in the process. They instructed the brothers to call if they did end up with some concrete evidence.

As word of the "siege" got out, it attracted the attention of the Oklahoma Department of Wildlife Conservation. After a brief investigation into the situation, officials urged the Humphreys to stop shooting at the creatures and instead address the underlying problem, which seemed to be the availability of venison. If the brothers would refrain from deer hunting on the property and remove the meat from the shed, perhaps it would diffuse the situation, whether it be hungry Bigfoots or any other animals. The Humphreys complied and soon the sightings, vocalizations, and other incidents became less and less frequent. Perhaps the creatures, realizing that food was no longer available, moved on as they normally would, roaming to other parts of the Kiamichi Mountains.

As far as the BFRO involvement, the story pretty much ends there. But according to Mike, the story of the siege had one final, dramatic scene. One year later, Tim's wife was pulling into the driveway one evening with the children when huge rocks began to fly towards the car. Moments later several creatures appeared and started screaming at them. She immediately turned the car around and drove to Mike's house in Talihina for help. Tim was at work, so it was her only option.

"My nephews were hysterical and my niece was in shock," Mike told me. "She was three years old and I had to help her out of the car because she had climbed up under the passenger-side dash of the car."

Realizing they were back with a vengeance, Mike and two friends raced to Honobia. When they arrived, Tim was already standing by the driveway looking down at the big rocks. He told Mike that he and his father-in-law had seen a "massive creature" standing across the road as they pulled in moments before.

It was the last straw. Tim loved the beautiful countryside that was their home, but he could no longer endure the risk to his family. A short time later he packed up his family and moved away. Bigfoot, in his eyes, was not a gentle beast. It was something straight out of nightmares, to be feared and, hopefully, forgotten.

SCARS

One of the most disturbing cases of an alleged Bigfoot attack I've come across was reported in 2002 by a woman from Paris, Texas, a mere 70 miles southwest of Honobia. The woman, whom I'll identify only as Debra for privacy reasons, told investigators from the Texas Bigfoot Research Center that she and her husband were driving one evening near Lake Crook north of Paris when their truck became stuck in the mud. Her husband did not have a radio or cell phone, so the only option was to walk to the nearest town so he could summon a wrecker to pull them out. Under the circumstances, Debra decided it would be best to wait in truck while he hurried. It was a decision she would come to regret.

After her husband departed, Debra rolled down the windows, kicked back in the seat, and settled in for the wait. It was a warm Texas evening and the air seemed peaceful and relaxing. She eventually started to doze off but was jolted awake by a loud scream. It sounded as if it had come from a large animal; one that she was not familiar with.

The scream was unsettling, but after five minutes with no further sounds, she relaxed again. That's when she caught sight of three figures walking towards the driver's side door. They were large, bulky, and covered in hair. Judging by the anatomy, one was male and the other two were females. They all looked fierce and ape-like, yet there was something strangely human about them.

When they reached the truck, the male quickly reached through the driver's side window, grabbed Debra's leg with its massive hand, and tried to pull her out of the truck. Fortunately, the animal was so bulky it could only fit one shoulder through the window so he was limited to one arm for pulling.

Debra fought for what seemed like several minutes, beating at the creature's arm with one hand and grasping the steering wheel with the other in a desperate attempt to keep it from pulling her out of the cab. During the struggle, one of the female creatures let out a scream. Debra was convinced they would soon join in, making it impossible to hold her ground within the safety of the truck.

In a final effort to fend off her assailant, Debra grabbed an empty soda bottle from the floorboard. She hit the creature with it as hard as she could until it finally released her and pulled its arm from the cab. As soon as it did, Debra rolled up the window and locked the door. She huddled inside, shaking violently from the fear and adrenaline. She was certain they would make another attempt to get her. However, as quickly as they had come, the creatures suddenly turned and ran back into the woods.

Debra collapsed on the seat, her leg bleeding where the creature's fingernails had scratched her. A short time later, she heard the welcome hum of a car motor. It was her husband returning with a wrecker. When he reached the truck, Debra frantically told him of the experience. Stunned, he pulled the car from the mud and rushed her to the nearest hospital in Paris. There she was treated and released within hours.

Following her recovery, Debra did some research and came across the TBRC website (one of the few places to report such a thing back in a 2002). She first reached out with an email and then spoke to investigators by phone. Long-time TBRC investigator, Jerry Hestand, remembers the events well. He told me that Debra showed them the scars on her leg and submitted to an extensive video-taped interview. Her story, though absolutely incredible, was convincing and never altered during subsequent conversations. They could not prove its absolute validity, of course, but most members of the group felt strongly that something strange had indeed taken place. According to Debra, the ordeal only lasted a few minutes, but it's something that will haunt her for the rest of her life.

The same thing could be said for a man in Mississippi who reported an even more violent encounter in 2016. According to researcher Don McDonald—who interviewed the witness on several occasions—the man was hunting one afternoon in the forest of central Mississippi. He was sitting quietly when a tall, hairy, bipedal creature walked into view approximately 50 feet away. At first the creature didn't see the hunter, but it finally turned its head and looked right at him.

The hunter watched the creature for several seconds, trying to decide if he should run, shoot, or just be still. About the time the creature started to move on, however, the man heard a twig snap behind him. Seconds later, another hairy creature rushed from the woods, grabbed him by the arm, and hurled him towards the nearest tree. The hunter felt himself collide with the hard wood before everything went black.

Sometime later, perhaps 30 minutes, the man finally awoke. There were no creatures in sight, but pain was shooting through his body. His side hurt and his collarbone felt broken, and he was bleeding from the head. Fighting back the pain, the hunter managed to hobble out of the woods and drive home. When he arrived, his wife immediately rushed him to the emergency room where he was treated for a broken collarbone, broken ribs, dislocated shoulder, fractured skull, and a punctured lung.

Needless to say the experience resulted in an extended hospital stay and a new fear of the woods. A creature he once thought to be a harmless legend was now a dangerous reality. He was reluctant to tell anyone what actually happened—and asked that his name be kept from this record—yet he feels he must warn others of the possible dangers lurking out there. Like Debra, the scars are an everyday reminder.

4. NATIVE GIANTS

In a land rich with Native American heritage and tales of Bigfoot, one should naturally expect the two subjects to intertwine. In other words, if these hairy giants and shadowy ape-like figures exist today, then surely the original caretakers of the Southern expanse would have encountered them. Without an extensive written history it's hard to say for sure, but upon examining their language, story traditions, and modern day beliefs, it certainly suggests they may have been familiar with the same creatures we now refer to as Bigfoot.

One such tribe, the Caddo Indians, lived along the Red River basin in Texas, Arkansas, Louisiana, and Oklahoma.[34] The Red River is, as we've learned, relevant to our starting point of Boggy Creek as well as other accounts we've explored so far. Upon examining the language of the Caddos, we find an interesting term. According to Kathy Strain, archaeologist and author of *Giants, Cannibals & Monsters: Bigfoot in Native Culture*, the Caddos used the word *ha'yacatsi* to describe a race of "lost giants" said to live in the region. "Lost giant" doesn't tell us whether this race was covered in hair, but it certainly brings to mind the huge, man-like apes reported in the very locations where the Caddo Indians once roamed.

The similarity is further supported by other tribes, including the Choctaw whose language included the phrases *Nalusa falaya*, which translates to "big giant" or "black giant," and *shampe*, which refers to "giant monster." *Nalusa falaya* is the more common term among the Mississippi Choctaw, while in Oklahoma the term *shampe* is more widely used. In both cases, the name is associated with a hairy giant who lived deep in the forest and harassed hunters, who are then compelled to leave a portion of their kill for him.

The Creek tribe, found throughout parts of Alabama, Georgia, Florida, and North Carolina, used a term that undeniably evokes images of Bigfoot. *Honka,* which means "hairy man," was a large, dark "man" who lived at the tribe's perimeter. Honka was said to be elusive and favored privacy, which the tribe duly respected. The Seminoles, who once inhabited Arkansas and Oklahoma and later, Florida, likewise had a word for a "tall hairy man" called *Ssti capcaki.*[35] A similar entity called *Eeyachuba* (wild man) was known to the Alabama Coushatta tribe.

Admittedly there's a gray area between what the natives considered "spirit beings" or "boogeymen" characters and those we know as flesh and blood animals, but it's hard to overlook the similarities between their tales of giant, hairy wild men and modern day Bigfoot reports. This doesn't prove that Bigfoot exists now, or then, but the fact that this concept was part of their collective history is noteworthy, and certainly more in favor of unknown primates than if there were absolutely no mentions of huge, hairy forest dwellers at all.

The creatures are still known to modern-day tribe members, having carried down beliefs from their ancestors, or in some cases having experienced a personal encounter themselves. Their beliefs range in concept from the creatures being flesh and blood mammals to being extraordinary entities who possess supernatural powers. Depending on the tribe and the individual, I've heard many perspectives on the subject, but one thing seems to be common: that there is some sort of hairy, man-like creature who has always lived in the forests of North America and who has, to varying degrees, interacted with the Native American peoples.

A logical place to explore the Native American's relationship to Bigfoot is Oklahoma. Prior to European contact, the state was home to the indigenous tribes of Wichitas, Caddos, Apaches, and Quapaws.[36] Following European arrival, the Osages, Pawnees, Kiowas, and Comanches migrated into Oklahoma, displacing most of the earlier peoples. When the Indian Removal Act was enacted by the U.S. government in 1830, all Eastern Indians west of the Mississippi River were forced onto reservations in Oklahoma, which became known as "Indian Territory." As a result, the land is rich with Native American heritage, one that includes stories of hairy, man-like giants passed down through the years.

In an article published in the September/October 2005 issue of *Oklahoma Today*, Riley Donica, a 72-year-old woman who grew up riding horses in the mountains around Honobia, recounted a story she heard long ago from a local Choctaw woman. According to Donica, trappers along the Red River basin often traveled along the Kiamichi River with the help of Choctaw guides. "This Choctaw woman told me there were giants up there and that evidently the Choctaw guides wouldn't go any further up the Kiamichi because there was something there beyond their willingness to deal with," she stated.[37]

Another Choctaw woman, Charlene Cusher, told reporters from *The Oklahoman* that she remembered hearing similar stories from her grandparents. One of them involved a small boy who wandered into the forest and got lost. "When they found the boy he was fine," Cusher recalled. "He said 'that thing' took care of him," implying that the "thing" was the large, hairy creature said to live in the Kiamichis.[38]

The presence of Bigfoot is also backed up by encounters with current residents of both Native American and Anglo decent. The town of Honobia, cite of the infamous "siege," is a prime example where not only countless sightings have been reported, but the resident tribes still acknowledge and respect the ongoing presence of these mystery animals. In fact, Bigfoot is so ingrained in the local culture that all around Honobia you can find visual reminders by way of road signs, souvenir shops, and wooden silhouettes of Bigfoot standing along the winding mountain roads. Honobia even hosts an annual Bigfoot Conference featuring well-known Bigfoot researchers and local historians who remind the attendees that Oklahoma, believe it or not, is truly a hotbed of man-ape activity.

It's a common misperception that Oklahoma is mostly a flat, barren wasteland so devalued by the federal government that they were willing to set it aside as a reservation. The state is, in fact, home to marvelous mountains, rich farmlands, twisting rivers, and dense hardwood forests where an unknown primate could easily find a suitable home. It is not surprising then, that some of the most in-triguing cases of the Southern Sasquatch come from this very state.

BIGFOOT WAR

One of the most fantastic tales involving Oklahoma natives is that of the so-called "Human-Bigfoot War." First circulated on the internet by a gentleman known as Dr. Tuklo Nashoba, the story re-lates an Oklahoma legend from 1855 in which a group of Choctaw Cavalry riders confront a horde of aggressive, cannibalistic "man-beasts."[39] As the story goes, farmers in the area of Leflore County (near what is now the McCurtain County Wilderness Area) had been suffering raids by shadowy bandits. The bandits had not only been taking large quantities of corn, squash, and beans, but had also kidnapped several children. To resolve this serious situation, 30 Choctaw Cavalry "light-horsemen" were assigned to flush them out and bring home the children. Among others, the team includ-ed Choctaw tribesmen Hamas Tubbee and his six sons, along with Captain Joshua LeFlore. Leflore was said to be part French and part Choctaw, but he commanded a deep respect from his men due to his incomparable honesty and legendary bravery.

The troop set off from the tribal capital of Tuskaloma on a hot July day, riding up the Glover River, and eventually to the loca-tion where the bandits were thought to be hiding near Little River. After resting, LeFlore led his troop within 500 yards of the bandits' camp where he halted to survey the layout with a "ship's eyepiece" (telescope). When he was ready, he ordered his horsemen to charge full speed ahead. As the troop neared the camp, an overwhelm-ing stench of death "assaulted both men and horses," so much that the horses began to buck and throw the riders into the heavy pine thicket.

Tubbee and his sons, along with Captain LeFlore, were the only ones who managed to keep their mounts under control, allow-ing them to ride into the outlaw camp. What they found there was horrifying. The clearing behind the initial tree cover was actually a "large, earthen mound." Upon the mound lay the corpses of human children in varying states of decay. The bandits themselves had apparently fled, leaving "three really large, hairy ape-like creatures" standing by the mound.

Captain LeFlore quickly charged the creatures, brandishing a sword in one hand and a pistol in the other. The closest creature hit his horse with a massive blow, killing it and sending LeFlore to the ground. The captain immediately emptied his revolver into the creature, but to no avail. He then advanced with his sabre, delivering several bloody blows before the monster grabbed him and literally ripped his head off.

As LeFlore's body collapsed, the Tubbees opened fire on the beasts with "50-caliber Sharp's buffalo rifles." Two of the creatures fell as bullets penetrated their heads, but the third managed to escape by running for the trees. Eighteen-year-old Robert Tubbee, a massive young man himself at "six feet eleven inches," chased down the wounded beast and finished it off with a hunting knife.

The Tubbees surveyed the horrific scene, counting a total of 19 dead children who appeared to have been partially consumed. The overpowering stench of the decaying bodies and the ape creatures themselves caused the men to wretch, but they managed to bury the children and their beloved Captain. At the end they gave him a solemn, 21-gun salute.

As for the strange man-beasts, the Tubbees piled them up and burned their bodies in a huge bonfire. "As they rode back into Tuskahoma, each man struggled with emotions and thoughts he never before imagined."

The story is fascinating, but is it true? There was indeed a Choctaw by the name of Joshua LeFlore, according to the Indian Territory's Dawes Roll Registry Card #4174.[40] (The Dawes Roll lists individuals who chose to enroll and were approved for membership in the Five Civilized Tribes: Cherokee, Chickasaw, Choctaw, Creek, and Seminole.) However, he's listed as full blood Choctaw. There's also a Robert Tubbee on the list, as well as other Tubbee men. This doesn't authenticate the story but provides a possible link to reality. The specifics of a "50-caliber Sharp's buffalo rifle" are questionable, as fine details such as this are typically lost when stories are passed down through the years. Not to mention, the 50-caliber model wasn't available until 1871.[41] So either this is smoking gun for fabrication or Dr. Nashoba enhanced the original legend. Regardless, the big question has to do with "man-beasts." Are these truly giant, hairy apes or simply bandits that didn't deserve to be called humans? The conclusion that these were actually Bigfoots can only be presumed.

Before completely writing off the tale as complete fiction, however, there are cases where archeologists have apparently found "giants" in the vicinity of Oklahoma. According to Sherry Cottle Graham, author of *Blood Brothers: The Forgotten Children of the Mound Builders*, two giant skeletons were reportedly unearthed at the Spiro Mound, one being seven-foot-tall and the other eight-foot-tall.[42] The Spiro Mound is an important Mississippian-era archaeological site located near the town of Spiro, Oklahoma, less than two hours from Little River (which was near the bandit's camp). Perhaps at the very least, the man-apes were in fact huge, brutish humans that defied normal explanation.

Whatever the case, the Little River is also the site of modern reports. According to an article in the August 2005 edition of the *Oklahoman*, a Choctaw man by the name of Billy Ludlow claimed to have seen a "gigantic, bipedal creature" on Little River in 1951.[43] Ludlow, who was 11 years old at the time, said he and two friends were playing beneath an unfinished bridge one night when they heard the sound of metal snapping above. "I looked up and saw this large, hairy animal stand up on two legs like a man," Ludlow said. "I'd guess it to be 9 or 10 feet tall with broad shoulders and hair all over."

Frightened, the boys turned and ran towards Ludlow's grandmother's cabin. As they ran they could hear the animal—or whatever it was—pursuing them through the woods. When they reached the cabin, they quickly got inside and slammed the door. Moments later something walked onto the porch and attempted to get in.

"Something came and pushed the door two or three times, and

then went away," Ludlow explained. It was an experience he will never forget.

According to an old article from the *McCurtain Sunday Gazette*, a rancher was hunting along the Little River in June 1975 when he encountered a similar creature.[44] He said he was walking along the bank, downstream from Yashau Creek, when a "manbeast" emerged from the brush on the opposite side. When it saw the hunter, it "broke into a sort of loping run" and disappeared from sight. The rancher said the beast was approximately eight feet tall with long arms and grayish-black hair. He observed it walking upright on two legs with a "shuffling gait" until it began running.

Startled, but apparently unfazed, the rancher began to look for evidence of the creature's passing. He managed to find strands of hair on a nearby branch and a 17-inch-long track in the soil. He collected the hair sample and took several photographs of the track, which he sent to a Bigfoot research group based in Portland, Oregon. The group, however, could draw no definitive conclusion about either the source of the hair or the maker of the tracks. The

One of Oklahoma's many scenic rivers
(Photo by Lyle Blackburn)

rancher had shown diligence, but whatever it was he saw along the Little River remained a mystery.

NOWATA MAN-THINGS

Further north in Nowata County, the native peoples also told of a large, hairy creature that lived in the forest. Former ranch owner Jim Strong heard the stories many times from his grandmother, who grew up there. But it wasn't just legends of the past. She had an interesting tale of her own.

According to my colleague Jerry Hestand, who interviewed Strong in 2005, his grandmother was 10 years old in 1917 when their neighbors claimed to have caught a strange animal in their barn and wanted her family to come see it. When she and her family arrived, whatever was inside the barn was banging loudly, trying to get out. The men standing guard outside became frightened and started shooting through the barn door. As wood splinters and gun smoke filled the air, they heard a huge crash on the backside of the barn. When they went around to investigate, they found a gaping hole in the wall where the thing had busted free. It was nowhere to be seen.

The neighbor was so distressed he instructed everyone to say it was one of his bulls that made the hole in the barn. Strong's grandmother was never sure what was really inside, although the native legends always haunted her when she thought of the bizarre incident. The bullet holes were definitely there. Strong had seen them himself, but like his grandmother, he had never personally seen anything that fit the description of Bigfoot... that is, until 1990. In the fall of that year Strong was at the ranch house one afternoon when a dark storm began to brew in the distance. As the storm neared, thunder and lightning increased and eventually knocked out the electricity.

To restore power, Strong had to replace a fuse in the electrical box located on the front porch. After doing so, he turned on the perimeter lights and looked around. That's when he caught sight of a tall, dark figure standing near a grain bin at the end of their driveway about 100 yards away. A chill went down his spine. The figure was so strange and out of place, he ran to his truck to grab a gun.

When he returned, the thing was no longer visible but reappeared within moments. Strong immediately fired six rounds, aiming as best he could in the overcast conditions. As soon as he started shooting, the creature moved away so quickly he doubted that any of the shots hit the target.

Strong's family members, and even some neighbors, heard the commotion and came to see what was happening. As he was telling them what he had seen, they heard something running through the nearby woods. Strong's father quickly jumped into the truck, while the rest gave chase on foot until they came to a large alfalfa field. They couldn't see the creature until Strong's father drove in from the opposite side of the field, shining his headlights across dusky expanse. As soon as the truck lights hit it, the thing jumped up and began running at an incredible speed. At that point they could see it had the general form of a human, but was covered in hair. It was also much faster than a human, as it covered a long distance in a very short time before ultimately escaping into the woods.

Nothing further was seen until several years later. One night Strong and a friend were fishing in a nearby creek when they shined a spotlight into the woods looking for animals. Catching some eyeshine, they focused the light to see a "large, man-like creature" — perhaps the same one — stand up and bolt through the woods. The creature ran until it approached a small group of cattle a short distance away. Again, Strong shined the light in its direction as the cows began to bellow. The beast then made a strange gesture with its arm and ran into the woods out of sight. Strong and his fishing partner quickly packed up their gear and fled the area. It was apparent that something more tangible than legends were living in those woods.

And perhaps they were. In 1974, several people claimed to have seen a similar creature near the town of Watova.[45] They described it as being tall, hairy and man-like. Nowata County was also the location of the infamous "Noxie Monster" hunt of 1975. Just before La-bor Day that year, a local farmer named Kenneth Tosh reportedly found himself face-to-face with something he would never forget. According to an article from the *Coshocton Tribune*, he was out walking when he realized something was standing a mere 10 feet away. He looked up to see a creature he described as "seven feet tall, hairy, foul-smelling and with eyes that glowed like a cat."[46] As soon as he saw the thing, it growled, sending Tosh into a panicked run in the opposite direction.

When he reached his house, Tosh immediately phoned Nowata County Sheriff Bob Arnold, who agreed to meet Tosh at the scene. The sheriff found nothing on his initial search, but he later came across an unusual track approximately one mile south of the site. "The print appeared to be eroded in the toe area," he stated. "It was about 6 inches wide and 11 inches long."[47] He made a plaster cast for safekeeping.

Following Ken Tosh's initial sighting, others had their own run-in with the alleged creature. Apparently Tosh's wife, son, and broth-er all saw it in the vicinity. Like Tosh, they described it as a Bigfoot-like animal. They also heard strange noises coming from the woods surrounding the farm. Jim Tosh said he was in the front yard when they heard a strange scream. "It was a high shrill scream," he said. "I could see these two big eyes just staring at me. It turned and looked away. When I looked back, it was gone."[48]

Outside of the Tosh family, 11 other Noxie residents observed—and in one case, shot at—a creature fitting the same description. The witnesses ranged in age from 15 to 72 years old and were "all considered reliable, responsible people by other Noxie residents."[49] The situation put the entire town on alert. Some residents even took up arms and attempted to track down and kill the shadowy monster.

As news of the events began to leak out, hordes of monster hunt-ers and Bigfoot researchers descended on the town. Much like the case of the Fouke Monster earlier in the 1970s, the ruckus quickly got out of hand with a mix of beer, guns, and monster fever threat-ening to injure people as much as the creature itself. In an attempt to avoid any such tragedy, Sheriff Arnold asked people to stay away. He already had an unconfirmed report that one horse and two dogs had been shot by monster hunters.

"A young person in this day and age, with long hair and a lot of stuff on his face, might at night look like a Wolfman and one of these guys that are drinking their beer might want to blow him to bits," he quipped at the time.

Needless to say, the chaos—which was covered by representatives of Canadian, English, and Japanese media outlets—did not result in any dead specimens or other proof. As soon as monster hunters poured into the woods, any such large animals no doubt made their way for high ground or thicker woods to avoid being caught in the fray.

CASINO CREATURE

While a majority of sightings in the Native lands occur near thick woods or remote mountains, there are other accounts which suggest these creatures may occasionally venture into the open Cross Timbers region of central Oklahoma. Given the potential for detection in such a place, it seems unusual, but nonetheless credible sighting reports and a dramatic video recorded near a tribal casino in 2000 offer potential verification.

In one report, a young man who lived on Cheyenne and Arapaho tribal land in Canadian County said he was driving with his father and brother when they saw two huge, upright animals walking along a railroad track.[50] "They were at least all of eight foot tall," he said. "They were black, hairy, and kind of hunched over when they walked."

The men were on their way to a hunting area when they spotted the creatures at a considerable distance down the tracks. The men used their binoculars to get a better look. The incident was so alarming, the man said his brother refused to ever hunt in the area again.

The report went on to mention that other tribe members had

recently seen these creatures in the vicinity, and their "tribal owned casino" had captured video footage of one such animal on its outdoor security camera.

Similar reports were being sent to the Bigfoot Field Research Organization. According to former BFRO investigator Alton Higgins, the BFRO received half a dozen reports from tribe members who mentioned the alleged video. Not all of the individuals had actually seen the video, but there seemed to be no question it existed.[51]

After verifying the reports were legit, several BFRO investigators from the Oklahoma area were dispatched to interview witnesses and, hopefully, get a look at the footage. One of the first to arrive was Roger Roberts. Roberts, who would later investigate the "Siege of Honobia," incidents, lived close enough to the casino that he could be on the scene within a short time. He first made contact with the wildlife manager of the tribal land, who allowed him to look around the casino and the property surrounding it. As far as the video, the casino owners were reluctant show it to outsiders for fear it might attract unwanted publicity or trespassers, but Roberts convinced them he was only interested in research and would not call in the media. The owners finally agreed to let Roberts and two other investigators see the film. They were the first people outside of casino personnel to view it.

Roberts and the other men were led into the security room of the casino where images on the surveillance cameras were monitored and recorded. The camera in question had a view from the rear of the building where it overlooked an employee parking lot containing a grease trap dumpster. Next to the dumpster stood a pole with a mercury light mounted on top. Beyond the parking lot was a fence and an open area that eventually dropped off into a ravine. The investigators sat down to watch what amounted to several seconds of footage recorded on this camera.

When the footage was played, the men could see a very large, bipedal figure walk from right to left across the far end of the parking lot. Details were hard to discern, but there was no doubt the subject was massive. It walked past the mercury light, ducking briefly as it did, before looking into the dumpster and then moving off frame. In an interview with the Bigfoot Information Project podcast host, Brian Brown, Roberts described exactly what he saw:

> It was a nine-or-ten-foot, 700-pound animal illuminated by the mercury light. What struck me was the size of this animal and the speed that it covered the back of the parking lot. In four or five strides, it was from one end of that parking lot over to where that dumpster is.
> When it got to the grease trap, it seemed to duck underneath the mercury light and it leaned over the grease trap.[52]

One could surmise it was simply a human, but Rogers didn't get that impression. It was just too huge, a fact that was verified when the investigators measured the light pole and calculated the figure's relative height of at least nine feet. The security officer played the video numerous times so the team could examine the details, one of which was perplexing. According to Roberts:

> On the top of this animal's head was a kind of a green glow, almost like something you'd see in a nightvision scope. So they backed it up several times, and we observed and tried to speculate what this green glow could have been. The only thing I could think of was that the mercury light reflected into this animal's eyes at the top of his head, and the eyes are so powerful that it reflected this light back in some way.

In conversations with other casino employees, the investigators learned this wasn't the only time the creature had apparently been seen in the area. A bus driver, who transported people to and from the casino, claimed to have seen it one evening. According to this individual, he had parked the bus behind the building after unloading passengers. As he was cleaning up inside, he noticed the creature looking in one of the windows. It frightened him so badly, he hid on the floor until the creature was gone.

Other employees claimed to have seen it lurking behind the

casino and often digging around in the grease trap. One of the local residents said the creatures had been seen in the area for decades. Tribe members told Roberts they acknowledged the presence of the creatures, which they considered to be another tribe. They would, on occasion, leave food out for them, but would not go into the fields behind the casino after dark. They respected the creatures but also feared them.

To further corroborate the video, a trackway of huge footprints had been found in the fine soil leading up to the parking lot, along the same path the creature had walked. Roberts and his team examined them carefully. They were impressed not only by the size of the foot but by the stride. According to Roberts, the stride measured 55 inches from heel to toe on average.

The BFRO investigators made casts of the prints and asked if they could have a copy of the video, but the casino owners denied their request, saying they did not want it to go public. However, someone had already leaked the news to the media. A short time after Rogers arrived, television reporters descended on the casino. They were denied access to the video altogether and promptly escorted off the property. The incident did not help in the BFRO's efforts to obtain a copy of the video, but at least it showed the casino was not purposely seeking publicity by staging a Bigfoot hoax. If they had, then surely they would have jumped at the chance to have their casino featured on the news.

After the investigation, Rogers and his team remained in contact with one of the non-tribal employees who worked on the casino's computers systems. They were still hoping to get a copy of the footage. The employee promised to try, but the connection went dead when he suddenly moved to Canada. To this day, no one knows whether the video was erased or whether a copy still sits on a shelf somewhere collecting dust.

Whatever the case, a series of photos taken in November 2000 on the same tribal land offer support for the premise that Bigfoot roams the area. According to Alton Higgins, who submitted a formal article about the photographs to *The Relic Hominoid Inquiry* publication, they were taken by Russell Lumpmouth, a member of the Arapaho tribe.[53] According to Lumpmouth, he and several men were cleaning up after an outdoor tribal function when they began taking photos to document their efforts. When Lumpmouth's supervisor posed for a photo in front of some trash, Lumpmouth noticed a dark object step into the background of the camera's viewfinder. The figure—or whatever it was—appeared to be standing behind the foliage just beyond the clearing. Lumpmouth hurriedly snapped the first photo then advanced several steps to take a second one. Whatever it was disappeared back into the woods at that point, and the men chose not to pursue it.

The photos, which show a dark shape behind some branches, were later printed on high quality 8x10 photo paper and examined by the tribal members before informing Higgins. The photos are by no means clear enough to prove anything, however, after careful analysis, Higgins feels they could depict the same creature described by the locals, and perhaps even the one seen on the casino surveillance video.

In an effort to validate the photos, Higgins interviewed Lumpmouth and visited the exact location where the photos had been taken. Believing the tribesman to be telling the truth, Higgins set out to create simulation photos that could be compared to the originals in order to assess the relative size of the subject. For this purpose, he positioned a person behind a distinctive tree visible in both original photographs. "Photos were taken using a human model positioned near the small tree so as to derive a conservative estimate of the subject's size," stated Higgins in the report. "The man in the comparison photo held a 2.3 m (7.5-ft) pole draped with an Army field jacket. This photo was cropped and enlarged to enable side-by-side comparisons with the subject depicted in the original photographs."

In the resulting side-by-side comparison, the subject "towers" over the man with the pole. "Extrapolations indicate the possibility of a stature in excess of 2.3 m (7.5 ft)," Higgins explained. In other words, whatever it was in those photos was massive when compared to the human stand-in. Higgins could only conclude that it was either a clever hoax—which he did not believe after interviewing

Native Giant by Joshua Foster

the subject—or it was some sort of unidentified species fitting the description of Bigfoot.

CROSS TIMBERS SNOW APE

It's hard to imagine such a creature would be bold enough to roam the open prairies of the Cross Timbers, but sightings in this area are not completely out in left field if we consider the principle of "They Always Follow The Creeks." As in many of the cases we've examined so far, the sightings in central Oklahoma tend to correspond with natural waterways. The casino location, for example, is just north of the Canadian River, a major U.S. drainage basin that slices diagonally across Oklahoma as it flows toward Arkansas. The casino is also in proximity to the smaller North Canadian River, which carves a twisting, parallel course several miles north of its counterpart. Along the way it passes close to El Reno (site of the infamous "El Reno Chicken Man" case of 1970) and other reported sighting locations, including one in nearby Edmond where eyewitness Matt Berger experienced a chilling incident in January 1982.

According to an interview I conducted with Berger, he was working at a fast-food job one day when a heavy snowstorm dropped a blanket of white on the area. He was 15 at the time and had no car, so he was forced to walk home when the restaurant shut down early.

It had stopped snowing by the time he began his trek, but he seemed to be the only person moving around, judging by the complete absence of tire tracks or footprints in the pristine snow. He had walked approximately one mile towards a heavily wooded area, when he passed a thick line of trees to the east. As he cleared them, he observed movement to his left. When he turned to look, he was surprised to see a figure playing in the snow.

Berger first thought it was child wearing a dark snowsuit. But as he continued to observe the figure, he came to the stark realization that it was not a child—and perhaps not even human. "I had a very clear view of it and could see that it was black, or very close to black, and covered with long hair or fur from head to toe," he told me. "It was probably around five feet tall, and weighed about 160 lbs."

As Berger watched unnoticed from a mere 30 yards away, the creature continued to frolic, bending at the waist, scooping snow, and throwing it into the air as if it were having fun. It also began rolling in the snow, giving Berger the opportunity to study it further. But the more he did, the more he felt a growing sense of alarm. "I felt stark terror at the sight of the thing," he said. "I was also very unnerved knowing that I was very far from any residential area, in the early morning, and that there was absolutely no traffic on the road."

At that point, Berger began to weigh his options. He thought about running but felt such an action would catch the creature's attention and perhaps cause it to give chase. The thing seemed playful, but in the surreal, snowy isolation, Berger didn't want to take any chances. "I continued walking the same route, my eyes on the ape, until I figured I was out of hearing range," he told me. "Then I ran as hard and fast as I could all the way home."

The area where the creature was spotted has since been turned into a park, but at the time it was a wooded area with the ravine running through it. The ravine flows eastward until it dumps into Arcadia Lake, a short distance from the North Canadian River. Berger, who is now a police officer, maintains that it was some sort of animal; one that he cannot not explain. If so, it must have been using the ravine as a way to travel, stopping for a moment to enjoy the strange white crystals that had covered its native land.

5. Mountain Monsters and Valley Apes

On a cool October afternoon I stood atop a mountain in eastern Oklahoma not far from Honobia. I was only a few hours from my home in Texas, but it seemed like a world away. From my vantage point, I could see an endless fabric of green as it stretched across the distant peaks and valleys below. It was both breathtaking and refreshing to see that such a vast tract of land could still exist beyond the clutches of human progress.

As I sat atop the peak enjoying the view, I tuned into the myriad of sounds around me. Squirrels jumping between trees; birds flitting about; trees creaking in the gentle breeze. Each added to the relaxing serenity of the scene, but not as much as the sounds I couldn't hear. There was no whir of a highway, no airplanes, or even the pumping of oil derricks I was used to on our hunting lease in Texas. It was truly a wild world where I was but one element of a great, organic order. Perhaps one that includes a rare animal who remains one of its best kept secrets.

The place where I stood was deep within the Ouachita Mountain Range, an area that includes both the mountains and 1.8 million acres of national forestry, which blankets the border between eastern Oklahoma and western Arkansas. It's one of several mountainous areas in the southern United States where Bigfoot activity has been reported. And it certainly made sense from my perspective. The location where I had ventured was remote and required a considerable amount of driving and hiking to reach it. If there were places in the South where mysterious creatures could hide, this was surely one of them.

View from the Ouachita Mountains
(Photo by Lyle Blackburn)

The western end of the Ouachitas includes the Kiamichi sub-range where we have already learned of Bigfoot encounters and stories dating back to the Native Americans. But that's just the beginning. This trend of sightings continues eastward as the range rises above the Arkansas Valley and the South Central Plains. All across this wild and untamed region, people from all walks of life have reported encounters with mysterious, ape-like creatures.

One of the earliest tales appeared in the 1941 book *Ozark Country* by folklorist Otto Ernest Rayburn.[54] In this account, Rayburn documents a tale from 1865 in which a "giant wild man" was captured in the Ouachita Mountains near Saline County, Arkansas. According to the story, the wild man was often seen in the area near the Saline River where he was thought to live in caves. He was said to be seven feet tall and covered with thick hair, a frightful vision to anyone who had encountered him.

The locals, worried what might happen if the wild man were to attack someone, decided to send a posse to capture him. One afternoon they approached a cave where he was hiding, lassoed him, and transported him back to the town of Benton where he was confined to the jail. The locals tried to dress him in clothes, but apparently he didn't take kindly to it, since he tore them off and attempted a great escape. The wild man was recaptured, but the story doesn't explain his ultimate fate. Rayburn's account simply ends there.

In recent times, reports with far more credibility and sobering facts have emerged from the Ouachitas. One of the most intriguing originated from a place not far from where I stood gazing across the valley that day. It had come from Terry Davis, a skilled outdoorsman who had been turkey hunting near Big Cedar, Oklahoma, in 2004. In a report filed with the Texas Bigfoot Research Conservancy and later dramatized on the television show *MonsterQuest*, Davis said he was hunting with his girlfriend and brother in the Ouachita National Forest on April 17.[55] It was early evening and they had all spread out, with Davis having set up his portable hunting blind along a creek bottom. As he settled in, he blew a locator call that mimicked a screaming hawk. He then sat back to wait for turkey.

After about 15 minutes Davis said he noticed a dark shape about 50 yards away he hadn't seen before. He thought it might be a burnt tree, but just to be sure, he raised his gun and looked through the scope. He was shocked to see it was actually an ape-like creature standing upright on two legs. It was approximately eight feet tall with dark, charcoal-colored hair about three inches long all over its body. It was bulky with huge biceps, arms, and legs, and had a pointed, dome-shaped head. Overall it reminded Davis of the subject seen in the famous Patterson-Gimlin Bigfoot film.

As Davis observed the creature, he could see it was fully aware of his presence and, in fact, looked right back at him with reddish-colored eyes. During the time he watched it, Davis also got whiffs of a strong odor much like "a fox den." The creature stood there for a few minutes, he said, before it finally walked off on two legs and disappeared from view.

Davis felt the creature had been attracted by his initial locator call and was merely curious. But no matter why the creature had come there, its presence spooked the seasoned hunter so badly he no longer wanted to be in the woods. Subsequent events didn't help matters. A week after the sighting, Davis said he and his nephew were sitting outside his sister's home when they heard "loud screams" coming from the mountain where he had been hunting.[56] It sounded like a large animal that he nor his nephew had heard before. The screams were so unsettling, his sister's cows panicked and ran under a light for safety.

The following January, Terry's brother, Jim, received word that a road crew was working on a bridge east of Big Cedar when the inspection engineer discovered a set of large, man-like tracks 50 yards from the site. Jim and their nephew, both interested in proving what Terry had seen in the woods, immediately drove to the location and examined the fresh tracks. The ground was dry, so whatever had made them must have been quite heavy. The two men could see evidence of a pliable foot in the way the toes separated and varied among the tracks. In their opinion, the prints did not appear to have been made from wooden stamp or any other type of device typical of a hoax.

My colleague Jerry Hestand followed up a short time later. When he arrived on the scene, only two tracks were still visible, but from what he could see they resembled human feet, except broader and much longer. A measurement revealed they were 16.5 inches long by 8 inches across at the ball of the foot.[57] He and several other investigators scoured the area but found no further trace of their maker. It was disappointing, but things were just getting started, as a research effort of unprecedented magnitude was mounting in the Ouachitas.

AREA X

Beginning in 2011, the group now known as the North American Wood Ape Conservancy (NAWAC) began a dedicated scientific study in the Oklahoma portion of the Ouachita Mountain range to determine whether Bigfoot creatures are indeed present. It isn't the only Bigfoot-related study that's ever been conducted, but it's arguably one of the most intensive, lengthy, and meticulously documented endeavors that's been undertaken for this purpose—not just in the South, but anywhere.

According to their *Ouachita Project* monograph, a 228-page document posted by the group in March 2015, the purpose of the on-going study is "to facilitate official recognition, protection, and conservation of what [the group] believes is a rare unlisted North American anthropoid species."[58] The location for the study was chosen by NAWAC for both its long history of encounters with a possible undocumented primate—classified by the group as a "wood ape"—and its remote seclusion. The area of study is on a large tract of private land deep within the Ouachita range. I've visited the site myself and can attest to its isolation. Only a single, unpaved, and often rocky road leads to the property where a few old hunting cabins provide a base of operation among heavily forested peaks and valleys.

NAWAC's interest in the area began in 2000 when group member and wildlife biologist Alton Higgins led a small team there to investigate several sighting reports. While searching the surrounding wilderness, Higgins and the team discovered several footprints of what appeared to be a large, humanoid type animal. According to the monograph, the "tracks were complete with toes, and measured sixteen inches in length, seven inches at the ball, and four inches at the heel."[59]

Higgins later made contact with a man who owned a cabin near the location where the footprints were found. The man told him of several strange incidents that had taken place while he stayed at the cabin, including loud vocalizations and rocks hurling from the woods. Higgins and other members of the group were invited to stay on the property where they too began to experience anomalous occurrences over the course of the next several years—including unfamiliar vocalizations, flying rocks, banging on the walls of the cabins, and the discovery of more footprints.

Dubbing the location "Area X," the group began more formal

operations in 2006 with a concerted effort to obtain photographic evidence. They placed high-quality game cameras at locations around the cabin and in the surrounding woods. The effort was a move in the right direction but fraught with challenges inherent to the remote location. Bears frequently destroyed the cameras and batteries failed, not to mention the difficulty in maintaining units that required a day's trek through the mountains just to check.

By 2010, the team hadn't captured a photo of the elusive species they were now convinced lived there, but they did notice a trend that influenced their future research. The longer the group members remained on the property, it seemed, the more frequent the strange incidents. It was almost as if the creatures grew more bold or agitated the longer they experienced human intrusion.

As such, the group moved ahead with a new strategy that would yield astounding results. The official study, known as The Ouachita Project, began in June 2011. According to the monograph, "The project has consisted of annual field surveys lasting between 60 and 120 days through the spring and summer months. Beginning in 2011, multiple teams—tasked with documenting direct observations—were deployed in consecutive one-week shifts over periods of several months during each calendar year."

Over a period of four years, more than 60 individuals participated. Their activities ranged from scouting the area, surveilling in concealed blinds, attempting to invoke responses through "wood knocking" (striking trees or other objects with wood or rocks), maintaining audio recording equipment, and utilizing thermal imaging devices. During the process, members maintained detailed field journals and submitted after-action reports that became the basis for the thoroughly fascinating monograph.

While NAWAC has yet to obtain conclusive proof of an anthropoid species, they seem just short of such a discovery. As illustrated in the document, the study has amassed a mind-boggling amount of circumstantial evidence and visual sightings that strongly suggests some type of ape-like creatures are inhabiting the Ouachitas. This is based on documented events that include countless unidentified vocalizations, numerous rock-throwing incidents, copious banging and wood knocking, bizarre disturbances at the cabins, and 49 visual contacts.

It would be impossible to cover every incident reported since 2011 (and beyond, considering the project has continued since the monograph was published), so I will highlight a few as examples of the activity. During my own visits to the property, I never personally experienced anything I could attribute to an unknown animal, but having met most of the individuals involved and heard their stories firsthand, I cannot dismiss the results of their combined effort that has been considerable for a subject most scientists would barely give a chuckle.

In one of the early visual encounters, team member Daryl Colyer—a trained survivalist with a background in Air Force airborne intelligence—was sitting in a mirrored hunting blind on the afternoon of May 10, 2012, when he caught sight of a large, bipedal animal 50 yards away. He described it as approximately eight feet tall and "gray with light-colored feet (possibly the soles), and some sort of light or white coloration in the buttocks area." As Colyer watched, it quickly and smoothly stepped from a mossy green boulder to a small bank before it disappeared into the thick vegetation. Later, when one of the team members tried to reenact the sequence he "had trouble even climbing onto the boulder where Colyer had seen the large gray animal step with ease and agility."

On May 13, 2012, team member Ken Helmer, a Houston trauma surgeon and biologist, was sitting in the same mirror blind at 6:10 p.m. when he "saw a black, upright figure step out and look toward him for a few seconds before it disappeared back into the foliage. Within a few seconds, the figure re-emerged, again curiously looking toward Helmer, perhaps directly at him. Helmer could clearly see its arms dangling on the sides, and could see clear separation between the legs. Helmer noted that the subject was entirely black, 'face and all.' After standing there facing Helmer for approximately four or five seconds, the figure again disappeared into the foliage." It was approximately 80 yards away.

The following day, one of the most significant sightings occurred in full light. At 6:30 p.m., several team members were gathered at the base cabin when they heard an object strike another cabin 50 yards away. (There are three cabins total at the site.) Three team members immediately headed toward the cabin to investigate, followed by a fourth. While they were gone, investigator Kathy Strain—archeologist, author, and native culture historian—heard a rock hit the base cabin, followed by what appeared to be some kind of animal peering at her from behind a clump of trees.

When the rest of the team returned, they searched the area where the animal had "peeked" at Kathy. They found no sign of an animal but noticed a trail leading away from the location which would provide a potential get-away route. Shortly thereafter, they heard what sounded like footsteps to the east. Within seconds, Kathy stood up and pointed toward the north slope. Team members Brian Brown, Mark McClurkan, and Bob Strain, along with Kathy, observed two "upright animals" moving quickly up the embankment. They moved with a swiftness unlike anything they'd ever seen.

The report states that: "[Kathy Strain] was able to note 'well-defined muscles' and she could see that the animal was leaning into its stride as it ascended the mountain. She also noted that its feet were 'splayed for traction.' [There] had been 'hesitation,' particularly in the smaller one of the two, before the two animals bolted up the mountain in an enormous burst of speed and agility."

Brian Brown confirmed he saw "two black streaks proceeding at a high rate of speed up the mountain." From another vantage point, Bob Strain saw the same two figures "partially obscured by foliage, moving rapidly up the side of the mountain, like they were 'on a cable.'"

McClurkan, who turned his head a few seconds later, only observed the legs of one animal as it ran. However, as he was watching the slope a few moments later, he observed an ape-like animal walk across the plateau above the clearing.

The event is significant in that it's rare for so many individuals to experience a sighting concurrently. I know all the individuals involved, which for me accentuates the likelihood that what they observed cannot be explained by accepted wildlife standards.

In a final Area X example, I offer an incident which harkens back to the Fouke Monster's classic playbook. It occurred in July 2012, as four of the group slept in one of the cabins. (Just to give you a visual, these "cabins" are not the cozy kind found in travel ads or ski resorts. They are small, dilapidated buildings full of dust, dirt, spider webs, and furnishings that would not look out of place in the *Texas Chainsaw Massacre*. In other words, rundown structures suitable for little else besides shelter.) That night three team members were sleeping in other parts of the cabin, while Ken Helmer slept in one of the bedrooms alone. His old creaky bed was shoved next to an open window covered only by a thin screen.

At 3:45 a.m. the men were awakened by calls for help coming from Helmer's bedroom. This was followed by "several loud impact noises, presumably on the wall" and some "indecipherable vocal sounds." They thought perhaps Helmer was dreaming and talking in his sleep, so they dismissed it. But the doctor wasn't sleeping... he was wide awake by now. Something had just reached through

The author navigates a rocky creek bed in Area X
(Photo by Sandy Blackburn)

the window and touched him while he slept.

"I was immediately fully conscious and trying to move away... and I then felt a slight pressing down and a pull toward the window on my right hip," Helmer recalled. "I began to yell for help."

In a follow-up conversation, Helmer told me that's when he looked at the screen and noticed it was pushed in at the bottom corner. It appeared that something tall with a presumably long arm had pushed through the screen and grabbed for him. It was altogether unnerving even for a guy who is not easily intimidated or scared.

After calming down, Helmer went to the cabin's bathroom to relieve himself. "I went into the bathroom and saw two big, fluorescent green eyes outside the window," he told me. "It darted away immediately." Helmer grabbed a gun and clamored out the front door wearing only a red headlamp and his underwear. By the time he searched the perimeter, however, whatever it was had fled.

The following day the men found a long, coarse gray hair stuck on a nail beside the window sill. They immediately thought of the tall, gray-haired creature Colyer had seen previously. It was chilling to think a shadowy, man-like creature such as this had been so close. The perceived safety of the cabin was perhaps much thinner than they'd imagined.

While subsequent testing of the hair proved inconclusive, visual observations and other such occurrences continued to add up over the years, leaving the researchers with little doubt they are on the verge of discovering a previously undocumented species living in North America. To that end, the team has made efforts to harvest a type specimen (i.e., kill one) in order to formally document the species. This position is hotly debated in Bigfoot research circles, but it's one the NAWAC feels is necessary to solve the mystery.

With nearly 50 visual reports and a track record that suggest these creatures are consistently present during their visits, it begs the question "why hasn't the team been able to obtain some kind of proof... a photo, specimen, or otherwise?" This question is not lost on the group who explain that:

[The] NAWAC invested approximately 48,000 man-hours in the project over the 4-year period. This translates to 980 hours per visual contact, or 40.8 days per person, per visual contact. Thus, on average, it took one individual six weeks to have one visual contact.

Considering the average visual encounter only lasts a few seconds, the prospect of proof seems daunting. This is perhaps reflective of "Bigfoot" research on the whole. When condensed down to consecutive summaries, the impression is that these beasts are running amok. But when viewed in light of the actual number of sightings over many years, it appears these sort of contacts are rare, unexpected, and, by all accounts, truly amazing.

ROAD WALKERS

Traveling eastward, the Ouachita wilderness crosses into Arkansas where the bulk of its rugged peaks and forestry are located. Here too we find a history of modern Bigfoot sightings that correspond to similar geography. In 1990, a group electrical linemen were working in Saline County when they reportedly saw one of these creatures. The witnesses were interviewed by long-time BFRO investigator, Tal Branco, who has spent the last 20 years researching such cases in Arkansas and the surrounding states. According to Branco, the first lineman was called out on a summer night to restore power to a transmission tower positioned at the top of Fairchild Mountain in the eastern reaches of the Ouachita National Forest.[60] At approximately 11:00 p.m., he arrived at the tower and began to troubleshoot the problem. He found that a breaker was being tripped in one of the legs down the line, so he drove his service truck along the power line (which ran parallel to the road) looking for damage with a spotlight. He eventually located a broken insulator and requested assistance to make the repair.

Two more linemen were dispatched and arrived within a short

time. One of them began repairing the insulator using a "bucket" truck, while the other two lineman stood below. As the two men talked, one of them caught sight of a "large hair-covered, man-like creature walking slowly off the slope on the north side of the road." [61] It was illuminated by the headlights of the truck, which was idling. The creature continued, walking across a ditch and onto the shoulder of the road. Stunned, the first witness asked his partner if he was seeing the same thing. The second lineman confirmed that he too was watching it. "The animal then turned away from the men and slowly walked west on the road until it passed over the crest of a ridge and out of sight," Branco stated in the report. "The animal never looked toward the men or the noisy vehicles, and seemed completely unconcerned about their presence."

The third man, high up in the bucket, did not see the creature and could not hear the other two men talking due to the truck noise. After the creature was out of sight, they yelled to the man in the bucket and told him to hurry with the repairs so they could leave the area. They were frightened by what they'd seen.

When the repairs were complete, the first witness drove back in the direction the animal had gone. He did not see any further signs of it but stated that he was still fearful even in his truck cab. The second witness told Branco that he too saw an animal that he could not identify and had been shaken by the whole experience.

In the same county of Saline, a woman told me she and her husband saw a seven-foot-tall creature in 2013. As they were driving along a dirt road in the early morning hours, they noticed something walking in the trees. It appeared to be ape-like, with dark hair and long arms, yet walked on two legs. It quickly turned into the woods and walked out of sight.

In nearby Montgomery County, a resident reported a similar creature in the winter of 2002. In this case, the 73-year-old, lifelong resident of the Ouachita Mountains was driving west of Mount Ida along a newly made logging road when he stopped to relive himself.[62] As he walked a few yards into the woods, a large animal suddenly came from behind a large pine log and began running across the road directly in front of the witness. It moved very swiftly on two feet as it headed down the mountainside.

The man was approximately 25 yards from the creature, which he was able to see in the clear conditions of late evening. He stated that it was "about five feet tall and covered in dark hair."[63] It had the "overall shape of a stocky human, except that it appeared to have no neck" and its head was very large. It also appeared to have longer arms typical of an ape.

The witness was most impressed by the speed of the animal as it fled. He stated "no human, nor any other animal he had ever seen could have moved as fast as this one." When compared to the eyewitness reports from Area X, this seems to be a common theme among the creatures living in the Ouachitas. Fast and stealthy.

According to a report from the now defunct Sasquatch Research Initiative (SRI), a woman saw a strange animal as she was driving in the adjacent county of Polk near the town of Mena one afternoon in 2005.[64] As she navigated along a single-lane road, she caught sight of a tall, brownish figure standing up ahead a few feet from the road. She immediately hit the brakes, worried that whatever it was might try to cross. When she came to a stop, she could see that it was a bulky, humanoid type creature that stood approximately seven feet tall and was uniformly covered in light-brown hair about three inches long. The creature merely stood there starring at her.

Afraid to pass it, the woman considered backing up but knew it would be risky since the road was narrow and curvy with a steep, 20-foot embankment on one side. She had almost made up her mind to continue forward when she glanced at the road behind her one more time to reconsider. When she looked forward again, the creature had disappeared.

An investigation conducted by members of the SRI group noted that the area where the witness claimed to have seen the creature was appropriate, with "high embankments and steep drop-offs, low human population, abundant water supply by natural creeks, and national forest boundaries."[65] The witness had lived in the area for 34 years and was a well-known person in the community. In the opinion of SRI investigators, she seemed very credible.

Remarkably, the location is close to one of the "Other Boggys."

Just east of Mena, a waterway called Boggy Creek crosses under Highway 370 as it meanders through the low country between the Ouachita National Forest boundaries. It's approximately 90 miles north of the legendary Boggy Creek in Fouke.

In 2012, an interesting footprint was found just south of Mena near Dierks, Arkansas. I became aware of the track when I participated in an episode of the Animal Planet show *Finding Bigfoot* titled "Return to Boggy Creek." During the filming, a young man and his high school teacher shared the details of the discovery. According to the young man, Aaron Eisenhower, he and his father often set traps for raccoons along a creek on the outskirts of Dierks. On January 12, 2012, Eisenhower was checking the traps when he found that one was missing. As he looked around, he noticed a strange footprint in the muddy bank near the location where he had originally placed the trap. He was familiar with the usual type of animal tracks in the area, but he could not identify this particular one. It clearly had toes, but the foot was too large to be that of a typical human.

The footprint was so strange, Eisenhower called his high school agriculture teacher, Shannon Bailey. Mr. Bailey accompanied the young man to the scene, where they found what appeared to be an additional print showing only the heel portion. The teacher examined both tracks, finding them to be very unusual. The distance between the two was also striking. It measured 66 inches from toe to toe, which Bailey felt was not possible for a human stride while ascending the steep incline of the creek bank.

Bailey had brought some plaster to cast an impression of the toe track, which also appeared to show dermal ridges. The resulting cast was impressive and clearly defied normal explanation. Given that it was reported by one of his students, Bailey had to consider the possibility of a prank, but after seeing the evidence and visiting with Eisenhower at length, he did not believe it was a hoax. I didn't get that feeling either as I listened to the two men tell their story in person. It reminded me of a scene in *The Legend of Boggy Creek* where a young boy finds a strange track while fishing down by a creek. The comparison was definitely appropriate given the subject of the *Finding Bigfoot* episode.

Track found in Dierks, Arkansas
Note the toes on the left side of the photo.
(Photo courtesy of Shannon Bailey)

Close Encounters

As the Ouachita Mountains stretch into the heart of Arkansas, they eventually give way to the fertile River Valley region to the north and the Mississippi Alluvial Plains to the east. Amid this cross-roads of ecological diversity we also find reports of elusive ape-like creatures who seemingly roam the extensive network of waterways and thick, forested landscapes indicative of the area.

One such report came to me via an eyewitness who grew up in the area north of Little Rock known geographically as the Arkansas/Ouachita River Backswamps. He had read my previous Boggy

Creek book and wanted to share his own experiences from else-where in Arkansas. The witness, whom I will call "Lee," is a promi-nent figure in his community, having worked as a firefighter, EMT, and constable. As such, he felt it would be best to withhold his real name from the record. I didn't doubt Lee's sincerity. Not only did his business card reflect his current occupation as an Emergency Medical Technician, I could hear the sounds of an emergency fire station in the background as we spoke on the phone.

Lee first told me of a few incidents that occurred near his home. On one occasion he and a friend found a strange track along a muddy creek. Later they saw a man-like figure gazing at them across a field. These incidents—which he readily agrees may or may not be con-nected to Bigfoot—were spooky to him a kid, but they were nothing compared to an incident that occurred in 1981 near the small town of El Paso, Arkansas. On the night in question, he and two fellow hunters (his cousin Matt and a female friend named Holly) arrived around 10:00 p.m. at a deer camp where they planned to hunt the next day. The camp included an old farmhouse that provided a suit-able place to sleep, albeit dusty and without electricity.

After checking out the farmhouse, the three hunters made their way to a pond where two deer stands had been placed on either end. They verified the stands were still in place and talked a mo-ment about their individual hunting strategies. As they were talk-ing, Lee's cousin shined his flashlight across the pond. As he was sweeping from left to right, Lee glimpsed a dark shape in the beam. He immediately told Matt to shine the light back to the same spot, where they could now see a faint silhouette with two reflective red eyes looking right at them. The shape of the creature was vague, but it appeared to be something other than a small varmint or a deer.

The shape eventually retreated into the woods and the trio re-turned to the farmhouse. As they were settling in for the night, they began to hear a "clapping" sound outside. At first it was faint but gradually grew louder and closer to the house. Curious, but not necessarily alarmed, Matt grabbed the flashlight and headed out the front door. Lee followed. The two hunters went to opposite ends of the porch and looked around but saw nothing. The clapping sound had stopped abruptly.

After a minute or two of listening and watching, Matt walked to the corner of the porch one more time and shined the flashlight down the side of the house. "Whoever it was just came out from behind this bush, jumped up on the back porch, and went into the house," he told Lee with obvious concern.

Holly had stayed behind in the house, alone in the dark since the men had taken the only flashlight. Lee turned to go back in the front door just as Holly hurried out. "We asked her what happened," Lee explained. "She said she could hear footsteps come through the house and heavy breathing outside the room she was in." Uncertain if the men were playing a joke or another person was in the old farmhouse, she got up and walked to the front door and out onto the porch.

At that point Lee suggested they leave. They all agreed, but Holly's purse was still inside. Matt volunteered to go get it.

"I was standing one step down off the porch and Holly was standing one step down from me," Lee said. "Matt started in the front door as I was starting to step up onto the front porch when something ran from the back of the house, through the house, and more or less tried to grab his leg." When it did, Lee could see Matt hit it with the flashlight. Batteries and pieces of the light went flying as everything went dark.

"When he came down and hit it with the light, he was hollering 'Lee shoot it, shoot it!' But I couldn't. Matt was in the way."

Finally, Matt got out of the doorway and Lee could see something furry standing in the threshold, illuminated by the sparse moonlight. "I could see its fur shake, but I could only see it from about mid-thigh down," he recalled. "It just stepped back into the darkness. It was on two legs."

In a panic, Lee tried to gather the pieces of the flashlight while Matt went for Holly's purse. They didn't see any further sign of the strange two-legged animal, nor could they hear it moving through the house. Perhaps it was still there, standing in the darkness just out of view.

When Matt returned with the purse, the three hunters got into their car and sped away. They drove until they got back to the main highway where they pulled over and stopped. After their nerves calmed, they discussed what they had seen. Both men agreed that the creature was covered in light-brown fur but was not an ordinary animal. It was not extremely tall, but it was bipedal. It could step quietly and run swiftly but was not human. Lee theorizes it could have been a juvenile Bigfoot, but of course there's no way to be certain. But whatever it was gave him and his friends the scare of a lifetime. And for me, another connection to *The Legend of Boggy Creek*: the incident is so eerily similar to what happened to the Ford family in 1971, I can't help but think of the movie's climactic scene.

I spoke to another man, Steve Bevins, who experienced a series of unusual incidents at his home just 30 miles to the west in Conway. His property is located near Cadron Creek and a heavy patch of woods that connects to the Ouachita Forest.

The incidents began around 2010 when Bevins stepped outside to make a phone call. (Cell phone reception is poor in the area, so his cell phone rarely works inside the home.) As he dialed the number, he heard several deep growls come from the darkness beyond his barn. These were followed by a loud, growling "whoop" he could feel in his chest. He immediately retrieved his rifle and a flashlight, but when he returned, he found no animal in the vicinity.

In the following months, Bevins noticed that his cows were becoming increasingly skittish. They would often huddle together rather than eat the sweet grain he would give them each evening. Even his blue heeler began to act strange. On several occasions, the dog simply refused to accompany her owner to the back pasture.

Bevins told me he continued to hear the growls from time to time—which were also heard by friends and family members—but had no idea what he might be dealing with until 2011. One evening about 11:00 p.m. his blue heeler was out back when she began barking very persistently. Bevins grabbed his flashlight and headed out to see what was wrong.

"I walked up to her and pointed the flashlight in the direction she was barking," Bevins said. "I saw an extraordinary animal on its haunches with red eyes the size of tennis balls. It stood up and walked off, looking back at me two or three times."

Bevins estimated the animal's height to be at least eight feet. He didn't want to rush to conclusions, but there was no getting around the possibility of Bigfoot. Unbeknownst to the witness, reports of a so-called Lake Conway Monster circulated in the same area during the late 1940s. According to an article posted by *The Saline Courier*, sightings of an ape-like animal with a terrible odor were reported frequently when the lake first opened.[66] Had such a creature existed all this time in the area without capture, or did the nightly visitor come from the outlying Ouachita Forest? Bevins has since found what appear to be 18 inch tracks in his back pasture, but so far the animal has not allowed him another glimpse. The case is still open.

Joann Hartman no longer questions the existence of such a creature in the Ouachita Forest. In November 2015, she was camping with her husband near Lake Winona when she got a glimpse of something she will never forget. In a personal interview, Joann told me they were sitting quietly one afternoon enjoying the fall weather and beautiful countryside. As she gazed into the treeline, she noticed a figure that had not been there moments before. Even though there was no wind, it swayed slightly as it looked directly at them.

"It was about seven or eight feet tall with broad shoulders," she said. "And it was covered in hair."

Joann focused on it for several seconds before she got her husband's attention and pointed toward the location. But the instant she motioned, the creature disappeared into the foliage never to be seen again.

"It really scared me," Joann said, as she recalled the event. "It was there and then it was gone."

I felt an air of sincerity as we visited. Like so many others, Joann had been extremely skeptical of Bigfoot stories prior to the experience. Now she finds herself on the other side, aware that people may be skeptical of her own account. But it doesn't matter. She's confident she laid eyes on something tangible; something that resembled a large ape in the shadowy woods of Arkansas.

The Ozarks

In the northern portion of Arkansas and into Missouri we find another mountainous region known as the Ozark Highlands. The Ozarks, as it's commonly called, is a lush landscape of hills, hollows (valleys), and plateaus initially formed when the Ouachita Mountains weighted down the edge of the North American continent causing the crust of the earth to flex upward. This geological activity exposed underlying Paleozoic rock to produce an ecological region that is partly forested and rich in karst features such as caves, sinkholes, and underground drainage.[67] With such a wide range of diverse and protective habitats, the Ozarks are perfectly suited for an amazing variety of Southern species.

Not surprisingly, the Ozarks are also reputed to be the home of several cryptids, including its most famous, the Ozark Howler. The Howler has been described as a massive, cat-like creature with glowing eyes, protruding horns, and an eerie cry that sounds like a cross between a wolf's howl and an elk's bugle. Tales of the creature date back many years and often straddle the line of folklore, a subject for which the Ozarks are also known. Even so, there have been plenty of modern reports that suggest the creature may be some sort of anomalous cougar species.

Aside from the Howler, the Ozarks boast several lake and river monsters, a few winged beasties, and of course, Bigfoot. One of the earliest documented tales of a possible Southern Sasquatch, in fact, comes from the area just east of the Ozark-St. Francis National Forestlands in Arkansas. As recounted in the May 9, 1851, edition of *The Memphis Enquirer*, a man from Greene county was out hunting when he reportedly saw a herd of cattle being chased by an "animal" that can only be compared to Bigfoot. The news article reads as follows:

> During March last, Mr. Hamilton of Greene county, Arkansas, while out hunting with an acquaintance, observed a drove of cattle in a state of apparent alarm, evidently pursued by some dreaded enemy. Halting for the purpose, they soon discovered as the animals fled by them, that they were followed by an animal bearing the unmistakable likeness of humanity. He was of gigantic stature, the body being covered with hair and the head with long locks that fairly enveloped his neck and shoulders. The "wildman," for we must so call him, after looking at them deliberately for a short time, turned and ran away with great speed, leaping from twelve to fourteen feet at a time. His foot prints measured thirteen inches each.
>
> This singular creature has long been known traditionally in St. Francis, [Green], and Poinsett counties. Arkansas sportsmen and hunters having described him so long as seventeen years since. A planter, indeed, saw him very recently, but withheld his information lest he should not be credited, until the account of Mr. Hamilton and his friend placed the existence of the animal beyond cavil.

The reporter goes on to speculate that the so-called "wildman" was a human survivor of an earthquake that struck the area in 1811. The individual, he theorized, had been cast into the wilderness as a boy due to the catastrophe and had grown up in a "savage state, until he now bears only the outward resemblance of humanity." The theory has merit since this earthquake did occur (December 16, 1811), but it doesn't account for the gigantic size of the individual nor the hair-covered body.

Dating back to 1865, a similar creature known as the "Blue Man" was being reported in the Missouri reaches of the Ozarks. While Missouri is beyond the reasonable boundaries of our search, no discussion of Bigfoot in the Ozarks would be complete without mention of the Blue Man, as the entity has become integral to the lore of the region. According to a 1915 article from the *Kansas City Star*, the first sighting occurred in the spring of 1865 when 60-year-old resident Blue Sol Collins of Upper Indian Creek set out on a hunt.[68] A light snow had fallen the previous night and an abundance of animal tracks were visible on the ground. Collins had intended to hunt deer, but when he noticed a set of huge, clawed tracks resembling that of a bear, he decided to pursue the larger game instead.

After hours of tracking, Collins was beginning to lose hope when he finally spotted a figure climbing above him on the north slope of Upper Twin Mountain. It was indeed the maker of the tracks, but it was not bear. It was a giant figure that looked very human-like although its body was covered in "blue-black hair."[69] Collins said it was nearly seven feet in height with a powerful, muscular build and "gorilla-like arms." It wore a shoulder piece and breech-cloth of animal skin, while its feet were covered with "deer hide moccasins, held together by thongs of buckskin that made the clawlike appearance in the snow." It also held a huge club in its hand. When it spotted Collins, it began to hurl rocks. The hunter was so frightened, he turned and ran for home.

Collins never saw the Blue Man again, but others claimed encounters between 1874 and 1890 in the vicinity of Douglas County. In one instance, a man said he came across the thing as it was carrying a cow near North Fork. When the creature saw the man, it began to chase him as it let out a roar. Others claimed to see it in Spring Creek Hills where it was apparently stealing livestock from the local farmers.

A drought of sightings between 1890 and 1910 caused many to speculate that the Blue Man was dead, but in 1911 a posse of men supposedly discovered the creature's cave and set a "large saw-toothed bear trap" inside. They discovered a few days later that the Blue Man had been snared but had escaped by cutting off two of its fingers. In 1915, the creature was spotted again at his old haunt in Spring Creek Hills when a man by the name of O.C. Collins saw it trying to catch a hog. Collins said that the Blue Man's hair was now white, possibly due to old age.

While some details are very human-like (breech-cloth, footwear, use of a club), it's interesting the individual was consistently reported to have dark hair or fur. The notion that its hair eventually turned white may seem to be a stretch, but it's not out of the question since there have been reports of Bigfoot with white fur. In fact, another Ozarks tale involves a bizarre creature of the very same coloration. This account, known as the Monster of Peter Bottom Cave, comes from a book by Phillip W. Steele titled *Ozark Tales and Superstitions*. The story claims that a murderous doctor fled into the forests near Peter Bottom—located along War Eagle River in Northwest Arkansas—in order to escape lawmen.[70] There he hid for 20 years until he was finally captured and arrested. He was then committed to an insane asylum where he remained until his death in the early 1960s. Just prior to his death, however, he called in reporters and told them of a "monster" he found living in the caves near Peter Bottom. It is uncertain what he told reporters in regard to the monster's features, but it was presumed to be some sort of hairy, man-like thing. Of course nobody paid much heed to a fantastical tale coming from a murderer, so it was disregarded.

That is, until 1966. On a warm afternoon that year, two men in their late 20s were riding horses near the lush meadows of Peter Bottom. Suddenly, a man riding a tractor came hauling out of the bottom at full speed, stopping long enough to warn them that there was "something horrible living there."

Paying no heed to the warning, the two men guided their horses down into the heavily wooded bottom where they spotted a large, white "clump" in the grass. When they "came within ten yards of it," Steele relates, "the clump of white fur stood upright!" The men were so frightened, they rode post haste out of the bottom and told their story to others in town. They described the monster to Steele:

> It stood upright like a man and its body was completely covered with snow-white hair about three inches long... its height was between eight and nine feet. The creature's body and facial characteristics seemed more human even than those of an ape. They also noticed a strong, offensive odor which... seemed to emanate from the creature.

Over the next few months hunting parties tried to locate the monster, but nothing was ever found.

Just three years later, in 1969, a strange incident was reported near the town of Springdale, not far from War Eagle. According to a report in the *Northwest Arkansas Times*, a woman called police to report that a prowler had been looking in her window.[71] When officer Ken Speedlin investigated, he found that the prowler would have had to be at least seven feet tall since there was no evidence that something had been placed below the window to allow a human to see inside.

A mobile home park on the north side of Springdale was the site of an even stranger event in which a "Bigfoot-like being," allegedly entered a mobile home park and tore up a vegetable garden in the early 1970s.[72] According to an article posted by the *Northwest Arkansas Morning News*, the creature horrified residents as it proceeded to hammer "large dents in the side of at least one mobile home" before leaving.

The same article mentions a separate incident east of Springdale in which two men came "face to face with Bigfoot in a secluded clearing." They were so unnerved by the encounter, they had to seek medical treatment. A few years later, some sort of "large and powerful beast" killed some livestock on a farm just across the border in Oklahoma. The culprit was thought to be yet another angry Bigfoot.

In 1970, Nathan Russell was walking through some woodlands at the southern end of the Ozarks when he noticed a strange animal in a tree.[73] Before he could react, the creature jumped down and stood up on its hind legs. It was covered in brown hair and stood around six feet tall. "From the neck down, there was long hair, and then halfway down, the hair was short like a hound's," Russell said of its appearance. It also had human-like ears and eyes like a hog.

For several minutes the two stood eying each other with a nervous gaze. When Russell finally panicked and ran, the ape-like thing came after him. Fortunately Russell was near a neighbor's home. When he reached the porch, the creature turned and ran back into the woods.

In more recent times, Ozark Bigfoot reports have been documented by a growing number of groups and individuals. Ron Boles is one such person who has concentrated his research efforts in the Ozarks. He's now a member of the BFRO, but long before he got serious about the phenomenon, he was merely a teenager with a passing interest in Bigfoot. That is until he had an unnerving encounter near his hometown in Greene County, Missouri.

In the summer of 1988, around 9:30 p.m., Boles and several friends decided to drive to a place called the Old Resort where people often "partied." The place was actually an abandoned hunting lodge left to ruin in a heavily forested near the James River. When they arrived, they found it to be deserted… no party, no people. Since Boles had never been there, they decided to get out and look around anyway. After 20 minutes of exploring the rather creepy surroundings, they began to walk back to their van. Two of Boles' friends were about 25 feet in front, with Boles and two other friends (Mike and Gene) following. Behind them was another group of three guys lagging at a distance of about 25 feet.

"As we were walking west towards the van in between the two hills with woods on both sides of the path, I started to smell the worst odor," Boles recalled. "That's when Mike stopped in his tracks and began looking to our right. We stopped as well and Gene looked where Mike was and said 'Oh my god, look!'"

Just twenty feet away, they saw a large figure standing in the moonlight holding a branch and swaying slightly. It appeared to be watching them, as it tried to stay hidden. When the trio realized it wasn't one of the other guys playing a joke, they took off running for the van.

"Whatever we saw was taller than both Gene and I by about a good half foot," Boles said of the incident. "I began to rationalize that maybe we just smelled a dead animal and maybe it was just a cedar tree. So Dave and I went back to the spot, and there was no smell and no tree at the spot where I saw it."

Boles told me he kept the incident to himself for over 20 years. However, as an adult he became more interested in the possibility of Bigfoot and delved into research on the subject. He's since documented sightings by a number of witnesses in the Ozarks area. In one of the most exceptional cases, he interviewed a gentlemen who claimed to have seen a trio of Bigfoot creatures in the vicinity of Hardy in Fulton County, Arkansas. In Boles' own words:

> I interviewed the witness on two occasions, February 25, 2013, and again on March 4, 2013. This is an amazing, rare sighting and I wanted to double check every detail.
>
> Early on a January morning in 2008 at approximately 7:30 am the witness was driving to the undeveloped property he inherited from his late father. As he came around a curve he saw a black furred animal sitting in the middle of the gravel road with its back towards the witness. The witness rolled to a stop approximately 10 feet away from the animal. He honked his horn then immediately saw a female approximately 7 ½ feet tall, covered in brown hair, swiftly walking bipedal out of the brushy, thick woods on his right to the small animal in the middle of the road. She scooped up the juvenile with her left hand and placed it on her back, and the juvenile then grabbed her around her short neck. The female glanced at the witness briefly as she exited into the woods downhill to his left.
>
> The witness stepped out of his car and stood in disbelief thinking he had just been hoaxed, but then a rock hit the roof of his Mercury Sable. The witness turned and saw a male approximately 6 feet from the back of his car. The male was approximately 9 feet tall with extremely large shoulders and broad chest. He was covered in black hair tinged with gray except for his flat nose and up to his wrinkled forehead, and he looked at the witness with intense, black eyes. The male then roared at the witness with a showing of its upper teeth. The witness jumped back into his car and watched in his rear view mirror as the male ran into the woods in the same direction as the female and juvenile.
>
> The witness then drove approximately 150 yards to the entrance of his property. He got out of his car and stood there in awe looking back down the hill. He could hear rustling in the woods and snapping of branches. He had small rocks thrown in his direction. He waited until the noises subsided and then got back into his car and

drove back the way he had come.[74]

Boles concluded by saying that the witness was extremely reluctant to come forward with the story, fearing that his reputation may be damaged. Certainly this is a remarkable claim, which many may dismiss as fabrication or hoax, yet it's not out of place among the timeless mysteries of the Ozarks.

6. LONE STAR SASQUATCH

Just seven miles west of Boggy Creek lies the border of Texas. The Lone Star State may not be the first to come to mind when contemplating the Bigfoot mystery, yet it boasts a staggering number of accounts, a few of which have already been mentioned. The state's massive size could be one factor in these numbers, but perhaps not the only reason.

Despite stereotypes that paint the entire state as a dusty expanse of ranches and scrub brush, Texas contains massive stretches of forestry, waterways, and even swamps that would be ideal for hiding large animals. Prairies, plains, and brush country are certainly present, but these generally fall into the western region of the state where Bigfoot reports are rare. Starting in the central portion of the state and growing progressively thicker to the east, Texas is enveloped in a surprising rich covering of mesquite, mixed hardwood, and pine thickets. In total the state boasts a whopping 60 million acres of forestland, which is more than any other U.S. State besides Alaska.[75] It is among these landscapes where we find the vast majority of the state's man-ape reports.

One of the earliest suspected cases comes from Lavaca County located in Southeast Texas. Known as the "Wild Woman of the Navidad," the details were recorded by early newspapers and later disseminated by author J. Frank Dobie in his book, *Tales of Old-Time Texas*.

As the story goes, settlers living near the banks of the Navidad River southeast of Hallettsville began to notice odd, barefoot tracks around their homesteads in the year 1837. These were usually two sets of human-like footprints with one set being larger than the other, as if to suggest a male and female. As time went on, the larger tracks ceased to appear, leaving only the smaller "Wild Woman" tracks, which increased in frequency. Numerous attempts to capture the Wild Woman failed as she was apparently able to move with great stealth through the darkness.

Finally, in 1845, the locals resolved to catch the mysterious prowler once and for all. On a moonlit night several hunters on horseback, along with their hounds, took up watch near an area where recent Wild Woman activity had been found. When one of the hunters heard a rustling in the brush, he looked up to see the "thing." He lurched forward on his horse, but the thing took off running toward a heavily wooded area. When his horse finally caught up, the rider tried to lasso it but was unsuccessful. Once the thing reached the woods, it disappeared within the trees.

The rider said the entity he pursued had long hair, no clothes, and brown fur that covered its entire body. It was also carrying some sort of object but had dropped it during the pursuit. The hunters later found a five-foot club in the field but no further signs of the Wild Woman. She had simply vanished into the realms of folklore and Bigfoot history.

In the following years other Bigfoot-esque reports were documented by newspapers. In 1871, the *Argus* announced that an "immense orang outang" [sp] had been seen near Gatesville, a town in central Texas.[76] It was described as being "seven feet high and covered from head to foot with a thick coating of hair." The creature had eyes that shone like "fire" and a "double row of murderous looking teeth." When it was last seen, the alleged primate was said to be carrying a large stick in its hand and a calf under its arm. A hunting party was organized to "capture or kill the monster," but no details about its success, or lack thereof, are included. Of course, this could literally be an orangutan, but even the largest variety of these don't stand seven feet tall.

In 1875, *The Statesman* out of Austin ran an article about a "Wild Boy" who was caught by men on horseback in nearby San Marcos.[77] The "strange being," who was described as being fearful and aggressive, apparently had a body "covered with hair about four inches long." While it's more likely this was a feral child (possibly suffering from hypertrichosis, a disorder that causes excessive hair growth on the human body), its hairy form does raise an eyebrow.

Tales of mysterious "wild men" continued into the twentieth century, some of them never reported by newspapers. I spoke to Josh Turner, curator of a small natural history museum in Cleburne, Texas, who told me of a frightening experience his grandmother had in the early 1930s. At the time, Pauline Beaty was a child living on the outskirts of Cedar Hill in Ellis County. The area was heavily wooded in those days and there had been several sightings of what her family referred to as the "wild man." One afternoon while Pauline and her classmates were having recess outside their one-room schoolhouse, two of the boys came running from the edge of the woods screaming in terror. They told the teacher they had seen a big hairy "man" lurking in the trees. The teacher, realizing it was no joke, quickly ushered all the students into the schoolhouse and locked the door. After some frantic discussions, two of the older boys volunteered to go for help. There was no phone at the schoolhouse, so this required them to bravely run on foot to the town. While the boys were gone, the teacher and students could hear thrashing, screaming, and ranting from the woods. But by the time help arrived, whatever had been there was gone.

In 1938 another incident was said to have taken place nine miles east near the town of Red Oak. According to a report originally submitted to the Western Bigfoot Society, four men were coon hunting one night in the heavy woods surrounding Red Oak Creek. As they sat in camp waiting for their dogs to sniff out a raccoon, they noticed the dogs weren't barking as they usually did on the hunts and were instead sitting close to the fire acting scared. "About that time they noticed a huge white haired figure standing about 30 or so yards from the fire," one of the witness' sons wrote. "It was just standing there watching them."[78]

The frightened hunters quickly grabbed their guns and dogs and fled from the bottoms. The next day they told others of the encounter, but no one believed their story. "My father was a very honest man... and I know his story to be true," the son affirmed.

The report is admittedly second hand, but it does support the notion that Bigfoot-like sightings have been occurring in Texas for many years. This report is also unique in that it specifies a "white-haired" entity. This is extremely interesting in light of monster accounts that would spill out of nearby Lake Worth some 30 years later. The Lake Worth Monster case, as it's known, was to become a pinnacle case among Texas Bigfoot mysteries, and ironically, one that occurred just miles from my childhood stomping grounds of Fort Worth.

LAKE WORTH MONSTER

On July 10, 1969, just after midnight, Bill Morris was sitting in a café near Lake Worth, northwest of Fort Worth. He was quietly enjoying a meal when a young couple burst into the restaurant looking for a phone. They were visibly upset and in a state of panic as the male dialed 0 and asked for the police. Morris couldn't help but overhear the conversation as the young man recounted a frightening incident that had occurred just moments before in a heavily wooded area on the north end of the lake.

The young man told the dispatcher that he and his wife had been out parking near Greer Island (a popular "Lover's Lane" hangout at the time) with two other couples when something leaped from a nearby tree and landed on their car. The thing, which he described as "half-man, half-goat with fur and scales," tried to grab his wife, but he managed to drive off before it got a hold of her.

The man hung up the phone and comforted his wife until four police units arrived. After a short conversation, they were escorted away by the officers. It was the beginning of a Texas-sized legend that endures to this day.

The following day, an article titled "Fishy Man-Goat Terrifies Couples Parked at Lake Worth" appeared in the *Fort Worth Star Telegram*.[79] In the article, journalist Jim Marrs explained that the police accompanied John Reichart and his wife back to the location of the incident. They found no evidence of the attacker there, but Reichart was able to show the officers an 18-inch scratch down the side of his car allegedly made by the attacker.

"We did make a serious investigation because those people were really scared," the patrolman told Marrs. The police had been receiving calls of a similar nature since June, but until that morning, they had simply been disregarded. After investigating the claim by Reichart and his friends, the police concluded it must have been the work of a "prankster."

However, that didn't stop the public from becoming enthralled. The article, along with radio and television reports, created such a stir that people began to assemble at Greer Island, hoping to confront the "goat-man" themselves. By the evening of July 11, there were as many as 30-40 people—including members of the Tarrant County Sheriff's Department—gathered near a landmark known as "The Pit" when the creature appeared on a high ridge above. In a second news article by Marrs, the creature was said to have "uttered a pitiful cry" before it threw a heavy tire (with the rim) nearly 500 feet above the heads of the awestruck assembly![80]

The "pit" where the Lake Worth Monster threw the tire
(Photo by Lyle Blackburn)

The crowd was so alarmed by the display of power, they began to flee. One young man reportedly backed his car into a tree as he tried to get away. What started as a rather innocent "monster hunt" ended in a frightening experience that left the locals questioning whether it was a real creature or a crazy, costumed prankster with a death wish. Morris confirmed that some of the would-be monster hunters were armed.

The general description of the thing was that it was big with gray or white hair like a goat on its body. Some, such as the original witnesses, said it was partially covered with scales, while some believed they also saw horns. Jack Harris, one of the eyewitnesses, noted that "the creature walked like a man but didn't look like one. He looked like he was 7 feet tall and must have weighed about 300 pounds."[81] These bizarre descriptions create a cryptozoological conundrum since some of the traits would place it into the "Goatman" category, while others would lump it into the "Bigfoot" category, if of course, it wasn't human.

In a *Star Telegram* article dated July 14, a representative of the Fort Worth Museum of Science and History stated that he believed the "monster" to be a bobcat.[82] A naturalist at the Greer Island Refuge and Nature Center backed him up, saying that a pet bobcat had been turned loose in the area at one time. A bobcat might account for the "pitiful cries," but by no means can a cat of any size throw a tire 500 feet over the heads of 30 plus witnesses. Another theory was offered by a local kennel owner who said he was "tracking a 40-pound runaway macaque monkey near the lake,"[83] but this too ignores the fact that witnesses had seen a much larger, bipedal type creature.

In the weeks that followed, more incidents involving the monster were said to have occurred. On one occasion the creature was reportedly seen running across an open grass field.[84] In another, five people claimed they witnessed it breaking the limbs of a huge oak tree. These accounts were either ignored or unknown to the press, but luckily a writer by the name of Sallie Ann Clarke saw the value of following up on the story, which she documented in her book, *The Lake Worth Monster*, published in 1969. The book includes interviews with numerous witnesses, including Ronnie Armstrong, who claimed the creature had been wounded by a gunshot that produced a trail of blood leading down to the water's edge. A set of tracks was also discovered by three individuals who showed them to Clarke and Armstrong. "We measured the ape like tracks," Clarke wrote. "[T]hey were sixteen (16) inches long with a toe spread of eight (8) inches. The tracks appeared to have been made by a real heavy animal or a being of some kind."[85]

Armstrong, who helped Clarke investigate the incidents, felt that it might be a "big white ape," based on his own sightings and interviews with others. Vic Franklin of Fort Worth also claimed to have seen the creature a number of times. He told Clarke it was at least seven feet tall and looked like a "real hairy" human. Another eyewitness, Jim Stephens, told Clarke the thing jumped on the hood of his car one night as he and two other men were driving around the lake. They had heard about the creature while fishing that day and decided to look for themselves. Stephens said the creature remained on the car's hood until he swerved and ran into a tree. At that point, the thing "jumped off and ran into the woods." He described the creature as "real big and human-like with burnt scars all over its face, arms and chest."[86]

Clarke's book is ultimately a semi-fictional treatment of the subject that includes both facts and interviews with witnesses, along with fanciful passages in which she imagines what it would be like to see the creature herself. This approach tends to muddy the waters in terms of accurate, cryptozoological research, but Clarke's intention at the time was to document the events while at the same time writing an entertaining book. Ironically, she would later have the opportunity to see the creature for herself as she continued her research after the book's publication.

In an interview with Sean Whitley, producer of the documentary film *Southern Fried Bigfoot,* Clarke stated that she ended up seeing the monster a total of "five times."[87] On the first occasion, Clarke said she was at the lake when she found a "big track." Later she was sitting in the back of a friend's camper when she saw the creature through the screen door. "I put a metal plate with some

Lake Worth Monster by Joshua Foster

shrimp in it on the back of the camper, and that thing come up and stood there, and carried off the plate," she recalled. "I watched it. Boy, I mean, that thing scared the devil out of me. It was just a big, tall white thing."

Clarke lamented that she didn't have a camera with her at the time, but fortunately someone did capture an image of the alleged beast. On November 19, Fort Worth resident Allen Plaster told a reporter from the *Star Telegram* he was driving west on Shoreline Drive with another couple at 1:35 a.m. when one of them saw a large, white figure stand up near the road.[88] Plaster managed to snap a Polaroid picture as it ran away. The resulting photo shows a blurry white figure that resembles a cloud with a head.

Plaster later downplayed the photo, saying that he believed whatever it was "wanted" to be seen. But regardless, it did show something big and white, which was not a fabrication by the photographer.

Just weeks before the photo event another man claimed to have been attacked while he slept in the back of his truck near Greer Island. On November 7, Charles Buchanan said he was in his sleeping bag around 3:00 a.m. when something began dragging him out of the truck's bed. Thinking fast, Buchanan reached for a sack of barbeque chicken he had left-over from dinner and shoved it towards the beast. The thing promptly let go of the sleeping bag and shoved the chicken in its mouth before running off towards the lake. It then plunged into the water and swam in the direction of Greer Island.

As 1969 came to a close, monster fever around Lake Worth began to dwindle as the sightings diminished. Some folks, such as Sallie Clarke and my friend Bill Morris, continued their research, but for the most part the newspapers moved on and so, perhaps, did the monster.

In the years that followed many speculated as to what had really happened at Greer Island that summer. A number of people claimed credit for a grand hoax, as often occurs in these cases. According to a 2009 article from the *Victoria Advocate*, back in 1969 police questioned several students from a high school in Fort Worth who were found with a "faceless gorilla outfit and a mask."[89] In 2005, the *Star Telegram* received a letter from an unnamed person who claimed he and two friends "decided to go out to Lake Worth and scare people on the roads where there were always stories of monsters."[90] The writer said they used "tinfoil" to make a home-made mask.

The tinfoil and faceless gorilla costume (which would have most likely been black or brown) don't reflect the white creature the majority of eyewitnesses reported, but other claims accounted for this by saying the creature frenzy was inspired by a goatskin or carcass that was being displayed on the hood of a car or, more dramatically, cast down from trees onto the parked vehicles of couples making out below.

To evaluate yet another rumor, a reporter from *Fort Worth Magazine* tracked down a man by the name of "Vinzens" who claimed credit for the tire-throwing incident. According to his article, Vinzens affirmed that he and two other guys had gone to Greer Island to party on July 11 where they ended up on the bluff overlooking The Pit and the throng of monster seekers below.[91] In an innocent attempt to "fire up the festivities" and impress some girls, he and his buddies rolled a tire down the bluff. He said it looked more like a "toss" because there was a "bump" toward the bottom of the bluff that launched the tire into the air. Vinzens said that "when the incident made the papers the following day, he and his friend decided to lay low" to avoid any repercussions from police or the armed monster hunters who were stalking the area day and night.

Interesting, but Vinzens is not the only person to take credit for the tire toss. A woman named Jan Galloway told a blogger at the Domain of Horror her brothers were responsible for all the "goatman" incidents. "They tied ropes and grapevines off in the day time and at night my younger brother Jack Shelby [11 years old] wore my rabbit coat and they would fly across the hoods of the cars and barely touch the hoods," Galloway explained. "One night my brother Billy Shelby [15 years old] decided to come across the ground on all fours like a monkey... he jumped on top of a car and scratched the windshield and made a Tarzan sound and jumped off."[92]

Billy's prank supposedly sent the first couple to call police. Later, she said, Billy put on cut-off shorts and a white t-shirt, then smeared a "black eye pencil" on his face, arms, and legs. After ascending the ridge at Greer Island, he and several boys used a giant slingshot to launch the tire across the pit while Billy beat his chest and made more "Tarzan sounds."

With so many ridiculous claims, it's hard to sift out the truth in the matter, be it man *or* monster. The only certainty is that strange things were going on at Lake Worth and there were witnesses who believed they had seen something not of human origin. To add to the mystery, sightings in the area didn't start in 1969, nor did they end there. The Lake Worth Monster of Greer Island, it seems, is just one piece of a larger, hairier puzzle.

STRANGE THINGS AFOOT

When the frenzy broke out around Lake Worth in 1969, it wasn't the first mention of a strange monster in the area. For years people had talked of a creature that haunted the lake. Some called it the "Mud Man" or "Mud Monster," while others simply referred to it as a ghost. A resident who had lived there for 40 years told Sallie Clarke he saw something fitting the description at least 20 years earlier.[93]

In 1963, the *Denton Record-Chronicle* reported someone near the town of Denton claimed to have seen a "hairy, eight-foot thing" which the locals referred to as a "monster."[94] The details are sketchy, but Denton is a mere 30 miles north of Lake Worth

In recent times, the wilderness surrounding the lake has given way to considerable development (save for a 300-acre nature preserve around Greer Island), but at the time it was a truly wild place. The lake itself is a reservoir created by the west fork of the Trinity River, a lengthy waterway that feeds it from the north and extends well beyond to the south. The area was sufficiently wooded, and all along the river's corridor we find a host of strange incidents not un-

The author at Greer Island holding a copy of Clarke's book
(Photo by Craig Woolheater)

like those that became famous in 1969.

During my research I spoke to a young woman by the name of Cynthia Dunston, who told me of a possible Bigfoot encounter she had just north of the lake when she was a child. At the time she was visiting her grandparents, whose house was located near Lake Worth and Eagle Mountain Lake. She spent many afternoons exploring the woods surrounding the home, and on this occasion she had followed an old cow path from their barn to Ash Creek. "I got about halfway down the path when I saw something," she told me. "There was a dark shape in front of the fence at the end of the path."

Cynthia, a rather experienced outdoorswoman for her age, felt there was no reason to be alarmed so she kept walking. As she got closer, however, the shape moved and she could see it more clearly. "Then I froze," she recalled. "I knew exactly what it was."

Standing before her was a hairy, man-like creature. "I remember that its hair was longish and a dark auburn color," she told me.

"It looked as tall as an average man but not freakishly tall."

The young girl was startled, but not terrified. To her understanding, Bigfoot does not eat people. "This was more like extreme apprehension and caution of a large animal when you don't know what it is going to do," she recalled. "This appeared to be a natural animal."

Despite her faith in the creature's benign eating habits, Cynthia promptly turned and started back towards the barn. She didn't want to run, thinking it might give chase, but hurried at a good pace nonetheless. "When I was almost to the barn, I looked back," she continued. "It had followed me but had stopped past the halfway point where I had been standing before. As soon as I had the house in sight, I made a wild dash for the gate to the backyard. Safely inside the gate, I looked back toward the barn. There was nothing there."

Although Cynthia never laid eyes on the beast again, she was confident it remained in the area. One night Cynthia and her grandmother were awakened by a bone-rattling "howl/scream" unlike anything they'd ever heard. At first the sound was very close to the house, but later it could be heard in the distance. The next morning they discovered two chickens missing from a fenced in area with a securely latched gate. As far as Cynthia is concerned: "There's no possible way any animal could open that gate, except for one."

Twenty miles northeast of Lake Worth sits Grapevine Lake, where another interesting incident occurred a decade before the Lake Worth Monster flap. Floyd Fry, whom I met during a book signing I did in Fort Worth, told me he and his family were picnicking at Grapevine Lake in the late 1950s when he discovered something unusual. As with Lake Worth, Grapevine is now developed, but at the time it was surrounded by woods. Even the picnic sites, which were new at the time, were simply clearings cut from the thick trees. Fry was about eight years old, and having no similar-aged playmates present, he was left to wander around by himself. "I wasn't paying attention and went farther than I thought away from my parents," he told me. "That's where I found some giant-sized footprints in the sand."

The footprints came from a treeline, crossed an open area of freshly cleared land, and disappeared into the trees on the other side. "Even as a small child, what struck me was the size of the prints," Fry recalled. "They were huge, barefoot prints and I knew they were too large for a normal man. My thought was they must have been made by a giant."

Apprehensive yet curious, Fry followed the footsteps into the woods along what appeared to be a game trail. "I lost the footprints there but continued following the trail for a short way among the trees," he said. "But I became too frightened."

Young Floyd turned and ran back to where his parents were still enjoying their picnic. He told them what he had found and urged them to look, but they brushed it off thinking he was joking or exaggerating. At the time Fry didn't connect the event to Bigfoot, but in retrospect he wonders if such a creature could have been responsible for the seemingly impossible imprints.

In 2013, I investigated an even stranger—if not disturbing—report from a horse breeder who once owned a ranch in Grand Prairie. The property was located along the west fork of the Trinity River, 17 miles south of Grapevine. In a phone interview, Floyd Ramsey (yes, another Floyd) told me he was working on his ranch sometime around 1974 when he noticed his dogs were chewing on something. Upon closer inspection, he discovered it was a huge, hairy leg severed at the knee joint. The ragged appendage was covered in dark, coarse fur similar to that of a bear, but it had a human-like appearance and a human-like foot with five toes. If the leg were standing upright, Ramsey said the knee would have come up to his mid-thigh. He estimated the foot would be a "size 22" in human terms. Ramsey assumed his dogs had dragged it up from the Trinity River bottoms.

Puzzled and concerned, he made a call to the Dallas police. In due time, two officers showed up and inspected the leg. They were equally puzzled. As per standard procedure, they confiscated the evidence for further examination, but promised Ramsey they would let him know about their findings.

Ramsey eventually received a follow-up call from the department, but it was only to report that examiners couldn't determine what kind of "animal" the leg had belonged to. They could only confirm it was not a bear, nor was it human. Ramsey never heard from the police again.

Nearly 40 years later, Ramsey was watching an episode of *Finding Bigfoot* when he thought of the bizarre incident. In 1974 he didn't consider the possibility of Bigfoot in Texas, but in retrospect it seemed like a possible explanation.

Like Lake Worth and Grapevine, Grand Prairie has been consumed by the greater Dallas-Fort Worth metroplex, but at the time it was still fairly rough and wooded. It's unimaginable that any sort of large animal such as a Bigfoot or even a bear could or would roam that area today, but back in the 1970s it's not out of the question, especially with its proximity to the Trinity River.

In order to check out the story, I wrote a letter to the Dallas Police Records Archive requesting a copy of the police report. I didn't have an exact date or case number, so it was a long shot, but worth a try. The Dallas Open Records Department eventually returned a letter stating they could not find the report. They questioned why the Dallas police responded instead of the Grand Prairie police, but Mr. Ramsey was positive it was Dallas officers who came to his ranch that day. "I don't know why I called the Dallas police, but that's who came out," he told me.

The hairy leg story sounds fantastic and unquestionably falls into a category of reports in which promising evidence seems to mysteriously disappear once in the hands of authorities. But even so, I found Ramsey to be very well spoken and credible.

Moving further south along the Trinity River corridor we eventually cross a long, snaking body of water called Chambers Creek. The creek, which spans 67 miles through Ellis and Navarro Counties, is said to be the home of a Bigfoot creature known as the Chambers Creek Monster. In the first public report, a man claimed that

City of Dallas

May 1, 2013

Lyle Blackburn
███████████████

Re: Public Information Request Number 20130-4205

Dear Mr. Blackburn,

The Open Records Team received your request for information pursuant to the Public
Information Act. (formerly the Texas Open Records Act). A search was made within the Dallas
Police Department by the respective Division(s) for this information and no records were found.

If you have any questions please contact the Open Records Team at (214) 671-3343.

Sincerely,

DAVID O. BROWN
CHIEF OF POLICE

Bryan B. Comish
Bryan B. Comish
Lieutenant of Police
Records/Legal Serv Unit
Support Services Division
Adminstrative & Support Bureau

Response letter for the Ramsey case inquiry
(From the files of Lyle Blackburn)

his father, Kenneth W., and a friend were fishing along the creek
between the towns of Avalon and Ennis in 1964 when "a large,
hulking, hairy creature, approximately eight to ten feet tall appeared before them and roared."[95] The men panicked and quickly
made their way out of the creek bottoms.

Aside from his father mentioning an old sighting from the 1930s
(there's that time frame again!), it was thought to be an isolated incident until researcher Larry Parks tracked down additional witnesses
who claimed to have seen something similar near Ennis. According to Parks, the first instance occurred around 1964 when several
people were camping near Chambers Creek's low-water crossing
at Ensign Road. While cooking fish, they heard something large
approaching through the brush. As it got closer, they heard a distinct growling and smelled a putrid odor. When the thing finally

emerged, the campers were startled by the sight of a big, hair-covered creature.

The second incident occurred a few years later, around 1969. In this case a group of young men were walking in the woods along a tributary of Chambers Creek when they heard a strange animal sound. When they looked around, they saw "an 8-9 foot tall, hair-covered creature drop down on all-fours and charge towards them with a strange gait." They said it had really long hair and definitely wasn't a bear.

While these anecdotal reports don't prove anything, it's hard to overlook the coincidence. By all accounts the Chambers Creek Monster witnesses didn't know each other, yet they reported seeing the same type of entity in the same general area and timeframe. This occurs in the Lake Worth Monster and surrounding cases as well. It's a synchronicity that comes up time and time again as one explores these type of stories.

Deep In the Heart

While the majority of Texas Bigfoot sightings come from the eastern half of the state, the western portions do boast a few classic incidents which deserve a mention before we ultimately traverse into the deep thickets. One of these comes from Hawley, a dusty town in the middle of Texas just north of Abilene. According to an article from the July 7, 1977, edition of the *Abilene Reporter*, three youths—Tom Roberts (14), Larry Suggs (15) and Renee McFarland (15)—were clearing brush on a ranch at approximately 10:00 a.m. when they were "startled by the breaking of tree limbs and a shower of rocks."[96]

Suggs was hit by one of the rocks while others whizzed by their heads. The three kids dropped their tools and ran for the safety of McFarland's parent's house nearby, but not before they caught sight of their assailant. "We got three good glimpses of him," Suggs told reporters. "It was kind of an ape, but still a man. He had huge arms.

They hung to his knees."

Next, the kids did what any resourceful Texas kid would do in those days... grab a .30-.30 rifle and head back to confront the ape-man. When they returned to the site, they could see the creature lingering about 40 yards away. Suggs raised the gun and took his best shot. The recoil sent him backwards as the creature ran into the brush. "That [illegible] brush is so thick you have to know where you're going and he just glided through it," Roberts reported. He also said they noticed a "rotten smell" just prior to the attack.

Authorities were doubtful that a "monster" was loose in the area, but "long footprints" were found in the sandy soil where the kids claimed it had been. In addition, the man who owned the ranch said he'd recently lost 21 goats from a pen without a trace, save for a couple of carcasses found in the brush a few days later. The Jones County Sheriff concluded that coyotes were to blame, but the rancher argued that it was unlikely since not a single goat was killed inside the pen.

This was not the first sighting of the creature either. Renee Mc-Farland told reporters she had seen it the previous October, but when she told her parents they dismissed her story as fantasy. Another resident, Mike McQuagge claimed to have seen the same long footprints, although he had never seen the beast.

When the incident made the news, reporters were quick to give it a monstrous moniker as they always do. Because Suggs had referred to it as a "him," it was officially dubbed the Hawley Him.

A year before the Hawley Him made headlines, a Bigfoot creature was spotted near Kelly Air Force Base south of San Antonio. *The San Antonio Light* newspaper reported the creature had first been seen by Ed Olivarri a few weeks before September 1, 1976.[97] Olivarri was preparing for work one morning when his dog began barking wildly in the backyard. Concerned, he went to investigate. As he looked over his back fence towards the woods, a whistle sounded from a nearby railroad track.

"The animal must have been hiding or lying down because when the whistle blew it started running," the eyewitness told reporters. "It looked like it was some kind of 'Big Foot' monster." Olivarri said it was "about seven feet tall with short brown hair over its body" and definitely ran on two legs.

On August 30, Olivarri's next-door neighbor, Rosa Medina, claimed to have seen a similar yet smaller bipedal animal, which may have been a juvenile Bigfoot. When her dog began barking at about 3:00 a.m., she went to her back window to investigate. In the glow of a security light, she could see an animal with light-brown fur sitting on her back step.[98] It was distinctly "ape-like" and about the size of a child.

Medina was too frightened to open the door so she tapped on the window pane. Around the same time another of the home's occupants opened a window. Upon hearing the noises, the animal jumped up and ran off on two feet. Medina estimated its height to be approximately three feet.

When Olivarri heard about his neighbor's sighting, he decided to search the woods behind their houses. There he discovered large, foot-like impressions along a creek bank. A game warden was summoned to analyze the suspected tracks, but unfortunately they were trampled by reporters and other curious people who were now converging on the location. Authorities could find no explanation for the events.

As one of the largest cities in Texas, San Antonio may seem unlikely for a Bigfoot sighting, but at the time there were considerable pockets of woodlands surrounding the outlying areas. Even today, Bigfoot-like activities have been reported there. In 2009, news of a strange 911 call made local headlines. In the call, a homeless woman named Jennifer—presumably using a payphone or someone else's phone—claimed she and her husband saw a "creepy scary very large creature devour a deer and run off clear across the road."[99] The call, which was made public, began:

911 Dispatch: 911 San Antonio. Do you need Police Fire or EMF?
    Caller: I'm not real sure ma'am. Um, I just watched the biggest creat-critter, but it smelled real bad. I'm a homeless female, I live right in the middle of the woods around 151 and Calebra. Just north where the light is.

This thing was 75 feet away from me, smelled awful, devoured a deer carcass and then took off and like screamed, screeched; and took off across the street. And I know you guys are going to think I'm crazy, but I'm dead serious, there was something very big. Bigger—a lot bigger than me—out here. So we thought it was something you should know.

Jennifer went on to explain that the thing they saw was as large as a grizzly bear, covered in fur, and ran on two legs. They watched it pick up the deer carcass and run from the area as it let out a blood-curdling scream. Judging from the tone of the call, the woman and her husband seemed sincere and decidedly frightened. Jennifer never used the word "Bigfoot," but her description fits firmly the category.

An officer was dispatched to the location where he met with the couple. He found them to be sober and outwardly shaken. He declined to search the area, however, and the police dismissed the case. A search of the area was conducted shortly thereafter by my colleague Ken Gerhard, but he found no conclusive evidence.

Being that the area is located within a rather busy intersection near San Antonio's Sea World resort, it seems rather unlikely that a large creature such as Bigfoot could roam the area without a considerable number of sighting reports, yet the caller seemed lucid and sincere. The case is another puzzling slice of the mystery.

PINEY WOODS

Moving eastward we eventually come to the most heavily forested area of Texas; it's known as the East Texas Pine Belt or "Piney Woods." The region consists of 43 counties extending from the Red River in northeast Texas to the southern Gulf Coast. Within its reaches we find most of the state's sanctioned forests and the greatest number of Bigfoot reports.

One area with a high number of reports is the Big Thicket located at the southern end of the Piney Woods. As the bold name suggests, the land here is full of heavy woods, thick brush, snaking creeks, and blackwater bogs. It's so thick, in fact, outlaws were said to have used it as a hideout, since only the most hardy of lawmen dared to challenge the rugged terrain, which is filled with alligators, snakes, wildcats, bears, and perhaps other more mysterious inhabitants.

According to my late colleague and Big Thicket expert, Rob Riggs: "For years people in the area between the Thicket's western edge along the Pine Island Bayou and the Trinity River swamp had occasionally caught glimpses of something large, hairy and not quite human," a creature the locals call "Ol' Mossyback."[100] In his book, *In the Big Thicket: On the Trail of the Wild Man*, Riggs recounts an alleged sighting told to him by a witness. The young man said he was at his home near the Trinity River swamps in Dayton one night when he heard a disturbance outside in his rabbit pens. When he went out to investigate, he saw a "large, dark form" in the moonlight as it fled into the woods with one of his rabbits. The witness impulsively chased the mysterious thief, following the squeals of its hapless prey. Upon reaching the river bank a short distance away, he watched "as what looked like a huge ape-like animal swam to the other side of the river, easily negotiating the strong current, and never letting go of the rabbit."[101]

Riggs also obtained statements from several young men who claimed multiple sightings of an ape-like creature in the Big Thicket Preserve close to the small town of Saratoga. The boys spent much of their spare time hiking through the Thicket—since there was little else to do—and were therefore very familiar with the local wildlife. This creature, they assured him, was definitely something out of the ordinary.

The first time they saw it, the animal was running on all fours across a rice field. They were in a truck at a distance of several hundred yards, so very little detail could be observed beyond the fact it looked ape-like. The next time they saw the creature, or one like it, it was creeping around an old bridge at dusk. This time they were much closer and could see that it walked in a bipedal fashion. The third encounter occurred near a sludge pit, which had been part of an old oil field installation. In this instance they saw what they believed was the same animal right around dusk. As they watched, it let out a long howl before slipping into the woods, never to be seen again.

The multiple encounters seem almost "too lucky," but Riggs heard similar stories from a woman in the area who claimed her family had also seen an ape-like creature on several occasions. One time they saw it near a sludge pit. By all accounts this woman and the boys did not know each other.

A computer systems engineer named James Hendrix told me of a more recent sighting. In the fall of 2003, he and his wife, Carrie, were driving near the Big Sandy Creek unit of the Big Thicket National Preserve in Polk County. Just after sundown, Hendrix caught sight of something running towards the road through his driver-side window. He immediately braked as he saw a bipedal figure leap a drainage ditch and run across the road in full view of the headlights. According to Hendrix, it ran fluidly with a bent-over posture, as if it had switched to all-fours once it hit the pavement. He noted that its long arms touched the ground, but only a few times. It was about five feet tall and covered in long, reddish-brown hair.

"It had a very broad build and looked somewhat like an orangutan except that it had a flat face and was proportioned more like a human with long arms," Hendrix told me. The creature paused when it reached the other side of the road. It looked back at the car before entering the dark woods.

Since the creature assumed a quadrupedal stance, a bear could be considered in this case. However, Hendrix feels strongly it wasn't a bear. "It was running on two legs faster than a person before it went to all fours," he explained. His wife, Carrie, also got a good look at the face from approximately 20 feet away as it turned to look at the car. She was sure it did not have the snout of a bear.

An almost identical incident took place in November 1972, only a few miles from where Hendrix saw the strange creature. According to Donna Gilchriest Grundy, who was 12 years old at the time, she was riding in the car with her grandmother and great aunt

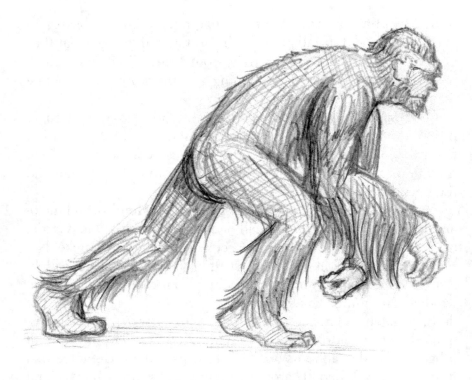

*Interpretation of the creature seen by James and Carrie Hendrix
by Cole Carter*

one afternoon around 3:30 p.m. The road—Segno Fire Lane in a heavily wooded area of the Big Thicket— was unpaved (as it still is today) so they were driving slowly. As Donna was leaning forward from the back seat talking to her grandmother and great aunt, all three saw a large, hairy, upright creature emerge from the woods and suddenly dart across the road on two legs. It missed the bumper by a mere three feet!

"It never looked at us, but we could see the body very well," Grundy told me, as we discussed the incident by phone. "It was covered in thick, long, shaggy hair that kind of shook on its body as it ran. It had long arms and a chest that was really thick."

The trio watched as it leaped over a drainage ditch at the side of the road and quickly disappeared into the dense thicket. The creature ran in a slightly hunched-over fashion, swinging its arms as it went, and stayed on two legs the entire time. Grundy estimated its height to be seven-to-eight-feet tall.

"We were stunned and shocked and pretty much afraid because we didn't know what we had just seen," she admitted. To her best recollection, she had never heard anyone talk about Bigfoot in that part of Texas at the time. It was only a year later that it seemed to make any sense.

"I remember the Boggy Creek movie came to Livingston [Texas] right after that and I wanted to go see it," she recalled. "And that pretty much confirmed what we saw."

Several miles southeast of the Big Thicket is another heavily wooded landmark of the Piney Woods known as the Sam Houston National Forest. The area is comprised of 163,037 acres, intermingled with privately owned timberland and farms throughout Montgomery, San Jacinto, and Walker counties. Named in honor of the man who ultimately liberated Texas from Mexican rule, Sam Houston Forest not only offers a world of scenic beauty within the heart of Texas but also the highest concentration of Bigfoot reports in the entire state.

In one of the oldest Walker County reports posted in the Bigfoot Field Research Organization (BFRO) database, a woman recounts an incident that allegedly happened to her late husband when he was young, around 1960. While he and his friends were hanging out at a cabin near Bedias Creek one night, they sighted a "six-foot-tall-plus being." The boys were familiar with a local legend that said a "hermit" lived in the woods, but the thing they saw didn't seem human— even by woodland hermit standards. According to her husband, it was very large, wore no clothes, and was "totally covered with long dark hair, about 4-6 inches long, all over." He also smelled a rank odor "like a moldy skunk."

In 1977, Gary Wiggins was camping at Lake Conroe in Montgomery County when he and several friends experienced a startling incident. The sun had just gone down, and they were setting up some lanterns around his camper, preparing to build a fire. As Wiggins was gathering wood, a loud crashing noise came from the trees, followed by crunching steps and guttural growls. It was enough to stop Wiggins in his tracks and alert the others. He stood there listening as the crashing became more intense. Something was moving in his direction.

"I could hear snaps and see branches moving," Wiggins told me in an interview. A half-moon hung overhead, but it was not enough light for a good view of whatever was causing the ruckus. "I could only see a dark shape," he affirmed. It was something large and it seemed to be moving on two legs. Wiggins turned and ran back to the group. They quickly gathered their gear, shoved it into the camper, and drove away.

While there's no certainty it was a Bigfoot, I do find it interesting that unrelated witnesses have reported sightings in the very same area over the years. In a case investigated by the North American Wood Ape Conservancy (NAWAC), a young man said he saw a Bigfoot-like animal just east of Lake Conroe in 2001.[102] This was the same location near the lake's north bridge where Wiggins heard the loud crashing sound.

In this instance the witness was driving along FM 1375 at 5:30 a.m. headed to work. Just after he crossed the bridge heading east, he pulled over to "unload" some of the coffee he'd been drinking. There was a spot where fisherman had worn a path from the road to the lake, so he walked a few feet down to do his business. As he did, he smelled a "really strange skunk odor" followed by a distinct "woofing noise." It made the hair on the back of his neck stand up. But that was nothing compared to what he saw next. When he turned his head in the direction of the noise, he saw something stand up.

"I had left my lights on in the truck and though they were not shining in my direction, the reflection was enough," he reported.[103] "It stood well over a foot taller than me and was still below me on the slope of the embankment." He went on to describe the figure as being approximately seven foot tall with dark-colored hair and a large head. It also had long arms and reeked of the horrible musky odor.

"It began to make a squealing bark kind of noise and in two or three strides was past [sic] me and headed for the road," he continued. "I don't know why it didn't turn and head back into the forest but it didn't."

As the thing crossed the road, a truck came around the curve and braked, presumably having seen the creature as well. The creature then walked up a hill on the other side of the road and disappeared into the trees. The witness got back into his truck and raced away.

"I have only told one other person about this because to be honest I don't want to look like some idiot seeing a ghost in the middle of the woods in Texas," he confessed. Obviously he's not the only one to cross paths with something like this.

In January 2016, NAWAC received another report from the same road. The witness said he was driving near the bridge one morning at around 5:00 a.m. when he noticed eyes reflecting in the headlights.[104] He first thought it was a deer, but as he got closer he could see the distinct shape of something standing upright on two legs. It was huge, much larger than a person, and perhaps as tall as eight feet. Startled, the witness swerved to the opposite lane as the thing watched him. He was certain it wasn't a human... not even one in a costume.

In a report filed with the Gulf Coast Bigfoot Research Organization (GCBRO), a man claimed to have seen a strange creature in the neighboring county of San Jacinto in 1983. According to the report, the man was scouting for deer signs when he and his fellow hunters saw an unidentified creature run out of the woods and cross a clearing. "It looked a lot like a monkey, in a way, but it ran on two legs, and never once to my knowledge did it ever use its hands to assist in its motion of travel," he stated. "It was black in color, approximately 4 [feet] tall, and was really fast."[105]

Canadian Bigfoot researcher John Green also has reports from the area in his extensive files. In a letter dated December 28, 1992, an individual recounted an incident from 1981 in which a woman by the name of Dee Hayes was driving to work through the Sam Houston National Forest at approximately 5:30 a.m.[106] As she rounded a curve in the road, she could see a seven to eight foot

Road through the Piney Woods
(Photo by Lyle Blackburn)

tall, brown animal standing on two legs near the side of the road 50 yards away. She stopped and watched the creature until it turned and entered the timber. She described it as having a "gorilla-like" head with no noticeable "snout."

In 2007, an uncanny series of events in Montgomery County further supported the notion that an unknown bipedal entity stalks the woods there. As documented by NAWAC, the first incident occurred on the morning of September 19, 2007.[107] At approximately 2:00 a.m., a construction employee working on a new sports facility in The Woodlands was taking a cigarette break when he noticed an upright, bipedal figure step from the woods surrounding the complex. He described it as exceptionally tall and covered in dark hair. The figure was only visible a few seconds before it slipped back into the trees.

A few days later, on September 21, two security officers were patrolling the same construction area at 2:20 a.m. when they spotted a huge, bipedal figure walking near the construction office trailers where some makeshift lights had been placed.[108] As they watched the figure from a distance of approximately 30 yards, they could see it stood at least seven feet tall and appeared to be covered in dark hair. It also walked with an unusually long stride, powerful gait, and a slight "slump," all of which did not look human.

After the thing moved out of sight, the officers reluctantly placed a call to 911, as per company policy whenever a trespasser was seen, regardless of its appearance. Police were dispatched—no doubt believing it was probably a human—but no further signs of the trespasser were found. In an interview with NAWAC investigators, the security officer that made the 911 call remained adamant that what he and his partner saw was not a person. He also claimed to have no knowledge of the previous sighting prior to his call.

Five weeks later, a woman reported a similar encounter just one mile from the construction facility.[109] As she and her husband were driving one afternoon they noticed a "hunched brown figure walking through the trees." As in the other cases, it appeared to be tall, hairy, and human-like. Had the new construction in The Woodlands uprooted an unknown resident? Given the corroborating reports, it's certainly possible.

East of Sam Houston lies the Angelina National Forest, another heavily timbered segment of the Piney Woods. Here again we find reports of curious ape-like creatures. In one of my investigations I spoke to Steven Woodson who told me of an experience he had in December 1991. At the time he was hunting near the town of Zavalla with his brother, Jim, and a mutual friend. They were walking along an old logging trail toward the Neches River at about 3:30 p.m. when they stopped for a bathroom break. Just as they were picking up their guns to resume the hike, the three men saw a large, hair-covered animal run across the logging trail approximately 15 feet in front of them. It was running on two legs and was visible for 1-2 seconds before heading into the woods on the other side of the trail.

"It was covered in gray hair and looked very muscular," Woodson told me. He estimated its height at around seven to eight feet and weight at around 500 pounds. He described it as having a coni-

cal shaped head, similar to a gorilla, and even compared its muscular form to that of a silverback. However, he said its legs were
definitely longer as it ran upright much like a human.

After the creature ran into the timber, they could see the top
of a large tree swaying back and forth as though the animal was
pushing it. The men followed it into the woods to get a better look,
but after a short distance they decided it might be best to leave the
creature alone.

The following year, Steve's brother, Jim, encountered a similar
creature in the same area. He told me he was hunting along a steep
levee embankment of the Neches River at the time. As he climbed
up the levee, he set his gun on higher ground so he could get better
traction. At the point where his head reached the top of the levee,
just enough to see the level ground beyond, he was startled by the
sight of a hairy bipedal creature walking just a few feet away. The
creature turned and looked directly at the him, although it kept
walking, seemingly indifferent to the human presence. Frightened
(and now without a gun), Jim ducked down and remained on the
side of the embankment where he watched the creature for another
20-25 seconds until it was out of sight. Jim then scrambled to the
top, grabbed his rifle, and high-tailed it out of the woods.

In our discussions, both Steve and Jim recalled a vague warning
their uncle had issued when they were younger. He wasn't specific
but was unusually stern when he told them to be careful in those
particular woods. Now they knew just what he meant.

7. BAYOU BEASTS

As the Piney Woods of Texas blend with Louisiana's South Central Plains, it's hard to draw definitive boundaries between the wooded landscapes and bottomlands that spread out along the border between the two states. The area here is forested, swampy, and webbed with miles of waterways owing to a high percentage of annual rainfall, which nurtures the great pine thickets and fills the sloping lowlands at the edge of bayou country. It's another of the South's most striking regions that not only beckons a weekend trip to the great outdoors but oozes with a steady stream of cryptid tales.

Stories of hairy, man-like beings date back many years, starting with the previously mentioned "lost giants" derived from Caddo Indian legends. In modern times, reports of would-be giants cluster around many of the area's watery landmarks such as Caddo Lake, a moss-draped, primordial paradise that straddles the border of Texas and Louisiana in equal measure. Earlier in the book we discussed the 1965 case of Johnny Maples, who was allegedly chased by an aggressive, man-like ape in Marion County, Texas. Marion is located within the Piney Woods, but it's also near Caddo Lake. The Bigfoot (assuming it was a Bigfoot) who harassed Maples that day could very well have come from the more remote regions of this sprawling wetland.

In my book *The Beast of Boggy Creek*, I briefly explored this area, noting that it's a mere 30 miles south of Fouke, Arkansas, and the Sulphur River Bottoms where the infamous Fouke Monster has been reported over the years. As part of the Red River watershed, it's a corridor where creatures such as Bigfoot could potentially roam based on the concept of "They Always Follow the Creeks." It's a connection that cannot be overlooked especially considering there was a corresponding rash of sightings near Fouke in the mid-1960s. One might argue Maples was influenced by newspaper coverage of these incidents, however, the Fouke Monster didn't make headlines until 1971. There would have been virtually no way for Maples to know about the sightings, which, at the time, were confined to a very small community south of Fouke called Jonesville.

While stories can and do spread, the creature tales of the bayou lands stand on their own, rooted in a history that goes back many years. The bottomlands that extend from the western border of Texas all across Louisiana are certainly comparable to those around Boggy Creek. And, as we shall soon see, just as rich with swamp-dwelling mystery beasts.

CADDO CRITTERS

With its network of shadowy coves, cypress trees, and Spanish moss, Caddo Lake seems like the perfect setting for monster tales. As such, sightings of a hairy, man-like creature referred to as the Big Cypress Swamp Monster or Caddo Critter would all but seem like characteristic folklore, if not for the modern eyewitnesses who have reported encounters time and time again.

One such witness is Charles Fason. He grew up on the west side of Caddo Lake, and as a boy he and his brother spent countless hours exploring its murky backwaters. They had their own boat and even constructed a treehouse where Big Cypress Bayou joins the main lake channel (in an area known as Devil's Elbow) to use for hunting and overnight fishing trips. It was their own private paradise full of wild game and boyhood adventures.

In the summer of 1969, however, the paradise took on a different tone. After a day of fishing around Devil's Elbow, the boys cooked up a big meal of fish and potatoes, and were now sleeping the night in their treehouse. Around midnight Charles was awakened by noises outside. He figured it was the usual "night critters" sniffing around but decided to have a look anyway.

Charles sat up and peered between the wooden slats of the tree-house wall. The newly risen moon was full and bright, giving him a good view of the immediate area. He expected to see raccoons going after their leftovers, but what he saw shocked him. It was a huge shape—like some sort of tall, upright animal—lurking just beyond the treehouse.

The startled boy drew back and quickly awakened his brother. When his brother awoke, Charles signaled him to be quiet and look outside.

"We're sitting there looking at this thing and it started moving towards us," Fason told me in an interview. They watched in disbelief as it walked to where they had thrown some leftovers, and it reached down to scoop them up. "Then it looked right directly back at us," he continued. "It started to move and then froze, like it all of sudden sensed we were looking at it."

For a few tense moments the boys remained frozen, wondering what the animal would do now that it was aware of their presence. But after a few seconds, it took off into the woods at an incredible speed.

"For something this big to move that fast was unbelievable," Fason recalled. "We could hear limbs snapping as it ran. Needless to say I didn't sleep the rest of the night. We were watching to see if it came back, but it never did."

The next day, in the safety of sunlight, the boys ventured out to investigate. As they looked around, they found several footprints left by the creature in the soft mud. "We were in awe because of the size of them," Fason told me. The impressions were huge and man-like with an incredibly large big toe. The boys didn't have a ruler, but they compared the impressions to their own feet. Fason estimates the creature's foot was at least 16 inches if not longer.

They attempted to gauge the height of the creature by placing an eight-foot 2x4 against a tree limb that was roughly the same height as the top of the creature's head when it lingered in front of the treehouse. By that estimate, the creature likely stood 7.5 inches tall. It was a staggering height that seemed consistent with the size of the footprints.

The Faston boys then followed the prints into the trees, noting a path of freshly broken branches where the thing had run. They also found several tufts of coarse hair clinging to the briars. Charles remembers it being very dark brown in color and similar to that of a horse's mane. Of course, at the time, they didn't understand the potential scientific value, so they didn't collect the hair or return later to cast the footprints.

During our conversation Fason noted that the creature hadn't made any verbal noises, although they had heard unexplained high-pitched howls in the area on numerous other occasions. These mysterious calls did not come from any animal or bird they were familiar with, and after their sighting, he believed they may have been connected to the strange animal. He could tell there was more than one animal involved, since he could hear pitch distinctions among the sounds as they echoed in the bayous late at night.

As witnesses go, I found Mr. Fason to be of the utmost credibility. He has a lifetime of outdoors experience and has never gone public with his account. I was lucky enough to have stumbled upon it when I was talking to his daughter—whom I'm friends with—about Caddo Lake. His is one of those stories that leaves me feeling confident that some unknown animal may truly exist, or has existed, in the region.

Reports of Bigfoot-like creatures in the area date back even further. Several years ago I spoke to two witnesses—a brother and sister—who recounted a brief but harrowing incident they experienced around 1947 when they were children. At the time they were staying at their family's camp house, which sat on the edge of Caddo Lake near Mooringsport, Louisiana. One evening after dark, as their parents visited with relatives, they were looking out the front window towards the lake when they saw a man-like thing peer inside. It had hair on its face, and they could see hair on its arms as it placed a hand on the glass. The frightened siblings screamed and ran from the window.

After telling the adults what they had seen, several of them hurried outside to investigate, but whatever may have been there was already gone. They found no trace of tracks but estimated its height

Swampy terrain at Caddo Lake
(Photo by Lyle Blackburn)

to be at least seven feet tall. The house was on elevated on piers, and it would've been impossible for an average sized man to be eye-level with the window.

I spoke to another witness, Dick Tinsley, who had an even more distinct sighting south of Mooringsport along Highway 169. In 1979, Tinsley told me he was driving northbound on Highway 169 near the Paw Paw Bottoms. He was a teenager at the time and was driving home after an evening spent at a rural racing track. At approximately 1:30 a.m., he noticed another vehicle traveling toward him. The vehicle was moving rather fast, so he slowed down in order to pass. (Back then Highway 169 was rough and narrow, so it was hard for two cars to pass at high speed.) After the car passed, Tinsley noticed a figure standing in the drainage ditch on the left side of the road. It appeared to be some sort of unusual, upright creature, so he stopped to get a better look.

As Tinsley's car rolled to a stop, the creature began walking across the road directly in front of him. The animal was approximately 7.5 feet tall with reddish-brown hair covering a muscular body. Its weight perhaps 350 lbs. "As it walked, it took long strides and kept its eyes and face focused ahead, never actually looking at me," Tinsley explained.

When the creature was about 50 feet from the car, Tinsley said he could make out some features, including a "somewhat human profile with a protruding nose and conical shaped head." The creature had shoulder-length hair on its head, but the hair on its face was shorter, revealing dark skin underneath. It didn't seem to be in a hurry, as it crossed the road in 4-5 steps before walking into a field on the right. Tinsley quickly maneuvered his car so he could shine its headlights into the field. The creature, however, could no longer be seen. Realizing he had possibly seen a Bigfoot, Tinsley then drove to a friend's house and relayed the story. His friend commented that he looked "white as a sheet."

Like the previous witnesses, I found Tinsley to be of excellent character and his story among the most solid I've investigated. In my mind he was either subject to a daring and professionally executed hoax or else he saw an unknown creature. There's little else that could explain such a credible witness with a very clear sighting.

In the fall of 1987, a man was hunting along Big Cypress Bayou (not far from the Faston boys' treehouse) when he observed a strange animal. According to a report filed with the BFRO, he was in his deer stand around mid-afternoon when he noticed a dark figure moving approximately 50 yards away.[110] It stood up from a crouched position in the shallow, murky water of the bayou.

The animal "appeared to be 6 feet tall, covered with hair from head to toe," the hunter told investigators who followed up on his report. As the hunter watched, the creature moved its head from side-to-side, as if looking for something. After about two minutes, it simply turned and walked into the woods. The experience unnerved the hunter so much he decided to leave the area as quickly as he could rather than pursue the creature. As he made his way to his truck, he came across a large footprint in the loose soil. It reinforced his instinct to leave without further hesitation.

Just two years later, an amazing up-close encounter occurred in the same vicinity. The witness was Brad McAndrews, a person whom I've been acquainted with for several years. (I included his story in *The Beast of Boggy Creek*, but it's worth summarizing again as we discuss the Caddo Lake area in more detail.)

According to McAndrews, he was visiting his grandmother's cabin east of Caddo Lake in the summer of 1989 when he was ten years old. One afternoon, his grandmother and aunt offered to take him and his younger brother for a picnic on the property, so they ventured from the cabin and walked past an old barn searching for a good place to spread out the blanket. Remembering a good spot, McAndrews ran ahead. He was now beyond sight of the others. When he arrived, however, he found the spot far more overgrown than he'd remembered.

As McAndrews began walking back, he was startled by a rustle in the woods. Something was coming directly toward him. Thinking it might be a deer, he stopped to see if it would cross the path. As he stood there waiting, the noise of cracking twigs and crunching leaves became louder until an animal finally did emerge from the woods. But this was no deer. It was an ape-like creature seven-to-eight-feet tall with dark, reddish-brown hair and weathered looking skin. At first it was running on all fours, but upon seeing the boy, it stopped and stood up on two legs. It was less than twelve yards away.

"I had never been so scared in my life," McAndrews said. "When it reached me, it immediately stopped and squared its shoulders." McAndrews' heart pounded as he stood face-to-face with the creature. For several seconds it alternated between looking at him and looking away, as if it were unsure of what to do next.

McAndrews' brother suddenly shouted from a distance. When the animal heard the voice, it instantly sprinted off on two legs, using its hands to tunnel through the thick trees as it ran into the woods. Relieved, McAndrews ran toward his brother as fast as his legs could carry him.

"From its facial features and expression, body language, and walking/running gait, this creature was scarily human," McAndrews recalled. "Even at my age, I could tell that this was an intelligent creature by the way it seemed to be assessing his circumstances. I also cannot express enough how fluid this creature was in shifting from a four legged 'run' to a bipedal running gait." Interestingly, the description of the animal's speed and movement is quite similar to what Charles Faston told me. It's a trait that makes perfect sense. For these animals to have evaded discovery all these years, they must be able to move very quickly when required to do so.

More recent accounts come from a family living near Twelve Mile Bayou on the east side of Caddo Lake. I became aware of their experiences while participating in a Caddo Lake episode of the Animal Planet show *Finding Bigfoot*. According to family members, several Bigfoot creatures have been seen around their property, which consists of 200 acres of pecan orchards.

In 2008, Faye Allen said she was headed to pick up some bagged pecans in a tractor when she noticed a large figure bent over one of the sacks. It appeared to be eating pecans. When she got within 70 feet, the thing stood up. Much to her surprise, it was a hairy bipedal creature. She described it as being very tall, somewhat slender, and covered in solid black fur. Allen said she couldn't believe her eyes, as the animal turned and looked directly at her. After a few moments it simply walked off into the woods.

Donald Meeler claimed he was out hunting on a cloudy morning when he noticed a huge, hairy figure in the trees. When he raised his gun to get a better look through the scope, the thing turned and darted into the thicket. "Any normal human couldn't walk through it," Meeler said. "He ran through it." His observation of the creature's speed through the tangled brush is again reminiscent of previous area sightings.

In one of the most dramatic stories, Ben DuPont—who lives one quarter mile from Caddo Lake—said he was awakened one night by some noise. When he went outside to investigate he saw a huge, hairy creature shaking a metal trailer where he was keeping several hogs. The hogs were making a frightened fuss as the animal tried to force its way in. As DuPont approached with a hand on his gun, the creature turned and looked at him. When it did, DuPont could see that it was a female with breasts. The creature then made a huffing sound and walked bipedally across a field. When it reached the treeline, it made a short howl before disappearing from sight.

In speaking to other members of the family, they confirmed that strange sightings have been occurring along Twelve Mile Bayou for many years. According to Danny DuPont, his grandfather and two of his brothers were hunting along the bayou in the early 1940s when a terrible storm rolled in. They were a long way from home on foot, so they sought shelter in a huge, 50-foot log.

"During the night, they kept smelling this awful odor and would hear something moving in the log on the opposite end," Danny told me, remembering his grandfather's story well. "They thought it was a possum or skunk."

As soon as daylight broke, the brothers crawled out of the log and walked to the other end. If it were an opossum, it would make a good meal since they were all quite hungry by now. Hoping to scare it out, one of them started kicking the dead wood, while another stood by with his gun. Sure enough, something stirred within and crawled out a few seconds later. But it was not what they expected.

"They said it was about five and a half feet tall, covered in hair, and had breasts," Danny recalled. "And it smelled like death."

The brothers were stunned when the strange creature emerged from the log and stood up. It was apparently just as shocked. Within seconds it ran into the trees and disappeared from sight.

None of them had ever heard of Bigfoot at the time, so they could only describe it as a "wild person." As the years went on, they came to believe that a family of them must be inhabiting the lonely stretches between Twelve Mile Bayou and Caddo Lake. It was an idea that would later transcend the old timer's stories and manifest itself in modern-day cinema. As a testament of Caddo Lake's eerie splendor and monstrous history, several Bigfoot-themed movies have been filmed there including *Creature From Black Lake* (1976), *Boggy Creek: The Legend is True* (2010), and *Skookum: The Hunt for Bigfoot* (2014). As with *The Legend of Boggy Creek*, the spookiest stories are always the ones grounded in reality.

SABINE THING

South of Caddo Lake lies the Sabine River. The river, which originates in the prairies of North Texas, is an extremely long waterway forming much of the boundary between Texas and Louisiana as it snakes through miles of the lower Piney Woods and western bayou country. The river is revered by campers, hikers, and paddlers alike for its serene beauty, but for people such as myself it's also notable for the presence of a Bigfoot creature the locals refer to as the Sabine Thing.

Dramatic sightings of the alleged beast date back many years, and in fact, we've already been introduced to one particularly chilling account in which Paul Matlock claims to have seen a massive, bipedal ape pummel a hog on the banks of the river in 2003. This took place in Panola County, Texas, where many of the Sabine Thing reports originate.

An older account from Panola County dates back to the winter of 1969. In this case, Teresa Dixon, her aunt, and her little sister (all very young at the time) were exploring a patch of fire-damaged woods behind their grandmother's house near Beckville when they noticed some kind of animal crouching behind some trees. As soon as they made eye contact, it stood up on two legs.

"It was very tall, thin, and hairy like an ape, but was more man-like," Dixon told me in an interview. She's unsure of the exact distance they were from the creature, but distinctly remembers seeing its eyes. "It didn't look menacing," she recalled. "And it wasn't scared."

Maybe not, but the girls were certainly scared. Enough that they turned and ran as fast as they could back to their grandmother's house located beyond a big field and a barbed wire fence. "I don't remember how I got over that fence," Dixon said. "But I'll never forget what I saw that day. It's tattooed on my brain."

After telling her family of the experience, her grandfather admitted that he'd seen an ape-like creature several years before near their house. He kept it quiet so as not to frighten anyone.

Approximately two years after Dixon's sighting, around 1971, her uncle claimed to have seen a similar creature while camping in the bottoms between Beckville and Carthage. Other locals whispered of a strange beast responsible for many unexplained livestock deaths.

In 1986, just west of the Sabine River in Panola County, Jeff Stewart was camping with friends as they often did on weekends. He was 15 at the time and already a skilled outdoorsman, having grown up in a culture of hunting and fishing typical of that area. The spot where they camped was located on 580 heavily wooded acres owned by his family, of which he was intimately familiar both in terms of geography and wildlife... or so he thought.

Earlier in the day he and his friends caught a load of catfish in the river and cleaned them at an old pump-well present on the property. Afterwards, they intentionally threw the entrails on the ground so they could return at night with flashlights to harvest any fur-bearing animals caught eating the scraps. Stewart had done this plenty of times in the past with successful results.

Later that night, after eating their fill of fish, Stewart was volunteered to go check the trap. Chiding his friends for being lazy, he grabbed his flashlight and .22 rifle and headed off down the trail. As he approached the spot, he could see something there eating, dimly illuminated in the beam of his old two-cell bulb. It was rather large and hairy, so he assumed it was a hog. However, when Stewart got within 20 yards, the thing stood up on two legs.

"I never will forget," Stewart told me during one of several conversations we've had about the event. "It never made a gesture; it just looked me dead in the face."

His first thought was that someone must be playing a joke on him, perhaps one of his friends. He even called out to it, indicating he wasn't falling for the ruse. But the more he looked at the silent figure standing before him, the more he realized it was not a person in a costume, if it was even a person at all. He had heard stories about people living down in the river bottoms who had gone feral; people who had gone down there to live and were rarely seen again. But this looked more like an animal. It was beastly despite its anthropomorphic stature.

He described it as being approximately five feet tall and covered in hair matted down with a layer of gray, gumbo mud from the river bottom. The face was exposed, with very dark, oily and weathered skin that reminded him of an Australian Aborigine. It had dark eyes and a nose that was wide and almost ape-like, but still within human parameters.

Unsure of what the creature might do, Stewart leveled his gun at it. But he didn't have to pull the trigger. Seconds later the creature took three steps backward in a distinct "toe to heel" fashion.

"When it got to the edge of the bushes, where there was a pine thicket, it was still looking at me and it just kind of disappeared backwards into the brush," Stewart told me.

After it was out of sight, the stunned teenager ran back to camp where he told his friends about the encounter. Stewart was outwardly shaken, but they still dismissed his story with a laugh, think-

The Sabine River
(Photo by Lyle Blackburn)

ing perhaps he was trying to scare them. Realizing it would be hard to convince anyone he'd truly seen such a thing, he resolved to stay quiet for many years. Now, as the stories are gathered in one place, it's evident Stewart is not alone.

Not far from the location of Stewart's encounter, two hunters reportedly shot at such a creature in November 2001. According to a report by my research partner, Jerry Hestand, both were hunting at separate locations near the Sabine River when they saw a "large ape-man" step from the trees. In both cases, the creature began walking toward the hunter. This frightened the men enough to raise their rifles and shoot. In both cases they believed to have hit the creature, yet it simply moved back into the thicket and disappeared into its shadows.

In April 2006, two men were bowfishing on the Sabine River in Panola County when they saw a similar, unexplainable creature.[111] At around 3:00 p.m. on a clear day, they were floating along in their boat when they caught sight of a large, dark figure moving just off the bank some distance ahead. As they drifted closer, they could see that it was walking on two legs through the trees with its back toward them. The thing seemed unaware of their presence as they watched it for several tense minutes. It appeared to be at least seven feet tall and covered in dark brown hair approximately two-to-three-inches long, with longer, darker hair on its head. It was bulky and definitely walking upright as it slowly moved away from the stunned fisherman.

One of the witnesses told my colleague John Morley that he was uncertain what the thing might have done if it had seen them, and that was the most unnerving aspect of the experience. After it disappeared from sight, his partner started the trolling motor and began to head back upstream. As soon as they felt safe, he cranked up the outboard motor and they sped to the boat ramp. Whatever it was, they didn't want to see it again.

Further south in Newton County, three hunters saw something fitting the description of the Sabine Thing in July 1998. John West, his father, and a friend were scouting locations for deer stands in the bottoms when they heard an eerie scream.[112] It was so startling, the three men stopped in their tracks. After a few moments without any further sound, they began to discuss what kind of animal it could have been. But they had no answers. Eventually, they continued on but with the distinct feeling that something was watching them.

After another 15-20 minutes, West's father stopped abruptly and whispered: "What the hell is that thing?!" John looked up to see a large, dark figure step out from behind a clump of trees. The thing appeared to be at least eight feet tall with dark, brownish hair covering its entire body. Its head was slightly conical in shape and it was decidedly ape-like in appearance. As the three men watched, the creature turned and headed back into the trees, walking on two legs as it went. They were at a loss to identify the animal, but were absolutely sure it wasn't a bear.

In 2014, I went to the Sabine area to look around myself. My father's family is from Carthage in Panola County, so I'd been to the area many times for family reunions at my great-grandmother's house (she lived to be 106!), but I'd never spent much time in the woods there. I found the Sabine River to be as beautiful as any river I'd paddled in the United States. It was calm and serene, like a huge, olive-colored serpent winding its way through a thick wall of trees. I was camped only miles from the county road that had brought me in, yet it seemed a world away.

During my visit I saw many examples of wildlife there, but did not get a glimpse of the ape-like creature so many have reported over the years. The lack of a sighting during my visit doesn't eliminate the possibility, however. Within the dark pockets of bottoms and crowding trees, anything could have been hiding, watching me as it might watch a feral hog.

MONSTER CENTRAL

In November 1992, Jim Lansdale and his son Josh were driving the backroads of their family's property in West Louisiana. They had just enjoyed a holiday meal with the family and were taking in the peaceful night air of the wooded bottomlands. The roads were muddy so it was slow-going, but they were in no hurry. It was refreshing to be out in the open country.

After a bit of driving, they eased up a muddy section of road that led to a five-gallon feeder Lansdale kept there for hunting purposes. It was not out of the ordinary to find a deer there, but on this occasion they were shocked to see something far different.

"As the headlights flashed into the field towards the feeder we saw the strangest thing I ever saw in my life," Lansdale stated in an article about his experience.[113] "It was built like a man but dark in color... some type of fur bearing critter." Both he and his son eyed the creature with amazement.

"The buttocks were heavy with the calf area looking a bit disproportionate for the thigh and buttocks," he explained. "This, whatever it was, had its hands, paws, feet or something on the feeder and it appeared it was shaking it. After a few seconds, maybe ten to fifteen, this animal realized there were lights shining on it, turned, looked our way with huge red eyes and bolted to the near thicket on all fours."

Josh immediately exclaimed "what was that?" Lansdale had no answer. Though he didn't know it at the time, this was only the first of what would become a long series of the most perplexing mysteries and tense situations he had ever experienced.

Lansdale's property, which has come to be known as "Monster Central," is located on the east side of the Sabine River among the murky patches of bottomlands and unrelenting thickets. Lansdale is now the team leader on a television show called *Killing Bigfoot*, but long before he appeared in front of a camera he was trying to find explanations for the mysterious happenings on his property along with nearly 40 other researchers who joined him at one time or another over the years.

Following the bizarre incident at the feeder, nothing else occurred until the next hunting season when he and Josh were trimming brush along a road at the back of the property. It was one of their hunting areas and some corn milo had been tossed onto the ground to attract quail. As Jim and Josh were trimming trees and hauling the limbs to the side, they came upon the grain where they noticed a very unusual track in the middle of the pile. "[We] could clearly see what appeared to be a barefoot human track," Lansdale explained. "But what was even stranger, it only had three toes: a huge large toe with two smaller outside toes."

Adjacent to the first track, Josh discovered another. It measured a whopping 19 inches. At this point it all came rushing back. The unidentified animal at the feeder. The two incidents must surely be connected. Realizing something strange was afoot, Lansdale returned later to take photos of the tracks and ultimately to cast them with plaster. He had been hunting and fishing all of his life in the Sabine River bottoms and had never come across such an animal. His interest was piqued, to say the least.

But things were just getting started. When Lansdale returned to cast the first set of tracks, he and an employee who was assisting him began to notice other tracks in the area. These were just as odd in appearance, so Lansdale decided to cast these as well. Later, when he returned at night to retrieve the dried plaster, he left his employee at the truck and walked down to the bottoms by himself. As Lansdale was walking he began to hear something moving in the woods beside the road. At first he thought it might be an armadillo, but it sounded more like something walking. Lansdale stopped to listen. When he did, the movement stopped. As soon as he started walking again, the footsteps resumed. Now he was sure it was something walking, perhaps on two legs. In fact, it appeared to be matching Lansdale's pace.

"This, whatever it is, was stride for stride with me and would stop when I stopped," he explained. He shined his flashlight into the woods, but saw nothing. It was a spooky situation that was getting more unnerving by the minute.

Despite feeling vulnerable, Lansdale proceeded to locate the dried cast. He was shocked to find it shattered into countless pieces. As he shined his light on it, wondering how it could have been broken, the noise continued in the trees. Now, whatever it was, was breaking limbs and rustling the brush more intensely. And it was breathing heavily and loudly. Lansdale tried again to spot it with his beam, but it was in vein. "I have never heard anything like this before and know of no animal capable of doing this," Lansdale remarked.

For the next year Lansdale continued to find tracks and hear strange noises coming from the bottoms as he worked and hunted the property. Now that he was aware of an unknown animal, he was always on the lookout. He had not laid eyes on it since the initial feeder incident, but that would change the following year.

One winter afternoon, Jim was sitting in a tripod deer stand when he swiveled the chair to look to his left. "As I turned to look, there was one of these animals standing damn near directly under me looking up," he said. "As we got a glimpse of each other, this animal wheeled to its left and hit the ground on all fours and was out of my sight. This creature made less noise running off then a deer would have made and this kind of spooked me knowing something about five to six feet tall weighing maybe a hundred to one twenty five or possibly a little more could slip up on me during a dry winter."

Lansdale only locked eyes for a few seconds, but it was long enough to send chills up his spine. The animal—which he did not believe was a bear—was distinctly ape-like, with "short dark deep brown hair" and "a rather slender build and what seemed like narrow shoulders." It also had large eyes and hair that was "neatly parted." It was something that altogether perplexed him, spooked him, and set in motion a hunt that would last for years.

In 1998 Lansdale contacted Bobby Hamilton, founder of the Gulf Coast Bigfoot Research Group. Hamilton had a dramatic sighting of a frightening creature in Texas during his childhood (which beckoned him to come to the window!), prompting his later interest in the subject. As head of the GCBRO, Hamilton had experience in the field and several additional sightings, and was familiar with the various types of suspected Bigfoot evidence common to the South.

"This is the wildest place I've ever been to in my life," Hamilton told me as we discussed his experience in Monster Central.

Not long after he was invited to visit the property, he too began to experience strange noises and discover unusual tracks. "I saw some small tracks and some bigger tracks," he explained. "The longest was 22 inches."

The track lengths varied from this massive measurement down to eight inches at the smallest with the toe counts varying in number from three to five. Hamilton also noticed that some of the tracks had a peculiar curvature. These were theorized to be those of the female creatures since they were consistently found next to smaller tracks thought to be those of juvenile offspring.

On one occasion, Hamilton and four other men were staking out an area of the bottoms late at night when they began to hear sounds like footsteps stomping in the nearby woods. The men listened as the steps got louder and limbs began breaking. Finally Hamilton grabbed his light and charged in the direction of the noise. Something big ran in the opposite direction and the noise ceased.

Returning to the camp—where a fire was burning—the rest of the group tried to get some rest while Hamilton stayed alert in his chair. Suddenly he felt as though eyes were watching him, intensely. A cold chill raced up his spine as he got up and headed towards a Hawthorne thicket where he believed the animal was hiding. In route he encountered a wall of stench until anything he had ever smelled. It was strong enough to make him nauseated, followed by an overwhelming sense of fear and vulnerability. Hamilton, who had previously felt no fear in the presence of such encounters, quickly returned to the camp and grabbed his shotgun. The rest of the night he sat awake, watching the woods closely. Whatever had been there taunting him in the darkness never showed itself, but it was nonetheless a haunting experience that left him with the horrifying feeling that the creatures were potentially dangerous and far from benevolent. "I knew if the thing had come out of there, he'd be playing for keeps," he told me.

Over the next few years other researchers were invited to participate in what became a massive effort to solve the mystery at Monster Central by harvesting one of the males, if such a shot could be made with certainty and safety. For the purpose of the "hunts," tower blinds were constructed and a variety of other techniques employed, including ground blinds and active efforts to flush a creature from the thick bottoms where they hid.

During the hunts, the men experienced the same sort of bizarre circumstances and occasionally laid eyes on the elusive creatures, which seemed to have the ability to move in both a bipedal and quadrupedal fashion. In one instance, a man was positioned in a tower when the structure began to shake violently. He looked down to see what he perceived as "a young female walking bipedal with a young toddler on all fours at her right side" but it quickly moved away.[114] On another occasion, a hunter said he managed to get a shot at one the creatures. He was certain he hit it, but the creature still managed to cross a creek and escape into the bottoms. An extensive search was undertaken to find the wounded creature, but they only found a few drops of blood and a mucus-like substance on some leaves.

According to Hamilton, they estimated at least a dozen creatures were present in the area based on the different tracks that were found. The creatures were all dark in color and generally resembled apes The footprints they left were often consistent with other Bigfoot prints, having five toes, but were more often of the three and four toed variety. The anatomy may seem strange, but it matches other impressions on record for many of the surrounding areas including Arkansas, Texas, and Mississippi.

Another interesting anatomical feature of the tracks was the "bulbous" big toe. According to researcher James Kane, the largest set of tracks he ever followed were 19.5 inches long and 7 inches wide.[115] These had "four toes on each foot with a bulbous big toe on each."[116]

According to Kane, he followed the tracks for almost 200 yards before they stopped. "All that was left were a few scuffmarks," he recalled. "I assumed that the animal had gone down on all fours and continued on. Interestingly, this is the same general area that one of our researchers saw the silhouette of a huge animal upright on a road just after dark, watching him as he assumed a defensive position with three other animals growling at him from the nearby tree line."

The bulbous toe has also been noted in man-ape sightings elsewhere in the South. In the report I took from Charles Fason, who saw such a creature at Caddo Lake in 1969, he recalled that its tracks had an abnormally large big toe. Could the very same creature seen by Fason and his brother be the one seen years later at Lansdale's place? It's an interesting proposition to consider.

The strange activity and persistent hunting continued at Monster Central for several more years until the sightings began to decline. Did the creatures move on, or did they become wise to their own jeopardy? A decade later, there's indications that the creatures are sometimes present — or passing through — but answers to these and other questions remain. What are these creatures? Primate, Bigfoot, Skunk Ape, or something else? Perhaps in time we will learn the true nature behind the "monsters" of Monster Central.

LURKERS IN THE LOWLANDS

While Monster Central may exemplify a hotbed of activity, similar ape-like beasts have been reported throughout Louisiana. Several examples can be found in an article titled "Bayou Bigfoot no laughing matter" which ran in the September 15, 2000 edition of the *Gadsden Times*.[117] In the article, restaurant owner Hosea Remedies recounts a sighting he had that month outside his home in Sabine Parish near Zwolle.

The article mentions other incidents from the same time period, which were also covered by the *Alexandria Daily Town Talk* newspaper. The first was reported by loggers Earl Whitstine and Carl Dubois who said they saw a hairy, man-like creature at Boggy Bayou near Cotton Island, 20 miles from Alexandria.[118] Whitstine said he was cutting timber when he saw the creature on August 22.

"It was hairy and looked like a human in a way," Whitstine told reporters. He pursued it in his cutter vehicle, but it jumped into the bayou and escaped into the woods on the other side.[119]

Whitstine told several men on his crew about the incident but was mostly met with laughter. Carl Dubois was one of those who doubted the story but changed his mind when he saw the creature himself two days later. "Earl hollered at it, and it ran off," Dubois said. "I wouldn't have believed it if I hadn't seen it."[120]

The creature was elusive but apparently left tracks in the soft mud of the bayou embankment. These were examined by the Rapides Sheriff's Department, Wildlife and Fisheries, and firefighter/researcher Scott Kessler who arrived on scene shortly after the second sighting.[121] Kessler reported a total of 16 tracks, which measured 14.5 inches in length and 7 inches at the ball. They looked human-like but only had four toes. Suspected hairs were also collected from the site, but they were later determined to be bovine (cow)—an animal common on the property.

Kessler interviewed both witnesses himself and found no deviation in their stories. The news article also mentions a third sighting, which occurred a month prior. In this case Larry Satcher claimed he was fishing nearby when a similar creature walked up on him. He described it as seven feet tall, bipedal, and covered in black hair. It appeared to be holding a dead hog under its arm. The creature lingered briefly as it studied the fisherman before running back into the woods. Authorities dismissed the accounts as the work of a prankster, but those who saw the beasts thought differently.

On May 30, 1994, in nearby Avoyelles Parish, my longtime friend Craig Woolheater saw something that literally changed his life. That night he was driving with his girlfriend from New Orleans back to their home in Dallas. The weather was warm and clear so the top of his convertible was down. At approximately midnight, they were travelling along a dark, two-lane highway south of Alexandria (between Cocodrie Lake and Bayou Cocodrie) when they caught sight of a figure on the right side of the road. It was walking on two legs with its back to them in a sort of hunched-over fashion. It looked man-like but didn't appear to be a man due to its covering of grayish fur and its massive size. By Woolheater's estimate, it stood around seven feet tall.

As they passed, they both blurted out: "Did you see what I saw?"

Woolheater immediately asked his girlfriend: "What do you think you saw?" Without hesitation she replied, "It looked like a Bigfoot." Woolheater agreed. He wanted to turn around and go back for a second look, but she would have none of it. The first glimpse was chilling enough, and they were in an open convertible. Whatever it was, she did not want to see again.

After another 10 minutes of driving, Woolheater decided to pull off into the parking lot of a country church where they discussed the strange event. No matter how they rationalized it, they could not dismiss the fact that they had clearly seen something fitting the description of a Bigfoot. After a few minutes Woolheater resumed the trip to Dallas but would never forget the incident. Several years later he founded the Texas Bigfoot Research Center (TBRC) in an effort to discover just what kind of creature might be lurking in the Southern Woods.

When it comes to these mysterious sightings, most people don't get a second look. That seems to be the nature of the phenomenon. The creature appears suddenly without warning and then slips silently back into the shadows. Or, it frightens the witness enough they would rather not have a second look. This type of reaction is not limited to casual motorists or hikers; it includes the brave personnel of law enforcement.

In March 2003, a Deputy Sheriff from St. Martin Parish was on patrol one night when he saw a strange figure in his headlights. In a report filed with the Gulf Coast Bigfoot Research Organization, he explained that it was walking on two legs and was slightly hunched over as it entered the road from a swampy low area.[122] Once in the road, it stopped and looked right at him.

"I was traveling 20 mph due to the road being limestone and very curvy," he reported. "As I approached the creature, I turned on the white take-down lights of the light bar and noticed that it was from seven to eight feet tall." He could also see that it was covered in "reddish-brown" fur.

The officer slowly edged his car closer to the beast for a better look. Its eyes reflected red in the glare of the patrol lights. It was a sight that truly unnerved the policemen.

"I am a Deputy Sheriff and I work alone and I am by no means a small nor easily frightened person," he stated. "But when I realized what I was looking at, I sped up and left the area. I did not return."

One can hardly blame him. The bottoms can be very unsettling at night, especially if they harbor unknown, man-like apes.

The area where St. Martin Parish is located, in fact, boasts some of the swampiest stretches of the Mississippi Alluvial Plain, a vast drainage system that flanks the Mississippi River and spills southward through the lower portion of Louisiana. Miles of backwater and inland swamps here fill the map like thick, green soup. Roads and highways are often forced to run for long distances across bridges or even surrender altogether to the convenience of boats. It's a place where large creatures could easily avoid human contact, although there are times when locals and travelers find themselves confronting a beast at the edge of the mire.

In an example fielded by my late colleague Charles DeVore, a truck driver was stopped at a remote rest stop when he got the shock of his life.[123] That evening he was driving along the 18-mile Breaux Bridge over Atchafalaya Swamp when he decided to pull over for a rest. It was approximately 11:00 p.m. and the location was deserted. After parking, he got out of the cab to stretch his legs. As he did, the driver said he heard something walking in the nearby water. It spooked him so he got back in his truck and began working on his log book.

As he was writing he glanced up and saw something in the moonlight walking up a bank no more than 20 yards ahead. He immediately flipped on his headlights. Now he could clearly see a "very large animal walking on two legs carrying a deer across its shoulder."[124] The animal was covered in dark, "matted hair" about three inches in length and had a muscular frame. It stood perhaps seven feet tall. There was no mistaking the deer either. The driver could see its antlers and tawny fur. The deer was perhaps 100 pounds, yet the creature carried it as if were "nothing."

As soon as the lights hit it, the thing turned and looked directly at the truck. The driver could see its face. In the interview he told

DeVore that its expression didn't appear to be that of anger or fear, but more of a look that indicated it did not want to be seen.

After a moment the creature turned and headed back in the direction it had come. The frightened driver immediately started his truck and left the rest stop. Like so many others, he saw something he simply could not explain. It was as if a legend had come to life.

HONEY ISLAND SWAMP MONSTER

It's impossible to discuss cryptids in Louisiana without mentioning its most famous hairy legend, the Honey Island Swamp Monster. While the creature's profile isn't altogether ape-like, it's a case that's often mentioned alongside Boggy Creek since both creatures are associated with Deep South bottomlands.

Honey Island Swamp itself is located in St. Tammany Parish east of New Orleans at the southeast tip of Louisiana. It lies between the Pearl River on the east, West Pearl River on the west, and Lake Borgne to the south. In its rugged, undeveloped state, it remains one of America's most pristine swampland habitats, covering nearly 140 square miles.[125]

Sightings of a hairy, man-like creature in the area are thought to date back at least a century. Natives referred to it as "Letiche," while the Cajuns called it the "Tainted Keitre"[126] or "La Bête Noire" (the black thing).[127] The first modern sighting on record was reported by Harlan Ford and Billy Mills, who said they encountered a strange animal near Honey Island Swamp in 1963. The sighting wasn't made public at the time but was later featured on a 1978 episode of the television show *In Search of...* and since documented by Ford's granddaughter, Dana Holyfield, who has written extensively on the subject.

According to Holyfield in her book *Honey Island Swamp Monster Documentations*, Ford was employed as an FAA Air Traffic Controller.[128] On the weekends he loved to spend his time in the outdoors, often hunting or fishing deep in the swamp. In the summer of 1963, Ford and fellow hunter Billy Mills said they were walking to one of their hunting camps north of Bradley Slough near the Lateral Canal when they came upon a massive, hairy creature crouched on all fours with its back to them. Their first impression was "hog," but when it stood up on two legs and turned around they could see it was definitely not. According to Ford, the creature was approximately seven feet tall with slender legs and a broad chest. Its body was covered in a layer of short gray hair while longer hair grew from its head. It had large, amber-colored eyes, which focused intently on the two men.

Ford and Mills were only able to study the animal for a few sec-

Honey Island Swamp
(Photo by Lyle Blackburn)

onds before it bolted into the trees. The hunters ran after it, trying to get another look, but the creature was simply too fast. After a few minutes, they gave up the pursuit, bewildered and rattled by what they had seen.

In the years that followed, Ford and Mills kept the details mostly to themselves as they watched the swamps with a wary eye. Despite their vigilance, however, nothing else was seen until 1974 when Ford and his son Perry were duck hunting in the swamp. In the course of the hunt, they came upon two dead boars lying near the water with their throats slashed and their bodies mangled. Blood was trickling from the neck of one boar into the water. It appeared that something strong and massive had taken them out. Alligators would have been a good candidate, but gators typically drag their prey into the water, not maim and leave bodies. The hunters were perplexed until they discovered a set of strange footprints nearby that had three large, clawed toes and a smaller dewclaw. Harlan immediately thought of the animal he'd encountered a decade before.

Ford didn't have plaster at the time, so he returned later to cast several of the impressions, which appeared to be from more than one animal based on differences in size. Now armed with evidence, Ford phoned the Game Warden at the Louisiana Wildlife Commission and told him of his experiences. The warden examined the tracks and agreed they did not match any known animal. They were also evaluated by Louisiana State Naturalist George Stevens, who concluded the creature must weigh upwards of 400 pounds.

Despite vague endorsements by the authorities, the nature of the tracks and their authenticity has been highly debated over the years due to several factors. First, the three major toes appear to be long and finger-like with possible claws, which is not typical of Bigfoot tracks or even those of a primate in general. In addition, a "fake shoe" was brought forth several years ago by a local resident who said he found it in the swamp. The shoe, which is fitted with a three-clawed "foot" identical to the famous track, was presented to two independent researchers from Mississippi who concluded it could have been used to create the famous tracks.[129] Holyfield looked into the matter herself and discovered the shoe size was smaller than her grandfather's foot. Without casting dispersions, she simply stated: "anyone can take an existing plaster track and make fake shoe-tracks to trek through the mud and claim it was a hoax."

Whether the tracks are real or hoaxed, however, is ultimately beside the point when analyzing this case in terms of Bigfoot. Sure the Honey Island Swamp Monster has been described as hairy and bipedal—albeit with slender legs—but its alleged footprint is far from the typical anatomy associated with these creatures. There have been cases where man-apes appear to have three main toes—including the Fouke Monster and the creatures of Monster Central—but the basic anatomy of those tracks remains closer to human or primate than anything else. The Honey Island tracks are more reminiscent of a reptilian creature or perhaps something from a prehistoric era, placing it into a different category of cryptid, if it does indeed exist. In a 1970s interview with WVUE-TV in New Orleans, Ford himself stated he didn't believe the Honey Island Monster was "related in any way to the well-known Bigfoot, or the Fouke Monster."[130] Swamps are often shrouded in mystery and this legendary denizen of the bayou is yet another enduring example.

8. REBEL BIGFOOT

As we move eastward from Louisiana, the lands of the southern gulf coast continue to spread out with amazing ecological and biological diversity. Like Louisiana, the neighboring state of Mississippi contains coastal lowlands, river floodplain forests, hilly coastal plains with evergreen and deciduous forests, and a variety of aquatic habitats that spill into the adjacent states.[131] The lands here are rich, and what they may lack in sheer forestry they make up for in food and water resources, perfect for supporting an abundance of wildlife both known and perhaps *unknown*.

With a little digging, it's not difficult to find old accounts of wildmen and ape-like creatures in the region. One of the earliest accounts comes from the *Dubuque Daily Herald* newspaper June 27, 1868. The account—mostly described within a reprinted letter—states that hunters from the small village of Meadville in Franklin County, Mississippi, had seen a hairy, man-like creature in the nearby swamps in September 1867.[132] The huntsmen were "driving in the swamps some miles from the [Homochitto] river" when their hounds took up the trail of some unseen animal. As the hunters followed, they came upon strange tracks that resembled a human foot except that "the toes of one foot turned backward." Seconds later the apparent maker of the tracks stood before them. In the writer's own words:

> On coming up with the dogs, which were now baying, they beheld a frightful looking creature of about the average height of man but with far greater muscular development, standing menacingly a few yards in front of the dogs.
> It had long coarse hair flowing from its head and

reaching near its knees; its entire body also seemed to be covered with hair of two or three inches length, which was of a dark brown color. From its upper jaw projected two very large tusks, several inches long.[133]

When the huntsmen tried to approach the thing, it fled toward the river. Both dogs and hunters pursued.

> When the party came up with the dogs the second time, the monster was standing erect before them, none of them having yet dared to clinch with it. But when their masters urged the dogs, they endeavored to seize it, when it reached forward and grabbed one of them and taking it in its hands, pressed it against its tusks, which pierced it through and killed it instantly.
>
> Becoming alarmed at this display of strength, the hunters fired several shots at the creature, which caused it to leap into the river. It remained under the water several minutes and then raised almost its entire length above the surface uttering shrieks, which almost petrified the pursuers with terror. No similar sound had ever come to the ears of these men who were familiar with the howl of the wolf, the whine of the panther and the hoarse bellowing of the alligator. After sinking and rising several times, [the creature] swam to the Louisiana shore and disappeared.[134]

As "wildman" stories go, it's similar to others reported throughout the South, although the "tusks" are unique. It's impossible to know if this is merely a descriptive license for huge teeth, an exaggeration by the letter writer, or its actual biology, but as far as your basic man-like creature it's not the only one reported in the state that year. The story goes on to mention a sighting from the same time period near Vicksburg, Mississippi, 100 miles away. It was theorized the creature seen around Meadville might be the same or one like it.

A strange animal account dating back even further can be found in the memoirs of French explorer Pierre François-Xavier de Charlevoix. In one of his journal manuscripts from 1721 (reprinted in the book *Charlevoix's Louisiana*), François-Xavier recounts the tale of a creature seen in the area of Natchez along the Mississippi River.[135] According to François-Xavier, he was camped in a local settlement when the people there became fearful and sounded an alarm. When asked what was wrong, they told the explorer that "a beast of an unknown species, of an extraordinary bulk, and whose cry did not in the least resemble that of any known animal" was nearby. Though no one had actually laid eyes on the animal, it had presumably carried off several sheep and calves, and had let out some ungodly howl or cry that could not be identified. François-Xavier theorized it could be an "estranged wolf" but the settlers would not concede that it was anything but a monstrous beast. Large wolves were not native to Mississippi, nor do wolves typically have the bulk to carry off livestock. François-Xavier noted the creature's cry was heard again, at which time the settlers took up arms, but he did not describe the sound. Without specific details its admittedly a stretch to conclude it was any sort of ape-like creature, but it certainly is interesting all the same.

If we project back even further, native tribes of the area tell of Bigfoot-esque creatures roaming the lands. The Chickasaw tribe—prominent in the states of Mississippi, Alabama, and Tennessee—told of a being called *lofa*, which was sometimes described as a giant and other times as a large, hairy smelly man.[136] Again, it's impossible to pinpoint this as a Sasquatch, although it does support the logical conclusion that if these creatures exist today then they would have been known to the original peoples of the land.

In his groundbreaking 1978 book, *Sasquatch: The Apes Among Us*, the late John Green states: "The Mississippi [River] seems to have some significance with regard to the reports of hairy bipeds."[137] Looking at this area today, we still find that he was spot on.

DENIZENS OF THE DELTA

On June 22, 1971, the *Delta Democrat Times* reported that Mae

Pearl Young had driven to her daughter's house just east of the river in Greenville, Mississippi, at around 2:30 a.m.[138] After waiting in the car a few moments, she got out and approached the house. She initially walked towards the front porch but decided at that late hour it would be best to knock on the bedroom window.

"When I went around to the side of the house and got almost to the bedroom window, I saw it," she said. "It was black and over six feet tall."

The figure had a large head and broad shoulders and stood with its hands near its hips. Mrs. Young thought at first it was a shadow, but when the shape moved she realized it was alive. Panicked, she ran back to the corner of the house where she turned around to see if it was still there. It was. She screamed.

"I have never seen anything like it before," she told reporters. "It was jet black… I couldn't see its eyes… [it] was the dreadfullest thing I have ever seen in my life."

Her daughter didn't have a phone, so the family locked themselves in the house for the rest of the night. When they looked out in the morning, it was gone. Only some "marks like something had been standing here" were left in the dirt.

The Greenville Police were eventually called. Chief W.C. Burnley said they had received several calls about such a "monster," but ironically the callers were trying to confirm rumors of a "monster" in Arkansas—Fouke, Arkansas. Young knew nothing of the Boggy Creek sightings, only that she'd seen a large, dark figure in the shadows of Mississippi.

In 1975, an even more disturbing encounter was said to have occurred further south in Warren County. The story was recently uncovered by Mississippi researcher Brian Sons, who got into contact with the witness only after the incident was mentioned to him by another person. In other words, the witness had never reported his harrowing experience.

The man, whom I can only refer to by his first name, Cecil, told Sons he was 12 years old at the time and remembers the story vividly since his dog was run over and killed the same day. It was morning when the dog was hit, and the family promptly buried it in the woods across from their home. There was a peaceful pond in the bottoms there with two hills rising up on either side. The dog was laid to rest part way up one of these hills.

Later that afternoon, around 3:00 p.m., Cecil walked back to the same woods carrying his pellet gun. He was feeling distraught, and he thought a bit of hunting would make him feel better. Except today things felt strangely different. Not just from losing a pet, but because of the woods themselves. When Cecil entered the thicker part of the bottoms, he noticed it was unusually quiet. Normally he would hear birds chirping and small animals moving about, but now there was only a strange stillness.

As Cecil continued to walk, he began to feel as though some-one—or something—was watching him. He was now very close to where his dog was buried.

Then he saw it.

"I just looked over there and all of a sudden it... it... I mean, it was there." Cecil explained. "It was straddling my dog's grave!"

The boy froze in horror as he looked up to see a huge, hairy creature standing on the hill. It had one leg on either side of the fresh grave and it was digging at it with its hands!

"He stopped about the time I focused in on him and he starts staring at me," Cecil recalled. "And it was, you know, wasn't a gorilla, it wasn't no bear! You could see the big crown of his head; big shoulders, big wide shoulders. It was just staring at me."

The frightened boy raised his pellet gun and aimed at the crea-ture, barely able to hold the stock steady. He quickly pulled the trigger and fired a shot. It struck the beast in the chest, causing it to grunt before it turned and ran off into the woods as Cecil fled the other direction.

Cecil estimates the creature was around seven feet tall and no more than 400 pounds. He remembers it was hairy all over, includ-ing its face, and its eyes were white with large, black pupils. "I was shaking to death," he stressed. "I had a scope on my pellet rifle so I could see his eyes real well. I just couldn't focus on the spot so I aimed at his chest."

The witness was so shaken by the event and so sure no one would believe him, he kept it to himself for six years. Then one night a friend called, screaming. The friend was a neighbor who lived down the road approximately one quarter mile. When he called, both Cecil and his father picked up at the same time since they had two phones on the same landline.

Between frantic cries, the neighbor told them "there was something in [his] garbage pit slinging through the garbage." He begged for Cecil to bring his father down with his deer rifle. The thing didn't look like anything he'd ever seen before, and he was too scared to confront it by himself.

"He hung up and I walked to my dad's room and I told him 'I think we need to go over there,'" Cecil said. But his father blew it off, stating that the kid's mother was a known alcoholic and it was probably some kind of nonsense. It was at that point Cecil decided to tell his father about what he'd seen in the woods the day he buried his dog.

After hearing the bizarre story, Cecil's father was still skeptical, but the neighbor called back, still screaming. "[You] could hear the fear in his voice," said Cecil. "My dad [was] finally like, 'get your gun too and we'll go over there.'"

By the time Cecil and his father arrived, however, the thing had already gone. After it finished digging in the garbage, the boy said it walked across the pasture and disappeared into the woods. Even though Cecil didn't lay eyes on it himself, he was sure what it was. Thirty-nine years later he's still sure.

Encounters of this kind are still being reported along the Mississippi. In 2003, a man claimed to have experienced a life-changing event in the neighboring county of Hinds.[139] He said he'd been fishing in a pond on June 3 when he decided to wrap it up during the late evening. After packing his gear, he took part of it to his truck, which was parked nearby. When he returned to retrieve the rest of his gear, he was shocked to see a hairy creature crouched down drinking from the pond.

"For some reason it seemed completely oblivious to my being there," he said. "I was standing right out in the open, why it didn't see me or chose to ignore me I can't say."

Either way, the creature remained in the spot drinking water for at least two minutes while the stunned fisherman stood by and watched. After the creature finished, it made a "snorting noise," stood up, and simply walked off into the woods. It was very surreal.

"I absolutely could not believe what I had seen," the witness recalled. "I never believed in the existence of 'Bigfoot' until then and at the time I wasn't sure exactly what I was looking at."

The witness described the creature as being about six –to-seven-feet tall and covered in hair. "I have seen pictures on the internet of the creature the man [Roger Patterson] took in California," he explained. "The creature I saw was not that husky. It was slender and its hair was not dark but a medium brown in color."

The description of a more slender Bigfoot creature is something common to many of the Gulf Coast reports. This is an important aspect since not only does it suggest the creatures here may be somewhat different than those reported further north, but that people

A lonely creek in Mississippi
(Photo by Brian Sons)

are truly seeing something. If people were merely aping Bigfoot reports heard elsewhere, surely they would not diminish the size of their own experience by describing a creature of smaller stature. Like fishing stories, one would naturally assume the opposite or at least a size that matches the pop culture image of Bigfoot. The fact that people in a specific area are reporting an animal of consistent size tends to support the case that people are truly seeing something rather than making up stories.

Admittedly, these are rough interpretations based on anecdotal accounts, yet on occasion there have been tangible elements offered in support of these denizens of the Delta. In one case, a video appeared online in 2013 that claims to show one of these creatures in the Mississippi woods.[140] Like most alleged Bigfoot videos, its content should be viewed with a wary eye, but as these type of film clips go, it's one of the more hotly debated examples.

The video was originally uploaded to YouTube on October 28, 2013, by a user named Josh Highcliff. In the description, Highcliff states that he was hog hunting about nine miles west of Tunica, Mississippi, on October 24, 2013, when he encountered a strange animal. At the time he was sitting in the swamp very quietly when he heard a noise. He then looked around and saw a "huge black thing crouched by a dead cypress about 50 yards away."[141] He thought it might be a hog until he saw its large shoulders, head, and hands. It appeared to be digging at a stump.

Highcliff explained that his first instinct was to run but instead decided to take out his iPhone and film the creature instead. That film, which lasts 2 minutes and 16 seconds, does indeed show a dark-haired, ape-like figure from the backside as it roots around in a tree stump. The figure is partially obscured by trees and foliage but moves enough to provide a decent view. After nearly two minutes, the figure stands fully upright on two legs and begins to move. At that point the videographer takes off running as the camera continues to record, showing the ground and the hunters legs as it ticks out the final seconds.

Says Highcliff, "…when it stood up I could not control myself and ran. That stump was huge and I'd guess the sucker was 7 feet tall; I am a hunter and am pretty darn good at guessing size."

The rest of the YouTube description makes a plea for someone to help evaluate what the hunter saw, admitting to the possibility he could have been pranked. He concludes it by saying: "I always heard stories of skunk ape and Honey Island Swamp Monster from these parts but never thought about it being real. Has anyone seen anything like this in Mississippi?"

We know the answer to the last question, but do we know if this video is real? Numerous researchers in the field have offered their opinion, both supporting it as real evidence or debunking it as a well-crafted hoax. Surely this could not be a prank played on Highcliff, since nobody in their right mind would sit in a swamp dressed as a Bigfoot with their back turned toward an armed hunter for two minutes. Granted, Highcliff was quiet, but regardless, who would sit around on a hunting property impersonating a creature that some have vowed to prove by any means necessary?

As far as the reality? The "creature" in the video certainly looks realistic and when it stands up, it does not resemble a bear. However, the hunter's decision to run seems typical, just when it's time for the payoff. A few more seconds might have been the tipping point for a definitive identification But that seems to be indicative of this elusive mystery. The answer always lingers just a few seconds ahead.

HOWLS IN THE NIGHT

On March 25, 1976, *The Valley Independent* ran the official headline: "'Big Foot' is reported now in Mississippi."[142] The accompanying article included information about some footprints found in Alcorn County in the northeast corner of the state. The prints were said to measure "nearly 15 inches long and 6-1/2 inches wide." No other details are provided except that similar huge tracks had also been reported five miles away near Hatchie Chapel. They were examined (or found?) by a local "photographer and naturalist" named Joe McKewen. According to McKewen: "At certain places the heel would dig in a little deeper. At some places its toes would grab in deeper. It looked just like tracks a human would make if he were walking." McKewen conjectured that the maker of the tracks would have to be "at least eight feet tall and weigh about 450-500 pounds."

The article also mentions that two boys reported a "big hairy creature" in Alcorn County two years prior. They claimed it tried to get in their cabin door but was unsuccessful. A farmer also reported seeing the same type of creature in his field.

A number of Alcorn County sightings originate from the Sharp's Bottom area. This swampy, wooded lowland—located on the eastern edge of Alcorn where it meets Tishomingo County—is said to be the home of a creature locals often refer to as the "Sharp's Bottom Monster" or "Gorilla of Sharp's Bottom." Over the years, sightings of this alleged hairy biped have been reported by deer hunters and other individuals who were driving along its maze of muddy trails.

In a report from the files of the Gulf Coast Bigfoot Research Organization, a witness claims that he and three friends were riding around Sharp's Bottom one night in 1991 when they pulled over to urinate.[143] Two of the group got out of the truck and walked to a small embankment while the witness and another man remained inside. Suddenly the two men on the embankment yelled for their friends to come quickly. When the witness joined them, he could see a large, human-like figure moving over a hill at a distance of 60 to 70 yards. "From where we were it looked to be about 6 to 7 feet tall and had a somewhat shaggy or matted hair," he reported. "We all just looked at each other and started trying to make excuses as to what it was."[144]

But there was no denying it looked like a Bigfoot. The witness had heard several stories about the Gorilla of Sharp's Bottom from older people in the area, but he had never put much stock in the tales. Now he was forced to rethink his position.

Located in the foothills of the Appalachian Mountain range, Sharp's Bottom is a primitive land full of creeks, hills, and vast bottomlands. In modern times it has become a popular destination for ATV riders who enjoy its miles of trails, yet it remains a rich habitat with an abundance of plants and wildlife. It's not out of the question that something large and unknown could make a home in the surroundings.

Around the same time, in 1975, several teenagers claimed to have a run-in with an unknown, upright creature in Lauderdale County, 200 miles south of Alcorn.[145] In August, around 10:00 p.m., they were driving on a country road when they stopped to "answer the call of nature." Three individuals exited the car and stood on the side of the road. In the words of the witness:

> While we were standing outside of the car talking, a loud noise started coming from up in the tree... it sounded like a grunt and a growl combined; the noise was repeated several times and one of the tree limbs started thrashing up and down. Our eyes had not adjusted to the darkness and we could not see what was making the noise. As we were looking we made out something large come out of the tree and land in the ditch running. As you can imagine this had us pretty shook up but that was nothing compared to the feeling we had when the thing ran into the area ahead of the car that was illuminated by the head-lights on bright. The creature was running on two legs, it was covered in grayish black hair and it was extremely well muscled, we could see the muscles rippling as it ran along the ditch, which was two and a half to three feet deep and my eyes were level with the back of its head. I am six feet tall, so I estimate it was 8 to 9 feet tall.[146]

When it reached a nearby bridge, it leapt down the embankment and went into the woods. They could no longer see it but heard its footsteps continue into the darkness. Completely unnerved, the men jumped back into their car and sped from the area. After several months the witness worked up the nerve to return to the site in daylight but found no remaining evidence or sign of the strange creature.

Lauderdale, it seems, has a history of monstrous activity that dates back even further. According to researcher John Keel, the small community of Lost Gap east of Meridian was seized by "monster mania" in 1962.[147] The frenzy kicked off when a group of teenagers claimed to see a tall creature with green eyes in the nearby woods. The police were skeptical at first, but when a dozen more citizens came forth with more sightings, Chief Deputy Alton Allen became convinced there was something to the stories. Soon a massive search party was organized, including bloodhounds and helicopters. Authorities searched feverishly but in the end found no trace of the creature.

In 1977, avid Bigfoot researcher Ramona Clark Hibner fielded an interesting report from Adams County near the Gulf Coast. According to her files, Dorothy Abraham and several other residents near Natchez called police on January 17 to report an "almost human" seen in the area.[148] An officer was dispatched, but the creature fled when the patrol car arrived. Upon further investigation, police spoke to three people who claimed to have all seen a "huge hairy creature well over 6 feet tall, dark, barefooted and naked." Police combed the area and found several large footprints and broken limbs, but they could find no sign of the strange entity itself.

A subsequent news report in the *Mississippi Leader* stated that on February 16 two boys—Ralph and Paul Case—found several huge footprints about 15 inches long in a wooded area of nearby Lincoln County.[149] Photos of the tracks, which accompanied the article, showed them to be very wide with five toes.

Another distinct contribution to the Southern Sasquatch mystery comes in the form of a haunting vocalization recorded in Forest County Mississippi. On December 19, 2004, at 11:00 p.m., researcher John Callender was investigating the area of a recent sighting when he managed to record a distinct moaning howl coming from an unseen entity. The "Mississippi Howl," as it came to be known, consists of at least six repeating vocals of a howling nature that span nearly 40 seconds. Within the vocalization can be heard other distinct audio elements, including a "falsetto shriek," "yahoo vocal," and "whoops."

The audio clip was cleaned up and examined by bioacoustics analyst, Monongahela, whose experience as a crypto-linguist for the U.S. military and current job position within the U.S. government require him to use an alias (which I verified). Monongahela noted the clip's resemblance to another suspected Sasquatch vocalization known as the "Ohio Howl" recorded in Columbiana County, Ohio, in 1994. Through this comparison and based on its own unique aspects, he offers the supposition that the Mississippi Howl comes from an unknown animal, possibility Sasquatch.[150] According to Monongahela:

> Moan howls have a characteristically long, gentle arch shape to them. Few other vocalizers routinely produce this shape. Coyotes are often more erratic and shorter. Wolves are often very flat and long. Cows can come close, they are deeper and shorter. This type of howl could be produced by man or canine, but the unique form is something to watch for when examining an audio clip. Combine that with other attributes (like frequency range) and the profile of the sasquatch moan howl becomes much easier to recognize.[151]

Admittedly it's hard to credit an unproven and unseen creature with a specific vocalization, but howls such as these remain a mystery to both wildlife experts and bioacoustics analysts who have examined them. Of course, one could assert these sounds are man-made and not animal at all, but to those who have had the rare opportunity to hear them in the field, it's just simply not a viable answer. I can tell you that first hand. In May 2014, at around 2:00 a.m., I was paddling a canoe on Mercer Bayou in southern Arkansas when Tom Shirley and I heard a repeating howl nearly identical to the Mississippi Howl. After hearing three repetitions of the vocalization on two occasions that night, both Tom—who ironically spent much of his youth trapping in Mississippi—and I agreed that the source was unlike any animal we had ever heard in our combined years of camping and hunting. And it wasn't human. Of that I can be sure. I still get chill bumps whenever I think back to that night and the sound that echoed over the lonely bayou.

DOWNEY BOOGER

Moving eastward from Mississippi, the Southeastern Plains continue into Alabama. Here too, in this environment of coastal lowlands and floodplain forests, we find a similar history of reports. In the 1880s a Bigfoot-like creature was allegedly seen by a fisherman near Bear Creek in Marion County. According to an article in *The Red Bay News*, a gentleman named Jade Davis was fishing near the confluence of Haithcock Branch and Bear Creek when he noticed a "hairy creature that looked like a man" standing only 30 feet away.[152] The creature was "covered with reddish brown hair" with tinges of grey on his head and shoulders. It was looking right at Davis.

Alarmed, the fisherman reached for his gun, which he always brought to this remote area. When he did, the creature jumped into the creek and dove under a rocky bank below a high bluff. Davis was so shaken, he never returned to the area again.

According to the same article, a "few winters later" some men were hunting in the same location when they came upon "barefoot tracks of man" in the snow. The tracks appeared fresh, so the hunters followed. At one point they could see where the track maker had stopped and turned around, presumably looking back at them. When the tracks reached the creek, however, they disappeared at the identical spot where Davis said it had jumped into the water. The men assumed the creature was living in an underwater cave beneath the bluff, but did not want to pursue it into the water.

A mere 20 miles east in Winston County we come across one of Alabama's most enduring creature legends. Known as the Downey Booger, stories of this half-human, half-animal creature began in the latter part of the 1800s when cousins John and Joe Downey were riding home after a Saturday night dance.[153] According to Vera Whitehead—a descendent of the Downey family—the event had been held at the log home of Oscar Tittle, which was located on a long stretch of desolate road surrounded by dense pines. As the Downey boys rode home reminiscing about their night, a creature resembling both man and animal suddenly leaped into the road. Just as the cousins spotted it, their horse reared up in a panic, snorting and stamping. It was all the boys could do to stay in their saddles as the steeds turned and ran full speed in the opposite direction.

The Downeys eventually calmed the horses and managed to get them back on track towards home. However, once they reached the spot where they had seen the strange creature, the steeds abruptly stopped and refused to move any further. With no other option, the Downeys had to return to Tittle's house by taking a much longer route through a small town seven miles out of the way. By the time they arrived home the sun had risen. They told their families what they had seen, but even though the boys were known to be truthful, it was too much for anyone to believe... at the moment.

Three months later a family was travelling at night on very same road when the creature emerged from the brush and stood briefly in the road before moving quickly out of sight. The encounter shook up the family so much, the children could no longer sleep alone.

Later that fall, a local beverage entrepreneur by the name of Jim Jackson was transporting several barrels of his best moonshine in a two-mule wagon. He was headed to the mining town of Galloway, where he often sold his product to the commissary who would in turn sell it to the miners. As he rode along he began to feel as though he were being followed. A cold chill came over him as he glanced over his shoulder. There, just several feet from the rear of his wagon, was a creature unlike he had ever seen. It was like an animal, yet it walked on two legs.

Jackson, knowing full-well his mules could not outrun such a thing, reached for his revolver, took aim, and fired. The bullet struck the creature causing it to scream and flee for the woods. When news of the event got out, the locals formed a posse to track down the wounded creature. Over the next few days they searched the entire area, following traces of blood presumably left by the animal, but the posse never found the beast.

The place where the Downey Booger story originated is close to a small community called Rabbittown within the Bankhead National Forest. Here, tales of the legendary beast can still be heard in conversation between some of the old timers. And, on occasion, from witnesses who have experienced dramatic, modern encounters.

In October 2013, a family by the name of Frye living in the Bankhead Forest said they were inside their rural home when their two small dogs began barking outside around 1:00 a.m.[154] When Mrs. Frye went out on their back deck to investigate, she saw both of their dogs running in the moonlight toward a larger group of dogs. The dogs were chasing a "dark, upright, huge figure" as it ran toward the woods. When the figure reached the trees approximately 50 yards away, it suddenly stopped, crouched on all fours, and jumped up while spinning around to face the dogs. It then let out a "growling screeching scream." The woman gasped, which caused the creature to look in her direction. It then stood up and walked into the dense woods as her dogs turned tail and ran back home.

Mrs. Frye was not sure what she'd seen, but as time went on she started to wonder if the same beast was still prowling around. On several occasions something had gotten into her chicken coup without tearing into it. She found hens with broken necks and noticed that others were outright missing. Whatever had taken them had apparently opened the coup by lifting two 2x4 crossmembers.

Several weeks later, her suspicions were confirmed in a startling way. On November 2, about one hour before sundown, Mrs. Frye was closing the back doors of their barn when she noticed some movement in the nearby woods. After securing the doors, she looked up again and this time saw a huge, anthropoid creature standing about 100 feet away. She estimated its height at nearly eight feet tall and the weight perhaps 450 lbs. It had longer, dark brown hair covering its body with its face having shorter hair of the same color. The arms hung down with long-fingered, human-like hands. It starred at the woman for a few seconds before bounding down a steep hill, which stretched out behind their property.

Having seen the creature in the evening light, Mrs. Frye now believed it to be a Bigfoot. This realization was further supported by the discovery of three footprints in the garden next to their house the following month. The strange tracks—two left prints and one right print—had five toes and measured 9 inches long by 5 inches wide. She assumed it was a juvenile version of the very same creature. Figuring no one would believe her, she cast one of the tracks with plaster. It was later analyzed by a BFRO investigator, who found possible dermal ridges.

According to Alabama researcher Paul Hulsey, who also examined the track and interviewed the Fryes, their home has an interesting back story that lends support to the account. While working as a minister in a nearby nursing home, Hulsey learned that one of the older female residents told several nurses she knew of the "Woods People" and had actually planted a garden on the side of her house specifically for them. The nurses didn't believe her story, but nonetheless they were all familiar with it.

As the old woman lay dying, she asked her grandson if he would plant a new garden for the Woods People. He couldn't fulfill the request but did return to the location of their old homestead to look around and to take his son fishing where he himself had fished as a boy. As they were fishing, his 9-year-old son kept saying he thought a man was watching them, but the father merely dismissed it as imagination.

While walking away from the fishing spot, however, the boy became adamant that a "man" was following them. When the father finally turned around to look, he saw a large, hair-covered creature standing on the trail behind them. They promptly fled the area and never returned.

As Hulsey began to unravel the tale, he realized the Frye's house had once belonged to the brother of the old woman. It was only a short distance from her own residence where she had long ago planted the garden!

Hulsey was intrigued so he set up a game camera inside the Frye's barn. For many nights the camera came up empty, but finally one frame caught his attention. There, standing in the shadows, appeared to be a face with two reflective eyes. Though the figure is extremely shadowed, the eyes are in a location consistent with a height taller than a man. Perhaps a decedent of the old Downey Booger had finally showed its face to a cynical, modern world.

Something in the barn
(Photo courtesy of Paul Hulsey)

SWEET HOME

Sightings of ape-like creatures throughout Alabama span the decades, inciting the gamut of astonishment, disbelief, and fear. In April 1938, officials reportedly formed a posse to hunt down a "hairy wild man" in the Choccolocco Valley east of Anniston. According to an article in the *Oshkosh Northwestern*, the situation started when a farmer named Rex Biddle claimed to have seen "hairy wild man" in the swamp. Biddle said: "He was about five feet tall, and had hair all over his body." He also said the thing moved on "all fours in the manner of an ape."[155]

Another farmer, Roy Storey, also claimed to have seen the beast. He said it followed him for some distance before it "dropped to all fours and chased [his] pet dog into the swamp." Other witnesses said they'd seen it in the presence of a female and child "both as savage in appearance and actions as the man." A hunting posse was organized by the local sheriff, but the group came up empty hand-ed after a thorough search of the district. Residents urged the sheriff to "catch this thing or we are moving out," but it was the beast that apparently moved on since it was no longer seen.

Walker County also had reports of a startling creature. Accord-ing to information relayed to me by resident Jeff Hart, his great un-cle Bart was working underneath his car one afternoon in the 1950s when he got the feeling he was being watched. After few minutes he pulled himself out from under the vehicle to observe a "gorilla-like" creature standing near the back bumper. It was slightly hunched over and looking directly at him.

Thinking it must be a trick, Bart briefly closed his eyes and re-opened them. When he did, the creature was running toward a wooded area about 25 yards away. (The family home was not in a remote area but was located in a rural environment with patches of woods and farmlands nearby.)

After the creature disappeared into the trees, Bart ran into the house and told his family what he had seen. He described the crea-ture as being similar to a gorilla, yet taller and more upright. It also had more of a "man's face." This strange description—prior to his or his family's knowledge of Bigfoot—might have been laughable except Bart's stepson had been claiming for some time that some-thing was peering in his bedroom window at night. The window was at least seven feet from the ground, so up until then the family had dismissed his earnest pleas as impossible. Now they weren't so sure.

Hart's mother (Bart's niece) was in the home at the time and has a vivid recollection of when her uncle burst in and told them of the incident. She remembers him being outwardly shaken. Bart has now passed on, but throughout his life he maintained that what he saw was absolutely real and out of the ordinary.

Police were involved with a case in 1960 in which a reverend and several other people saw an ape-like creature "bounding" along a rural road south of Clanton in Chilton County. Reverend E.C. Hand contacted Sheriff T.J. Lockhart who went to the location to investigate. There he found "two sets of tracks, one larger than the other."[156] The tracks were human-like in shape, except the big toe was sticking out at an angle. Measurements of the tracks were not provided, but as we know, the anatomy of a large or different type of big toe has been noted in other suspected Bigfoot cases in the South.

Believing it to be a creature worthy of pursuit, the police formed a posse and combed the area in and around Walnut Creek but came up short.[157] (Notice a trend?) Later, Reverend Hand saw the creature again near Liberty Hill at which time he grabbed his shotgun and gathered his hound dogs but was unable to run it down. In fact, the dogs simply refused to follow. "I can make my dogs catch a mule," the clergyman told reporters. "But I could not get them to venture out toward the 'Booger.'"

A 1965 article from the *Union-Banner*, noted that a year or two after the initial incidents more tracks were found in a peach orchard three miles south of Clanton near a swamp.[158] A cement cast was supposedly made of the footprint(s), which were said to be about the size of human feet, yet look more like "a hand."

An article in the *Birmingham News*, dated December 29, 1974, cites a dozen Bigfoot reports in the Guntersville-Albertville area located at the tail end of the Tennessee River.[159] In one case, a woman named Hazel Stephens was said to have seen a beast "six or seven feet tall" walking near her home one night. Guntersville is located in Marshall County where reports of a horrid, hairy creature known as the Guntersville Terror have continued to surface over the years, particularly near Guntersville Lake, a snaky waterway that runs for 75 miles. According to testimony filed with the BFRO, a family was driving along the lake's edge one night in 1992 when the father caught a glimpse of something walking in the shallow water.[160] It was well after sundown but the moon was full and bright. Having passed it, he slowed down and looked back to see a large, bipedal figure covered in long, dark hair, wading near the shore about 50 yards away. It was approximately seven-to-eight-feet tall and was carrying the head of what appeared to be a St. Bernard dog in its hand. "I saw the bigfoot from the knees up, carrying the head of the dog," the witness explained.

Noticing the startled look on her husband's face, the wife asked what was the matter. He tried to explain but by the time she looked back, they had passed some trees and the figure was no longer visible. The husband was too shaken to turn back.

Having driven the road many times, the witness was aware that one of the lakeside residents had two St. Bernard dogs who always hung out in the front area of the house. The witness didn't know this resident, but noted that he never saw these two dogs after the date of his strange sighting. Years later the witness finally met the resident and decided to ask what ever happened to the two big dogs. The dog's owner told him they had both died of natural causes and one was buried behind his house around that time. The witness could only theorize that the Bigfoot had dug up the remains of the dog and carried off its head, although he didn't share his rather gruesome theory with the dog's owner.

While it does seem like bizarre story, it's interesting in light of the previous report from Mississippi in which the boy saw a hairy, bipedal creature digging up his own deceased dog. The Guntersville Terror is apparently just as ghoulish, but its alleged behavior doesn't stop at graverobbing. A recent example of its more extreme, terrorizing behavior was recorded by longtime Alabama researcher Jim Smith. In the report, a female hunter said she had taken her young son deer hunting in the winter of 2015.[161] They had gone to a location near Guntersville Lake where they found an abandoned tree stand. After sitting in the stand for a while, they heard crashing in the woods, as if something big was approaching. After a few tense moments, a huge, hairy animal burst into view and ran on two legs straight towards them. When it reached the tree, it let out a frightening, "blood curdling roar."

The mother was quick to identify the creature as some kind of Bigfoot. It was like nothing she'd ever seen. Both mother and son were terrified, but she tried not to show it as she calmed her son. But it was not that easy. The creature was apparently agitated as it thrashed about below, rattling small trees and bushes amid angry growls and snorts. She was worried the creature might scale the tree at any time. The woman had a crossbow but was too scared to take a shot. Her only recourse was to sit still and hold her son as they waited in terror.

After what seemed like half an hour, the creature finally trudged off into the trees. They could hear it crashing through the bush for several minutes as it moved further into the distance. Finally the woods went quiet again.

Feeling it was safe enough to make a getaway, the mother and son quietly and quickly got down from the tree stand and ran for their lives. When they reached their truck, the mother started the engine and drove away as fast as she could. Having witnessed the rage of the Guntersville Terror, she knew they were lucky to have escaped with their lives. It was one of those instances where a Southern Sasquatch certainly seemed to live up to its dangerous, rebel reputation.

9. APPALACHIAN APE-MEN

One of the most impressive features of the North American landscape is the Appalachian Mountain Range. This amazing expanse of peaks and plateaus runs nearly 2,000 miles from southeastern Canada to the southern United States, making it one of three major mountain systems in the U.S.[162] As it crosses the lower portion of the U.S., the range spills into several southern states including Kentucky, Tennessee, Georgia, Alabama, and the Carolinas. The mountain environment has contributed a great deal to the regional culture of the area. Its foothills have also been known to produce tales of mysterious man-apes.

In the previous chapter we discussed the case of the Sharp's Bottom Monster located at the northern border of Mississippi and Alabama where the Appalachians begin in the South. The area just north of Sharp's Bottom enters Tennessee, a land famous for its contributions to country music by way of Nashville and its homegrown frontiersman including the hero of The Alamo, Davy Crockett.

While not as famous as Crockett, tales of other "wildmen" in the area date back to the late 1800s. In these reports—primarily extracted from old newspapers—people describe a hairy beast known regionally as the Tennessee Wildman. In one account reported in the May 5, 1871, edition of *The Hagerstown Mail*, witnesses claim to have seen "a strange and frightful being" in McNairy County (not far from Sharp's Bottom).[163] They described it as "seven feet high, and possessed of great muscular power" with large "fiery red" eyes. It's hair was said to hang in tangles to its waist, while its beard was long and its body covered with hair. By all accounts it was a frightful being that shunned men but was willing to approach women with "wild and horrid screams."

The wildman in this case seems human-like, but the article does go on to state that he/it can run with "astonishing swiftness, leaping the tallest fences with the ease of a deer, defying alike the pursuit of men and dogs," which is certainly animal-like. As usual, frightened locals scoured the woods en masse but failed to come up with the culprit.

In 1889, the "The Wild Man of Tennessee" was mentioned again by *The New York Times*.[164] This time he/it was identified a few miles southeast in Walker County, Georgia, where several people claimed to have seen a "being of gigantic stature, covered with a thick growth of hair" in the mountains.

A decade earlier, the *Louisville Courier Journal* ran a story about another wildman in Tennessee, but the "creature" described in this article was covered in "a layer of scales, which drop off at regular periods, in the spring and fall, like the skin of a rattlesnake."[165] Its height was measured at 6.5 feet, and it was noted to have "a heavy growth of hair on his head and a dark reddish beard about six inches long." This account has been referenced in Bigfoot books although it appears to be nothing more than a tall man—perhaps feral—with an extreme case of ichthyosis, a condition that causes the skin to become thick and scaly. The individual was being exhibited around the country in a sideshow and apparently didn't speak or behave like a civilized man, but this could be attributed to a feral life since in those times a strange appearance may result in the parents abandoning the subject as a child. Either way, it does not align with the other reports of a hair-covered creature in Tennessee.

Reports of a decidedly Bigfoot nature became more common to the area starting in the late 1950s. In 1959, the Knoxville *Journal* reported that a man by the name of Earl Taylor attempted to shoot a huge, bipedal creature after it approached the porch of his country home in Knox County.[166] The creature, which he described as being eight-to-ten-feet tall, was first seen from the window. When Taylor went outside, the creature ran into the woods. Fearful it might return, Taylor and a neighbor waited with a shotgun. When they heard a noise on the side of the house, they immediately ran to the spot and saw the same animal. Taylor fired, but it managed to escape into the woods unharmed. He told reporters: "I don't believe it was human, it was too big and moved too fast and quiet."

In 1965, the Nashville *Tennessean* reported two sightings of a man-like ape in Rutherford County.[167] In the first incident, two men summoned police after they saw a tall, hair-covered creature on Brown's Mill Road in the evening hours. Roy Hudson told reporters he and a friend were driving down the road when they saw the creature walking along one side. They proceeded to pass within several yards of it, then turned around to get a second look. When they did, the animal jumped over a five-foot fence and ran off. They promptly called the police and a deputy was dispatched. He found no signs of the creature, but upon leaving he was stopped by two other locals who also claimed to have seen it. Doris Barrett said she and a friend spotted the creature sometime after the first sighting and shined a flashlight in its face. It was described as having "long reddish-brown hair," large teeth, and a "pug nose like an ape."

In the 1970s, more strange reports emerged from Wayne County close to the Mississippi border. In a statement to a *Wayne County News* reporter, a 27-year-old man claimed to have seen a "hairy primate" along Indian Creek.[168] He said he was hunting for squirrels behind his father's farm when he saw the creature swinging in the trees. It quickly moved out of sight.

When taking into account all of these reports, descriptions of the so-called Tennessee Wildman seem to vary greatly from feral-like humans, to upright beasts, to tree-swinging primates. While the early wildman sightings suggest a more dangerous type of beast, the later sightings paint a more docile picture of a lone primate, even when fired upon by frightened citizens. But that was about to change when a heavily publicized case hit the Tennessee news in 1976. The aggressive Tennessee Wildman had apparently returned.

BODY SNATCHERS

On April 26, 1976, four-year-old Gary Robertson was standing just outside the backdoor of his home in Flintville with his mother, Jennie Robertson, right behind him.[169] They had just finished dinner and were headed outside to enjoy the late spring evening. Suddenly, Gary cried out with a fearful scream as Jennie caught sight of dark, hair-covered figure a few feet away. It reached for Gary with a long, hairy arm. Jennie acted instinctively, grabbing her son just as the thing's hand grasped his arm. She pulled him inside and slammed the door.

"Gary and I were standing just outside our back door when I heard a wheezing noise, like someone with asthma trying to breath… and smelled a terrible odor," she told reporters.[170] "I turned—and there was this huge black thing just a few feet from Gary and me." She described it as being at least seven feet tall with a hair-covered body and long, dirty claws on its outstretched hand.

Once inside, Jennie called to her husband, Melvin, who came running. She told him in a panicked voice that something outside had tried to grab their son. Melvin opened the door but saw nothing more than a "big black shape disappearing into the woods."

He might have dismissed it as delusion, but Melvin had seen the creature before in the nearby woods. He had also heard it scream. However, he had chosen to keep silent about the events so as not to scare anyone and, moreover, to keep people from thinking he was crazy. But now he no longer cared. The thing had tried to snatch his son right out of their own backyard!

The following day Melvin drove to nearby Fayetteville where he placed a notice in the *Elk Valley Times* warning others that an unknown and possibly dangerous creature might be living in the vicinity. This action inevitably brought attention from the media and also flushed out more accounts. After the Robertsons came forward, their closest neighbor, Houston Smith, confessed that he had also seen it. But like Melvin, he had chosen to keep a lid on it for fear of ridicule.

"I've been seeing this thing around the woods here for three years," Smith told reporters. "It walks upright but kind of bent over. It's not a bear and it's certainly not a person."

Another resident, Sarah Prostise, came forward with another story of the creature's alarming behavior. She claimed it had attacked her car when she stopped at a deserted intersection. Another man said he chased it down a gravel road in his truck after it surprised him. The beast, however, was fast enough to elude the vehicle and escape into the woods. Others said they merely caught a glimpse of it, corroborating the presence of a creature that was by all accounts, horrifying and unexplainable.

Following the outbreak of stories, the locals... yes, you guessed it... decided to organize a posse so they could track and down and kill the would-be body snatcher before it tried to grab another kid, or worse. The hunters took to the woods, looking specifically for a set of caves between Flintville and the Elk River where they believed the creature might be living. Stan Moore, one of the participants, said they found tracks and "droppings" but could not locate the creature nor the caves.

The story was so widely publicized it drew the interest of notable clairvoyant and paranormal researcher Lorraine Warren (famous for ghost investigations and demon hunts, including the Amityville Horror case). During a visit to the Robertson's home, she claimed to have made telepathic contact with the creature while walking in the woods behind the house. According to Warren, it simply wanted to be left alone. (A plea that seems inconsistent with an attempt to grab a human child, if I do say so.)

Psychic debates aside, the case by itself may seem like nothing more than the fevered imaginings of a small Appalachian town, but in context with similar reports in the region it doesn't seem out of place. This applies to the visual reports of ape-like creatures, but also to instances where children have disappeared from the Smokey Mountains vicinity under suspicious circumstances. After all, the creature seemed to be reaching for little Gary Robertson.

In the most famous case of a missing child in Tennessee, Dennis Lloyd Martin was visiting the Great Smokey Mountains National Park with his family in 1969 when he simply vanished. According to the *Knoxville News Sentinel*, Dennis was playing in Spence Field with several other boys—in view of his father and grandfather—when the boys split up and circled around some trees intending to jump out and startle the adults.[171] When Dennis failed to reemerge after a few minutes, the adults and other boys began calling out loudly and searching the area where he was last seen. A short time later, rangers and volunteer searchers joined in. They thoroughly combed the meadow and surrounding woods looking for the boy but couldn't locate him.

Over the course of weeks, the largest manhunt in the 36-year history of the park was launched, consisting of at least 1,400 searchers at its peak. But still Dennis could not be found. The family insisted Dennis must have been abducted, while park officials believed it was more likely the boy simply got lost and perished in the extremely rugged mountain terrain. Perhaps so, but there are some bizarre details that can't be ignored.

The same afternoon Dennis disappeared, Harold Key and his son were near Rowans Creek in the Sea Branch area—roughly 45 minutes walking distance from Spence Field—when they heard a "sickening scream." A few minutes later, Key noticed a rough-looking man moving stealthily in the woods near the location of the scream. He seemed to be hiding behind some bushes. This certainly lends merit to the abduction theory but takes on a whole new possibility in light of other details.

According to diligent research by David Paulides, who pieced together the entire story in his *Missing 411: Eastern United States* book, Key's son initially stated he'd seen a bear, but this was later changed to Harold's statement that he had seen a human hiding in the brush.[172] Absent from the public record was the fact that the Keys claimed the "rough-looking man" appeared to be carrying something over his shoulder. To add to the weirdness, the FBI would not allow the Keys to come back to the park to make their statement and show officials exactly where the bear/human was seen. Officials did not believe a person could have taken Dennis from Spence Field all the way to Sea Branch between the time the boy went missing and the time the scream was heard, although searchers had proved it was possible if an adult were walking at a good clip straight through the woods. To make things even stranger, former park ranger Dwight McCarter later admitted there were "wild men" known to live in the park at the time, but they were not readily acknowledged. He was presumably taking about human men and even stated they were possibly "criminals," but still, one can only wonder about their true nature.

There's much more to the story of Dennis Martin's disappearance, but for purposes of this book, the point has been made. We've got a vague sighting of a rough-looking human who was mistaken for bear in an area where a child has gone missing; an area with a history of mysterious ape-like animal reports. The implications are disturbing to say the least.

KNOBBY AND YAHOOS

Crossing eastward over the Appalachians we find ourselves in North Carolina, a state situated between the mountains on its western side and the Atlantic ocean on the east. Between these landmarks unfurls contrasting landscapes from beaches to rolling countryside, and from densely populated urban cities to isolated views atop the Blue Ridge Mountains. As we've learned, where there's mountains, there's mysteries, and North Carolina is no different. Among the mysteries here are the famous Brown Mountain Lights, a series of ghostly illuminations visible along the Blue Ridge Parkway, and Knobby, an ape-like creature said to live in the western part of the state.

Reports of the creature first became public in 1978 when residents in Cleveland County claimed to see an upright hairy creature lurking in the nearby foothills. The creature was dubbed "Knobby" because it had been seen on Carpenter's Knob north of Kings Mountain. In the first report, 88-year-old Minnie Cook said she saw a huge, black hairy creature prowling around her rural home on several occasions.[173] It frightened her so much she started carrying a rifle when she ventured outside.

Another woman, Sally White, also claimed to have seen the beast. On the evening of January 16, 1979, her dogs began barking wildly as if alerting her to a presence outside her home. She told a reporter: "I looked down the path and I saw it—something long and black coming up through the woods. It's the same thing I've seen twice before, once before Christmas and once right after."[174]

Prior to that, Forest Price found one his goats dead with a broken neck. Several nights before something had been creeping around his property and disturbing his animals, causing one of his mules to break its rope and escape. When Price discovered strange tracks and the dead goat, he could only wonder if it had been the same creature.

While Price never saw it, his brother Sammy apparently did. Sammy told reporters that he and his wife "spotted the creature after several nights of hearing animal screams."[175]

Other people reported hearing unfamiliar screams coming from the foothills at night. They described it as "a sound that varies in pitch from a low growl to a high scream, as being like a bull bellowing, but with its own sound."[176] They also noted that after the scream they could hear a yodeling type sound for a few seconds.

Those willing to venture into the woods around Carpenter's Knob discovered more strangeness. One man, Daniel Cooke, said he found tracks similar to those of an ape at the mouth of a cave. Others, who formed a small search party, discovered tracks and an animal den two miles from the Price houses. According to their statement, the tracks were "at least as large as a man's hand and similarly shaped, even with a thumb-like protrusion."[177]

The usual round of explanations were offered up, including a panther, an escaped "carnival baboon," and a bear. The authorities mostly backed the bear scenario, reminding folks that a bear had been seen in the area for close to a year. But of course bears don't walk upright, scream, or yodel. Panthers could account for the bizarre sounds, but are even further from the profile of an upright ape.

The events quickly reached a frenzy, resulting in a number of newspaper headlines and radio coverage. In one case, a radio station broadcast live from a campground at the base of Carpenter's Knob. This spawned the usual wave of monster hunters who poured into the area and tried to flush out poor old Knobby. By the spring of 1979 there were at least 16 reported sightings but still no concrete evidence.

Then, as quickly as it had come, the sightings ceased. Whatever had been haunting the foothills of Cleveland County had apparently gone into hiding or moved on (perhaps as a result of the monster hunting frenzy). It would be more than three decades before the legend of Knobby would return to stalk the countryside.

In June 2010, Tim Peeler said he heard screeching and grunting sounds coming from outside his cabin northwest of a Casar, a small mountain town in Cleveland County.[178] When he went out to investigate, he was startled to find a 10-foot-tall creature with a long beard and yellowish-blond hair menacing his dog. According to a news report on WCNC Channel 36, Peeler "rough-talked" the creature and told him to "get away" from his home.[179] This apparently worked, but only temporarily as the creature returned a short time later. Worried the creature would kill his dog, Peeler then called 911 to summon help from the authorities. An officer was promptly dispatched.

Peeler further described the creature as having "beautiful hair" and six fingers on each hand. He said it emerged from a path behind his home and had returned in that direction after he threatened it with verbal shouts and a walking stick. Sergeant Mark Self, who responded to the call, was aware of Cleveland County's history with Knobby but could find no evidence to support Peeler's claim. Given the rather bizarre description and lack of evidence, it's hard to say whether old Knobby had actually made a reappearance.

But Knobby isn't the only case of a Bigfoot creature in the Tar Heel State. Way back in July 1793, the *Boston Gazette* printed correspondence from Charleston, South Carolina, regarding a creature known to live around Bald Mountain in North Carolina.[180] The article states that local inhabitants call it "Yahoo," while the Indians refer to it as "Chickly Cudly." Researcher Scott McNabb determined that Chickly Cudly could be an English variant on the Cherokee term *ke-cleah kud-leah*, meaning *hairy man/thing*.[181]

An article posted in the January 3, 1878, edition of the *McK-*

ean County Miner told of "A Wild Man of the Mountains" spotted in Watauga County at the heart of the Appalachians. As the story goes, several men were prospecting in Globe Valley when they saw a huge, man-like entity at a distance of 40 yards. They decided to approach and came within "twenty steps" before they stopped to consider what they were looking at. As they were discussing the best course of action, one of the prospectors yelled and jumped toward the wildman. The wildman responded by lunging forward and pounding his chest with his fists. After the display of aggression, the wildman stood there for two minutes before he "turned and bounded off with the speed of a deer."[182]

The article recounts the wildman in detail:

> Our correspondent describes the wild man as being about six feet five inches tall, with broad shoulders and long apeish arms; smooth face and funnel-shaped head. His body is covered with dark brown hair, near two inches long. His head and a greater portion of his forehead is covered with long, luxuriant, dark red tresses.[183]

Following the encounter, the men hurried to the house of a nearby miner where they retrieved a "gun, pistol, and other articles of warfare" before returning to pursue the strange being. During the search they discovered a small mountain cave where they found a bed of leaves and bones indicating that perhaps the wildman had been living there. The correspondent mentions this was the first time such a creature had been reported in the area. No further articles can be found to determine if it was ever seen again.

In modern times, Bigfoot beasts have been reported in other parts of the state, including areas along the Cape Fear River. According to a 1976 article from the *Latrobe Bulletin*, people in the area of Chatham County reported sightings of a "seven foot tall, apelike creature with black hair" they called the "Thing."[184] In one case, a farmer named Brody Parker said he watched such a creature in his field for nearly 20 minutes. He said it was "sort of hunched over" and appeared to be looking back at him.

Jim Hollingsworth, a professional therapist who documented the reports in his spare time, stated that locals had also found unusual three-toed footprints measuring 18 inches long. The creature was also blamed for "unearthly screams" and reputed to cause tracking dogs to cower in fear. All of these elements (ape-like creature, three-toed tracks, spooky screams, hard to track) are undoubtedly reminiscent of the Boggy Creek case. Were people being influenced by *The Legend of Boggy Creek*—which was circulating heavily in drive-ins around that time—or were these creatures distributed much further across the South than previously imagined? If so, they seem to be roaming there even today.

In June 2015, Doug Dotson was sleeping in his travel trailer at an older campground within North Carolina's immense Uwharrie National Forest. The head of his bed was near a small window, which was propped open for ventilation. Sometime during the night he was awakened by a noise just outside the window.

"I was woken up by the sound of something outside breathing," Dotson told me as I interviewed him about his experiences. "It was a wet, deep, kind of breathing."

Dotson sat up and listened for a moment. He was startled but figured it was some sort of injured animal. Just to be sure, however, he grabbed his flashlight and went out the trailer door. He shined the light in every direction but saw nothing. Whatever had been there must have slipped quietly back into the woods.

Dotson all but forgot the incident until the following month when he was camped at the same spot. Again he was sleeping inside his trailer with the window open when something hit or tapped the screen and awakened him. As he did before, he slipped out of bed, grabbed his flashlight, and cautiously went out outside. He shined the flashlight around but didn't see anything until he approached the back of his camper. There, in the stark beam of his light, stood an ape-like creature.

"She was probably about 15 or 20 feet away," Dotson told me. "I was shocked and scared at the same time." The creature in front of him was outwardly female and was covered in a layer of mottled

A rocky creek near Bat Cave, North Carolina
(Photo by Cindy Lee)

brown hair about six inches long. "The face wasn't quite ape, not quite human, and not quite Neanderthal," he noted.

Dotson said he tried not to make any sudden movements as he stood for several seconds gazing in amazement. Then the creature made a "cooing noise" and simply stepped off into the woods and was gone in an instant. It's hard to imagine what such a creature might think of human contact, but for Dotson it's something he will never forget.

HULKING HIGHLANDERS

Traveling south from the land of Knobby, the Blue Ridge cuts a path through northern Georgia in an area known as the Highlands. Among the ridges and fertile valleys here, forested slopes and clear streams provide a backdrop for one of the richest centers of biodiversity in the eastern U.S.[185] Like other parts of the Appalachian foothills, it's also home to incredible reports of Bigfoot creatures.

The sighting history dates back to early settlers and perhaps even to natives that once inhabited the land. The Creek tribe of northern Georgia, for example, told of a strange entity called *Este Chupco*, whose name translates to "tall person." Este Chupco, they said, could be heard tromping through the forest slapping trees but was never actually seen. Some researchers have suggested Este Chupco could be the native's interpretation of Bigfoot, noting that the tree slapping could be "wood knocking," a supposed communication behavior associated with Bigfoot.[186]

As white settlers moved in, they began to record stories of ubiquitous wild men doing wild things. As mentioned previously, *The New York Times* declared that the infamous Tennessee Wildman stalked the mountains of Walker County, Georgia in 1889. According to additional details published in the *Atlanta Constitution*, a man was searching for mineral deposits at Lookout Mountain when he heard a loud scream.[187] He turned around to see a hulking "wild man" standing in the trail some distance away. The miner described it as being "7 or 7-1/2 feet high, hairy as an old bear, and... from his looks, 400 pounds." He also noted it "had a pole in one hand that looked to be ten foot long."

Frightened and presumably desperate, the miner tried to communicate with the thing. He asked its name, but the only response came in "the shape of a large stone" hurled in his direction. The miner promptly fled the area as a shower of stones followed.

This story is especially interesting in that it refers to another behavior commonly associated with Bigfoot: rock throwing. Time and time again researchers and witnesses have reported that these creatures have the ability and the propensity to hurl stones at anyone they perceive as trespassers. While it's rare that anyone reports being hit, it's a sobering thought nonetheless.

Early documentation of such behavior was noted in the infamous "Ape Canyon" incident of 1924. In this case, six miners claimed they shot an ape-like creature while working a mine along the east slopes of Mount St. Helens in Washington. Later that night, the miner's said their cabin was besieged by a group of these creatures, presumably intent on retaliation. According to the men, "the apemen hurled rocks onto their cabin that night and 'danced' and screamed until daylight."[188]

Rock throwing seems to be universal to all North American Sasquatch and has since been reported in numerous Deep South cases, including the "Siege at Honobia" and "Area X" discussed earlier, and many others that I've personally heard over the years. This case from Georgia is yet another example.

While not all encounters in the Highlands invoke such a violent response, there are a number of other cases that suggest ape-like creatures have and still do roam the region. In 1974, Les Alexander, Bob Martin, and Chris Stevens claimed to have seen a huge biped near Dahlonega south of the Chatahoochee National Forest. According to a vintage publication called *The Yeti Newsletter* out of St. Petersburg, Florida, the men were camped at the nicely named Blackburn State Park when they were surprised by an eight-foot beast rummaging through a garbage can.[189] It reportedly made a high-pitched scream before moving from sight. Park rangers confirmed the creature had been seen on other occasions by locals who dubbed it the "Billy Holler Bugger."

In nearby White County, an artifact hunter saw a similar beast in the summer of 1980. The witness told my colleague Matt Pruitt he'd been searching for Indian artifacts in the foothills of Horse Range Mountain in an area that had been recently clear-cut.[190] As he was driving out of the area, he noticed a tall, dark animal moving downhill towards a creek. The witness first thought it was a bear, but upon closer observance determined it was not. "It walked upright with a slight stoop for about 75 yards down a hill toward a small creek that was bordered by trees and brush," he stated.

After the creature entered the treeline, the witness drove his car across the creek and waited to see if it would emerge on the other side. It never did.

On the north side of the Chatahoochee Forest near Taylor Ridge, a man reported seeing another peculiar animal in August 1986. According to the *Bigfoot Casebook*, the man was looking for ginseng below Taylor Crest when he came upon a large, primate-like creature with a pointed head and arms that hung below its knees.[191] It was covered in "thick, long black hair falling in locks, and its face was monkey-like with thick lips to its mouth and a flat nose." The witness stood within 25 feet of the animal as he observed it for several moments. He noted that its left arm appeared to be injured and hung down as if useless. At the tip of its hand, he could see long, dirty fingernails. The left leg also looked injured but not enough to prohibit the creature from walking. After a few moments, it grunted and strolled away.

Just west of the Chatahoochee Forest lies the Cohutta Wilderness, another significant area of reports. In one example, multiple witnesses got a glimpse of the unexpected in 2001 as they were camping in Murry County. According to a report filed by Morris Collins of the BFRO, four campers were sitting beside their campfire at around 11:00 p.m. when they began to hear a series of high-pitched screams spaced approximately 20 minutes apart.[192] One member of the group suggested it could be a panther, but no one could agree as to what it was.

After at least three screams, the group was startled by the sound of limbs breaking on the other side of a nearby creek. "It sounded like whatever it was started getting closer," one of the witnesses stated. "When all of a sudden… out steps this figure into the firelight. It took two more steps, then we all could plainly see it."[193]

Standing there beside the creek, in full view of the group, was a huge, bipedal form. It had come down a hillside and stepped in front of the trees about 30 feet from the fire. The thing looked to be seven feet tall with a huge, broad chest perhaps three feet wide, and arms that hung to the knees. It's eyes reflected amber in the flickering firelight.

The sight was so shocking, one of the campers jumped into his tent. Seemingly unconcerned, the thing proceeded to squat down and dip its hands into the creek as it kept its eyes on the group. After about a minute, it stood up and simply walked back into the trees.

Morris interviewed two of the witnesses at length; they were adamant about the reality of their encounter. One of them stated that a child was with them at the time and had been crying prior to the appearance of the creature. Researchers have theorized that Bigfoots are attracted to the sound of young children, and if so, then perhaps this was the case.

Another of my colleagues, J.C. Williams, has been researching the area of Georgia as part of the Southeastern Bigfoot Research Group. In discussing the various reports he's investigated, he was able to supply another account of a creature in the same vicinity.

The incident occurred on October 13, 2013, at the home of a nursing student.[194] His home is essentially a cabin located in the woods of Pickens County, due south of the Cohutta Wilderness. That morning the witness had gone out for an early coffee and was returning to his home at 5:30 a.m. when he caught sight of something digging through his garbage. As he pulled into his driveway, he could see its reddish eye-shine glaring in the headlights.

"I thought at first it was a bear, but something about whatever it was made me think that it was not a bear," the witness said. "I sat in my car staring at it, while it sat perfectly still."

The animal's body was obscured by the garbage, but after a few moments it stood up, turned around, and ran into the woods. "It did this extremely *fast*, and I was so scared I immediately put my car in reverse and tried to get out of my driveway, but ended up crashing my car into the woods behind me," the witness confessed. "I sat there for a few moments because I was afraid that it was still out there, and seeing how fast it could move, I did not think I could make it to my front door if it really wanted to catch me."

The witness sat in his car for several minutes, trying to process what he'd just seen. The creature was large and grayish-brown in color with a pointed head and red eyes. He wished it were a bear, but knew it wasn't that simple. "This thing was definitely not like anything I have ever seen," he concluded. "I can only say that it looked like what people say a Bigfoot looks like."

It's a concept that many people question, but as with this witness and others like him, it only takes a moment for a legend to come to life.

TERROR ON THE TRAIL

When it comes to hiking trails, perhaps none is more famous than the Appalachian Trail. This 2,190-mile path, completed in 1937, has become a legendary American landmark winding its way from Mount Katahdin in Maine to Springer Mountain in Georgia.[195] Along its many stretches, the AT—as it's called—offers serious hikers and weekend nature lovers a chance to take in some of the finest scenic beauty and breathtaking views in a fiercely challenging yet rewarding environment.

For the millions who hike some portion of the trail each year, the undertaking is a memorable one full of good times, adventure, and accomplishment. For others it ends in defeat, but it's not something a bit of rest and recovery can't fix. For others, apparently, the trail can become a nightmare.

On March 5, 2014, Todd Kelley departed the Amicalola Falls State Park in Georgia on foot, bound for the Appalachian Trial.

Southern Sasquatch by Brian Sons

Kelley had always dreamed of hiking the full length of the AT and had come from California to Georgia to begin his journey. It was to be a new chapter in his life, starting with an accomplishment that few can boast.

That morning, Kelley set out on one of the "approach trails" originating from the state park. The trail he chose, Len Foote, eventually converges with the southern-most beginning of the Appalachian Trail in Springer. The approach is challenging unto itself, but by 1:45 p.m. Kelley made it to the Hike Inn where hikers can rest before the final ascent to the AT.

That day the inn was closed and no other hikers were present, so Kelley rested a short time then resumed his journey. As he walked, he relished the pure, natural surroundings. The forest here was filled with tall pines, laurels, and oaks that pushed to the sky like huge arrows. It was early spring, so there was very little leaf-cover, providing a great view of the remarkable landscapes.

After a short time, however, the strenuous hike started to set into his legs. His 42-pound backpack was getting heavier, and he began to trip over the tangle of roots that fanned across what had become a smaller, single-person footpath. Deciding it was time for another rest, he found a small outcrop with an inviting moss-covered boulder where he could stretch out.

As Kelley lay back, propping up his feet and relaxing, a sudden pop shattered the idyllic scene. He bolted upright just in time to see a large tree falling in his direction. It missed him by 10 feet as it crashed to the ground.

Kelley stood up and looked down the embankment. He wondered how a tree could fall so suddenly on a calm day, especially since he could see the tree was mostly green and alive. Curious, he followed the trunk towards its origin. But as he approached, the odd occurrence took on a whole new meaning. There, where the tree stump should have been, was a colossal, ape-like creature, partially obscured by a fern and highlighted from the back by the rays of the sun.

In a phone interview, Kelley told me what he saw. "The sunlight was hitting its fur, which was brown," he said. "It had a conical-shaped head with hair sticking up like a cowlick. I could see the shoulder definition and bulging muscles. It was at least as tall as I am; I'm six [foot] four."

The creature appeared to be eyeing him as Kelley tried to absorb what he was seeing. "It all happened so fast, it was like my mind was making a motion picture as I was sizing it up," he continued. "It was ominous and I knew this was trouble."

Kelley turned and started towards his pack. A few seconds later he looked back but the creature was gone. He paused and laughed to himself. Surely he hadn't really seen such a thing. There had to a reasonable, if not humorous explanation.

But the laugher was short lived. To his right he caught another glimpse of it. The creature was now a behind a large dirt berm where it appeared to be concealing itself. Kelley could see the dark shape of its head and shoulders as it moved. Whatever it was, it had apparently run with unparalleled swiftness to the second location.

Realizing this was no illusion, Kelley grabbed his pack and ran back to the trail. He momentarily considered backtracking to the Hike Inn, but at this point the next shelter would be closer so he decided to move on. Now he was no longer tripping over roots as his adrenaline rushed. He hiked with determination and speed while grappling with the notion that a huge, ape-like creature—a Bigfoot—was here in the mountain forest. It was thought that, prior to that moment, would have seemed absurd.

After another mile, Kelley came to the point where the Nimblewill Gap forestry road crosses the Len Foote trail. He was still on edge but could not go on without a rest. He hadn't heard any sounds behind him for a while, so he could only assume the creature had not pursued. Either way, he slung down his pack and sat on a rock overlooking the majestic Smokey Mountains.

A few minutes later, a snap echoed below, down a steep hillside. Seconds later, a tree fell. The tree was too far below to hit him, but Kelley instinctively jumped up. He immediately scanned the area where the tree hit, and there below he could see the same dark-haired creature—or one like it—looking up at him.

"It looked to its left and that's when I saw the other one," Kelley explained. It was a second creature, standing nearby. This one had lighter, more reddish-colored hair. "It was comparable, if not a little larger [than the other] with butterscotch-looking highlights."

Shocked and desperate, Kelley shouted "Ya hey!"—not knowing whether he was trying to communicate or warn them. The creatures looked briefly at one another then back at him. Kelley said he then pointed forward up the trail with an exaggerated movement and began to walk. Now the tree canopies below him started shaking as the creatures apparently moved along the bottom of the slope in the same direction.

Kelley trudged along the trail as fast as he could. Below him he could hear the brush rattling and a loud rock clacked behind him. It seemed as though they were pursuing or pushing him along.

"There was one behind me," he explained, "and I was expecting it to touch me any minute."

Kelley marched ahead, but he was near exhaustion, which forced him to rest every few minutes. He would stop briefly and lean his pack against a tree while catching his breath. Each time he did, however, a huge rock clack sounded behind him. It was as if the creatures were taunting him.

Finally, after several stops, Kelley reached the Black Gap Shelter. It was modest A-frame structure with walls on three sides and an open front. Like the inn, it was deserted with no signs of other hikers anywhere. Under the circumstances, the camp seemed creepy and unsettling as he faced the fact that he could no longer go on. It would be dark soon and he would have to stay here for the night regardless of the creature's intentions.

Gathering his wits, Kelley entered the shelter and cast off his pack. As he did, two barred owls let out a booming call. This was answered by more calls, which seemed to trail off with a "chimp sound." It could have been his imagination, but the calls were like nothing he'd ever heard. It only increased the eerie intensity.

Exhausted, Kelley assembled his tent and got into his bed roll. It was around 6:00 p.m. by this time and still light, but he fell asleep within minutes. It was not to last, however. At some point after dark,

Georgia forest near the Appalachian Trail
(Photo by Lyle Blackburn)

he was awakened by noise or movement outside the tent. The wind was blowing through the trees, but he could hear what sounded like footsteps. He listened for several minutes, hoping it was other hikers or a ranger, but there was no reflection of headlamps or talking. "I was desperately hoping it was a ranger," he confessed, "but that wasn't the case."

Without lights or talking he could only assume it was one of the creatures. Perhaps it was there to finish him off. At that point Kelley resolved to confront the situation and he moved to unzip the rainfly door. It was then that a strange feeling came over him. It was as if he could no longer force himself to move; as if fear or some external force held him paralyzed.

"That's when I really panicked," he said. "It could have had its way with me."

As he lay there, propped on his elbow, he could feel an overwhelming sense of fear crushing him. The feeling lasted for several minutes, until suddenly it was gone. Now he could hear footsteps backing away from his tent.

Kelley abandoned the thought of going outside and laid back down. But he could no longer sleep. The strange happenings had left him questioning his own reality. Had the creatures evoked some sort of infrasound or external force to make him feel that way? It seemed impossible, but Kelley is not the only one who's described such a feeling. Over the years, a handful of other Bigfoot witnesses have described a similar, overwhelming sense of fear during their encounters. Perhaps the creatures have some extraordinary abilities that are just as mysterious as their species.

Regardless of its nature, Kelley was relieved that the experience seemed to be over. For several more hours he remained alert inside the tent until finally falling asleep in the early morning hours. After the sun rose, he crawled out of the tent and looked around. There was no sign of any other hikers or strange animals, so he quickly packed his gear and headed up the trail.

When he arrived at the Springer Mountain Shelter, there were plenty of hikers and trail officials there. He told his story to several people before requesting that his guide to take him back down. The experience had left him drained and unable to go on despite his original plan to spend six months thru-hiking the trail.

Of course, none of the hikers, rangers, or even his guide believed his story. They reasoned that if they had been on the trail for years and never seen one, then Bigfoot did not exist. To Todd Kelley, however, the malevolent apemen were as real as the Appalachian Trail itself.

10. Coastal Creatures

"Shambling Beast Terrorizes Town" read the headline in the February 9, 1938, edition of *The Daily Gleaner* newspaper.[196] Locals in the South Carolina town of Rock Hill were apparently living in terror after a bipedal, hair-covered creature allegedly attacked a man and strangled two dogs. According to the article, "Constable Carl Hovis reported he saw the shambling beast in a dark back alley and shot at it twice but failed to bring it down."

Prior to the shooting, a man by the name of Sam Watts claimed the creature had chased him through a wooded area. Two other men told police that "a fierce, fur-covered animal accosted them on a lonely, dimly-lit street," while another reported "the beast had attacked him and ripped off his clothing before he managed to escape."[197] The police responded with gunfire when they themselves saw the beast shambling through the small town. However, it managed to escape unharmed.

In an effort to solve the mystery, officials asked a nearby circus if they were missing any bipedal apes. All of their animals were accounted for, but police did manage to link their case to similar incidents that had occurred in Mobile, Alabama. Apparently a beast by the same description had been seen recently near Marmotte Street, earning it the nickname "The Monster of Marmotte Street." The Marmotte Monster had also been spotted near a cotton mill by two men. One of the men, John White, said: "It was standing in the water. It was black and tall as a man. I threw a rock at it but it snarled and started after me." The other man, Bruce Neal, confirmed the story, saying that "the animal ran on two legs as it chased them." He also noted it "smelled terrible."

Though several aspects do align with the Southern Sasquatch

profile—including the aggressive nature and terrible odor—Sasquatch is not often associated with the Deep South coastal regions. Here among the rural farmlands dotted by Antebellum architecture and pastoral fence rows, the southern charm typically beckons one to stop for a glass of sweet tea rather than search for Bigfoot.

But alas, there have been dramatic reports of strange creatures and events within this coastal expanse that are worth exploration. The coast itself is populated with picturesque seaside towns, but to the west the Southern Coastal Plain offers a landscape where loblolly pine and oak-gum cypress stand among great rivers and marshy lowlands to make up the rich Piedmont region. There's plenty of swampy areas, thickets, and shadows where huge creatures can, and apparently do, lurk. Some of these have been described in terms of Bigfoot and some in a similar fashion. Creatures such as the Hidebehind, an upright, hairy beast of the woods, and the Wateree Walking Bear, a "bear" that prefers to walk on its hind legs, are among them. As in other parts of the South, the distinction between these alleged beasts and Bigfoot are minimal, and at the end of the day are probably one and the same, provided they exist.

One of the earliest accounts comes from the Tugaloo River, which runs along the border between South Carolina and Georgia. According an 1889 edition of the *Clarksville Advertiser*, a native hunting party was camped east of the Tugalo River (now called Tugaloo) "during the time the Indians were in the South," when their deer carcasses began to go missing while they were away from camp.[198] On the third consecutive night, they decided to leave one of their party behind to watch. As the Indian sat guard, he watched a "monster animal" walk in and carry off a deer carcass. He described it as being about seven feet tall, upright like a man, hairy all over, with great claws on the fingers and toes. Although he had the opportunity, the guard was too frightened to shoot it.

The following day, all seven hunters stayed in camp. When the monster returned to grab some free venison, they fired upon it with their guns, dropping it instantly. A few hours later, the Indians began to hear someone or something holler in the distance, making a "yahoo" sound. Alarmed that more of the creatures may be on the way, they broke camp and sought help from local law officials. The documentation doesn't state the lawmen's reaction to the monstrous corpse they presumably had, but they apparently found merit in the story since they formed a posse and searched the area with dogs. When they came upon another of the creatures, they chased it down and shot it. There was no mention, however, as to what became of these corpses.

Many years later in 1974, the Atlantic coast was the setting of another interesting news story. According to the *St. Petersburg Times*, Beaufort Chamber of Commerce Secretary Dean Poucher and four other men had planned a hunting excursion on one of the islands that dot the coast east near Savannah, Georgia.[199] The men had been warned by the island's owner that the interior was extremely thick and impossible to penetrate. This had been reported by a previous hunting party who could not work their way through the dense foliage and whose hunting dogs refused to hunt.

Undaunted, Poucher and his friends went ahead with their plans, arriving in two boats with two of their finest hunting dogs. The hunters immediately found evidence of deer rutting, but when they tried to set the dogs on the trail, the dogs refused.

"We proceeded to implement the game plan and it was then we noticed the strange behavior of our dogs," Poucher said. "They wouldn't get out of the boat. They sat shivering miserably with their tails between their legs."[200]

The embarrassed dog owner finally dragged them out of the boat and put their noses on the trail, but they turned tail and ran back to the boat. After a few tries, the men gave up and proceeded toward the interior of the island on their own. As they were looking for signs of game, Poucher and another man both came across something rather shocking.

"At opposite ends of the island, we had come across tracks," Poucher explained. "I will never forget their size, nor the depth to which they were sunk. My boot alongside, a size 11, was hardly half as large as the track."

The tracks were not only huge, but impressed so deeply in the blue marsh mud that Poucher could not reproduce the depth with his own foot. Poucher had discovered a set at one side of the island, while the other man found a trackway on the opposite side, independent of each other. They described the tracks as being "about 18 inches long, 7 to 9 inches wide." They had no "instep" and were flat-footed. By their estimate the animal would need to weigh between 600 and 800 pounds to have made the impressions, some of which were in hard, compact sand.

Poucher admitted he didn't intend to tell anyone about the tracks for fear of ridicule, until he found out his fellow hunter had also discovered tracks. The hunters only penetrated a small portion of the island, so they could not speculate as to what might be living there.

In 1977, another barefoot phantom made tracks across a farm in Saluda County at the western end of South Carolina. The *Rock Hill Herald* reported that the prints, which were found on February 6, measured 14 inches long and 7 inches wide with a four-foot stride.[201] Photos show what appears to be a promising Bigfoot track, one of many as the creature apparently left tracks for a mile as it wandered from a "pond down a little-used road, over a sawdust pile, along a creek bank, across a pasture and back to the pond."

As in other cases, people had reported loud screams in the area for years. The creature was also a suspect in the murder of several cows found "half-eaten" in Saluda County. But like the track maker on the opposite end of the Palmetto state, its identity could never be verified.

BOOGERS AND BUGGERS

In 1989, people living in Cold Point, South Carolina, just north of Saluda claimed to have laid eyes on something that would certainly qualify as a Bigfoot. The first sighting came in April from Martha Tollison (57), who said she was driving to work at 5:30 a.m. when she saw a "hairy, grayish-black giant" on the side of Indian Mound Road.[202]

"I slowed down at first, but when I saw how big and tall it was, I took off," Tollison told a journalist from the *Spartanburg Herald*. "I just went by and it just kind of turned and went back in the woods."[203]

Tollison told her husband and friends of the encounter but was not taken seriously. It wasn't until a few months later they learned she was not the only person in Laurens County who had seen something strange. According to the article, at least nine people including Arlene McCall, claimed to have seen a similar beast lurking in the roadways. McCall's sighting took place on Indian Mound Road where she saw the creature lingering for a few moments before it walked on two legs into the woods. No footprints or other evidence were recovered, but that didn't stop curious folks and monster hunters from gravitating towards Cold Point in search of the beast dubbed the "Cold Point Creature."

Details on the other eight sightings are not included in the article, so it's hard to judge the veracity of this case, but perhaps an-

Thick Carolina woods
(Photo by Lyle Blackburn)

other notable South Carolina case can help shed some light on the affair. Just one year prior to the Cold Point Creature sightings, the highly publicized case of the Bishopville Lizard Man hit the press like a bug on a windshield. The Lizard Man—which I discuss in detail in my book *Lizard Man: The True Story of the Bishopville Monster*—was an eerie entity reported in the vicinity of Scape Ore Swamp in Lee County, two hours east of Cold Point. The sensational reports involved everything from alleged attacks, to mauled cars, to the usual roadway glimpses, details of which were plastered across countless media outlets including regional newspapers, radio, *People Magazine*, *Good Morning America*, and the *CBS Evening News*, just to name a few.

Descriptions of the creature were primarily that of an anthropomorphic, reptilian-skinned humanoid, but in several cases the witnesses told police they encountered an upright creature with hair. In my research, I came across police documentation (witness affidavits) that suggest a Bigfoot-like creature could account for at least some of the Lizard Man sightings from 1988 to 1990. If this is true, then perhaps the Cold Point Creature is the same entity seen in Lee County at times.

For example, one year after the Cold Point sightings, at 10:30 p.m. on July 30, 1990, Bertha Blythers and her five children were driving west of Bishopville near Scape Ore Swamp when a large figure appeared out of nowhere and lunged toward the passenger side of the car. Bertha's oldest daughter, Tamacia, was sitting in the passenger seat with the window rolled down, and when she saw the creature, she screamed. According to a statement given to the Lee County Sheriff's Office shortly after the event, Ms. Blythers wrote: "I was looking straight ahead going about 25 mph, and I saw this big brown thing, it jumped up at the window. I quickly sped up and went on the other side of the road to keep him from dragging my 11-year-old girl out of the car."[204]

Once they passed the animal, Bertha slowed down as she tried to calm her daughter. Her son Johnny, who was sitting in the back seat, looked out the rear window and saw the bulky figure as it continued across the road. It walked on two legs, like a human, but was

210

slightly hunched over and much, much larger.

In her statement, Ms. Blythers described the creature as being tall, wide, and having "two arms like a human." She could only see it from the waist up, but there was no question that it was big. She was not able to make out any clear facial details, but she was quite sure the body was covered in brown hair. "I never seen anything like it before," she wrote. "It wasn't a deer or a bear. It was definitely not a person either."

Johnny agreed. In his own statement to police, he described the creature as being "6 feet tall or more" and brown in color. "I certainly don't think it was a human dressed in something" and "was definitely not a bear," he concluded.[205]

Based on their statements, the creature more closely resembles a Sasquatch than a reptilian humanoid, which is closer to the description of the Cold Point Creature. Having read the Blyther's witness statements, I have no doubt they saw something that night. The question is whether it was an actual ape-like creature. If so, this would support other regional sightings such as Cold Point.

Another case with ties to the Lizard Man is that of the Belt Road Booger. The Booger was first reported in 1979 in Coweta County, Georgia, by a woman who claimed to have seen it on Belt Road in the city of Newnan. According to the August 9, 1979, edition of *The Newnan Times-Herald*, Mary Strozier was at her home on Belt Road one evening when her children ran inside hollering about a "monster" in the road.[206] When Mrs. Strozier walked into the yard, she saw a dark, five-foot-tall thing with a face like a monkey, a bushy tail, and eyes that looked like "diamonds." She wasn't sure what it was, but it was enough to send her and the children running back into the house.

Strozier immediately called police, but by the time they arrived they could find no trace of the thing. Newnan Police Chief Jerry Helton examined tracks found by a creek near the Strozier home but could not determine what had made them.

Things died down until the following week when another local woman, Nancy Jackson, said she arrived home from work at

7:00 a.m. to find "the ugliest looking thing" she's ever seen on her patio.[207] It was four-to-five-feet tall and covered in black hair with a face like a dog and a long, bushy tail.

"[It] dug in my flowers," she said. "Nobody can tell me I didn't see that thing."

Police responded again but found no evidence. However, a larger picture was starting to develop. Several locals informed the media that the creature had been seen in the area for at least nine years. One of the men said that seven or eight years earlier he and his brother were driving in the early morning when they saw "a large animal the size of a cow standing on its hind legs." As they approached, it disappeared into a marshy area.

The following week the police received an anonymous report from a caller who claimed to have seen the Belt Road Booger— as the media dubbed it—in the Sargent area of town. Once again the police investigated but found nothing. Despite the lack of evidence, they did feel there was enough credibility to the eyewitness reports to warrant an attempt to capture the creature. They planned to place traps in the surrounding woods, if they could determine a probable location where the creature may be hiding. However, as suddenly as they had started, reports of the Belt Road Booger died down and eventually stopped altogether.

In hindsight, various townsfolk and officials offered opinions on just what might have been stalking the streets of Newnan back in 1979. Eddie Ball, director of the Coweta County Emergency Management Agency who was on site for some of the original investigations, told reporters in 2005 he believes the Booger was "a man, now deceased, who was very large and a bit strange and shy about being seen walking down the local roads. When cars approached he would duck into a ditch, then reappear and continue his trek to nowhere. He wore a water faucet handle around his neck... and was totally harmless."[208]

Journalist Winston Skinner, who also investigated the Booger sightings at the time, told author Jeffrey Wells he heard mentions of a hoax but believed there might've been something to the sightings besides a "man in a monkey suit."[209] He stated that several credible people had confided in him about their own sightings, but didn't want their stories publicized for fear of ridicule.

In support of the hoax theory, an individual was eventually fingered as a suspect. In 2015, longtime Newnan resident Rucker Orr told the hosts of a radio show that his brother Kenneth Orr was the man behind the Belt Road Booger. He said Kenneth was a boy at the time and had created a suit for fun. But things turned serious when the police "shot" the Booger with a .22 rifle. According to Rucker, his brother was hit in the arm and had to go to the hospital. Following the shooting, the police showed up at the Orr's house and questioned Kenneth. Thereafter the Booger was "retired."[210]

Considering the creature was described as five foot tall with a dog face and a bushy tail running around the streets of a city, it's possible the creature was truly a prank. It's curious, however, that the shooting by police was not mentioned in the newspaper coverage. There were articles coming out on a weekly basis, yet no mention of the police or anyone taking a shot at the thing with a gun.

To take the monstrous plot even further, Rucker said his brother was also the man behind the Bishopville Lizard Man. He told how Kenneth allegedly used a creature mask to scare one of the major eyewitnesses (Christopher Davis) at night near Scape Ore Swamp. This is quite interesting since Kenneth was in fact stationed at Shaw Air Force Base 30 miles from Bishopville at the time and did come forward to police in August 1988 claiming he had "shot" the Lizard Man.

According to the August 6, 1988, edition of *The State* newspaper, Orr claimed he was driving along a road when the creature ran toward his car.[211] As proof, he presented some fish scales to the sheriff, which he said were left on his truck when the wounded creature leaned on it. The sheriff recognized common fish scales and immediately dismissed the wild claim. Orr never said anything else about his supposed involvement in the sightings.

While it can't be ruled out that Orr was dressing up in a costume and running around in Scape Ore Swamp, it seems unlikely he could be responsible for the attack on Chris Davis or for all the sightings that spanned from at least 1986 to 1990 when the Blythers saw the mysterious hairy creature in the road. I visited the site where Davis claimed he was changing a tire on the night in question, and it seems doubtful a car could drive up and park without Davis seeing or hearing it. Not to mention there were others who also claimed responsibility for the Davis incident, while the young man himself maintained he was chased by some sort of large, "green wetlike" creature.

As with the Lake Worth Monster events discussed previously, the case becomes a confusing tangle of claims that are never backed up by anything physical, such as a monster suit or photos of the "prankster" in such a suit. While there's little doubt folks saw *something* in these cases, the question remains: what was it?

Road near Scape Ore Swamp where Davis said he was attacked
(Photo by Lyle Blackburn)

The Nightmares Continue

Nearly a decade after lizardmania broke out, strange things were still being seen in Lee County. In 1997, two fishermen claimed to have seen a huge, hairy creature at Lynches River, not far from Scape Ore Swamp. In an interview with my colleague Mike Richberg, James Spires and Daniel Livingstone said they were fishing from the bank during the late evening of July 12 when they heard something large moving in the brush on the opposite bank.[212] At first they thought it might be another fisherman, but concluded it must have been a deer since a person never emerged.

As dusk began to set, they decided to head home. They gathered their poles and other gear and started walking to their truck when they heard a tremendous crash across the river. They both turned around to see "an upright animal of large proportions." It was covered in reddish hair and stood perhaps seven feet tall. Visibility was diminishing in the twilight, but there was enough light to see it was not a person or a bear.

After a few moments, Jim blurted out "what the hell is that?" and both he and Dan turned and ran out of the woods. As they approached their truck, the men heard what could only be described as a "blood curdling scream" that lasted several seconds. They jumped in the vehicle and immediately left the area.

Richberg interviewed the men at length and found them to be credible in their matching statements. "Both described the animal in exactly the same fashion," Richberg noted. "Tall, very muscular, thick and heavy set, with rusty red hair over the entire body with the possible exception of the chest area, where the hair was much thinner or not present at all."

The men were unnerved by the encounter but decided to return a few weeks later to look for evidence. However, storms had moved in and washed away any chance for such a discovery. As for the fishing, they would try their luck somewhere else.

In April 2005, more than two decades since the Belt Road Booger roamed the streets of Coweta County, strangeness returned there too. It started when *The Newnan Times-Herald* received a handwritten letter from an anonymous "hunter" who stated he'd seen an "enormous... very hairy beast walking upright in a field on Happy Valley Circle."[213] He said the incident scared him and he wanted to know if anyone else had seen such a creature in the area.

Naturally the letter conjured memories of the Booger, but since no other sightings had been reported and the writer was anonymous, the matter was simply dismissed in a tongue-in-check news article that christened the new creature the "Happy Valley Horror." Readers in the vicinity of Happy Valley got a good laugh, including Donna Robards who remembered the Belt Road Booger case well. However, Robards laughter soon ceased.

According to the September 15, 2005, edition of *The Newnan Times-Herald*, her son, Jeff, got the first shock on August 22. "He had just dropped his sister off at her east Coweta home and was heading west on Cedar Creek Road near its intersection with Happy Valley Road just after 2:30 a.m." when he was "startled to see a huge, hairy creature strolling down the middle of Cedar Creek Road toward his vehicle."[214]

"At first, [Jeff] thought it might have been a bear, but he didn't stick around to see," Robards told reporters. "When I asked him about it later, he said it couldn't have been a bear because the face was flat and didn't have a snout."

Robards wasn't sure what he'd seen but found out soon enough. Three nights later she was driving home after work around midnight when she reached the same intersection. Suddenly she could see two upright figures standing in the road ahead. She slammed on the brakes and skidded to a stop within 20 feet. She was now face-to-face with two uncanny creatures, one approximately eight feet tall with coarse black hair and one about a foot shorter with reddish-brown hair.

As Robards' car came to a stop, the smaller creature turned and ran into the woods west of Happy Valley Circle. The big one, however, advanced toward her. "I thought oh, dear God, that thing is

216

going to come in the car after me," she recalled. "And I was scared to death."[215]

Finally, after a few tense moments, the creature turned and followed the smaller one into the woods. As soon as it was out of the way, Robards stomped the gas pedal and drove home in a blur. She recalled that "It wasn't human, but you could call it ape-like. It stood upright but the hair on its face was shorter than on the rest of its body. And the eyes didn't bulge like an ape's. They were set back like human eyes." It was an image that would haunt her forever.

While the Coweta creature sightings tend to be associated with roadways rather than deep woods, the county does have a significant portion of Georgia forestry within it, and certainly did at the time of the Happy Valley Horror incidents. Expansion has been occurring all along, but this could contribute to animal sightings as their homes are stripped away in favor of asphalt. What was once a game trail or favorite hunting ground becomes thoroughfare with cars. But old habits are hard to break. Though the hard surface of the road reveals no footprints, residents of the former woodlands may still walk there in the dark cover of night.

ELKINS CREEK

When it comes to purported Sasquatch footprints, the South offers one of the best examples. Known as the "Elkins Creek Cast," this huge, five-toed track is considered by many experts to be an authentic footprint of an unknown primate.

The intriguing story of Elkins Creek dates back to 1994 when an elderly man living near Elkins Creek in Pike County, Georgia, called the Pike County Sheriff's Office to report a violent intrusion at his rural home. This wasn't the first time the man had called to complain about strange disturbances, and in fact, he was considered a nuisance caller by the police due to his frequent calls over the previous six months. This time he said the door to his shed had been ripped from its hinges and demanded that an officer be sent to the location.

Deputy James P. Akin, who was on duty at the time, was dispatched to the scene. He had been to the man's home on several occasions to investigate the complaints but thus far found no explanation for the increasingly bizarre happenings. In a phone interview with Akin, he told me of the situation, which had been unfolding since the fall of 1993. He said at first the calls were prompted by a "tapping sound on the side of the home" late at night. The man claimed he and his wife had even seen a shadowy figure lurking outside.

"Initially we would go out there, mostly me, and wouldn't find anything," Akin explained. "The man had a big oak tree above his residence and he would hear tapping and things like that. I attributed it to acorns falling off the tree, although I did encounter some really nasty smells when I exited my car."

As things progressed, however, the tapping turned into a forcible pounding. Volumes of dog food and corn began to go missing as well. The couple had several outside dogs that not only became agitated by whomever or whatever was coming around, but they eventually started to disappear one by one. Even more bizarre, the man said he perceived some kind of crude voice, as if the intruder was standing outside trying to call to someone in the house.

After responding a number of times, Akin came to the conclusion that a human trespasser was to blame. The secluded area of Elkins Creek at the time would make a tempting spot for a moonshine still or marijuana grove, so perhaps it had something to do with that.

"I thought, okay, there's someone that for whatever reason is trying to get the old guy and his wife out of the house," Akin told me. "Maybe we got some moonshiners, somebody who wants them out of here so they can move their product in and out without being discovered."

During the response calls, Akin would use his handheld spotlight to survey the area but could never spot the intruder. It seemed as though the man and his wife were hallucinating or making up stories, however, the physical evidence suggested otherwise. Akin explained:

> I knew the guy wasn't bullin' me, something's going
> on here. I saw the dents [in the metal siding] where
> something had hit the house. Something pulled the door
> off his shed out there. I looked for pry bar marks, but
> something had pulled the Master Lock and hasp straight
> off. And something threw a heavy tractor tire up in a tree
> about 30 feet. On nights when I smelled the smell, I had
> an eerie feeling someone was watching me.
>
> The harassment was ongoing... maybe every three
> nights or so. But catching them was hard because I
> was the only deputy on [shift] at night and by the time
> I got out there obviously whomever or whatever it was
> could hear my engine coming down the road and it had
> forewarning that I'm going to show up.

After seeing the tire in the tree and inspecting the shed door, it was obvious to Akin that whomever was perpetrating the damage was strong and powerful. At that point, he started to entertain a theory that it could be something other than a person. "I knew by the time of the shed and the tractor tire that we're dealing with something bizarre now," he explained. The idea was reinforced by related incidents. According to Akin, another person claimed to have seen a large, bipedal creature crossing in front of their truck on nearby River Road.

Finally Akin asked the man if he could return during daylight hours to conduct a more thorough search. Thus far he had only been there at night when darkness limited his capacity to investigate. The man agreed, so Akin returned the following afternoon in his personal vehicle. The deputy was "off the clock" but willing to use his own time to get to the bottom of the situation.

As Akin looked around the home that afternoon he located a small game trail near the house and followed it to Elkins Creek. Both he and the homeowners surmised that if someone were coming to the house from the woods, this might be a likely route. When he arrived at the water, he followed the creek for a short distance, looking for anything that would indicate the path of the intruder. It wasn't long before something caught his eye.

"I got to a place where there was a mud bank in the center of the creek, and I saw, plainly, that something had scuffed along there," Akin explained. "So I went down it to look. And sure enough, from the top of the bank, I could see that there was a big footprint in the middle."

He descended the bank to get a better look. When he did, he could see four more prints submerged in the clear water. Something had apparently walked along the water and left a print on the mud bank before climbing out of the creek bed.

The shape and size of the print immediately alarmed the deputy. It was massive, perhaps three times larger than a human foot, yet had five toes. And it appeared to be fresh, probably left within the last few hours. Akin put a hand on his firearm as he looked around. "It could have been a reaction to what I'd just seen," he told me. "But I really did have this feeling I wasn't alone out there."

Despite feeling spooked, Akin knew it would be a good idea to cast the print just in case the situation progressed. So he retrieved some plaster from his vehicle. When he returned to the creek, he no longer felt something was watching him, but nonetheless kept a wary eye on the surroundings as he waited for the plaster to dry.

"Once the thing had dried up enough to where I could remove it safely, I backed out of the creek. And that's what transpired," he noted. "From that point on I never heard anything else. I got hired in another jurisdiction and just put the cast up in a closet at the house."

The bizarre case may have ended there, but as it happens, Akin became friends with Georgia Bigfoot researcher Steve Hyde. One afternoon in 1997, Akin, Hyde, and some other acquaintances were gathered at a gun shop in Griffin, Georgia, when Hyde mentioned to Akin that he was interested in Bigfoot studies. Akin proceeded to tell Hyde of the strange events at Elkins Creek. Hyde was intrigued, of course, and asked Akin if he could see the track. When Akin presented it, Hyde was amazed. By all appearances, it was one of the best examples of a Sasquatch print to ever surface. It was not only massive—measuring 17.5 inches long and 8.5 inches wide— but it appeared to show evidence of dermal ridges, which are indicative of a real footprint.

Recognizing the value, Hyde convinced Akin to ship it to Grover Krantz, a respected anthropologist at Washington State University who was willing to consider the possibility that an undocumented ape might be living in parts of North America. After concluding the cast was authentic, Krantz shared it with Jeff Meldrum, professor of anatomy and anthropology at Idaho State University, and Jimmy Chilcutt, former Latent Fingerprint Examiner for the Conroe Police Department in Texas.

Both Meldrum and Chilcutt conducted a detailed analysis of the track and agreed that the footprint was likely that of an unknown primate species. Chilcutt, who has a long history of fingerprint studies, including those of primates, found evidence of primate-like dermal ridges and even sweat pores that could be seen with magnification. He documented his finding in an email to Meldrum:

> I have come to the conclusion that the dermal ridges in Areas "A" and "B" [located in the toe area of the cast] are definitely the ridges of a non-human primate. This conclusion is based on the fact that humans have creases running perpendicular to the lateral ridges on the first joint of the toes where the toe meets the foot. No such

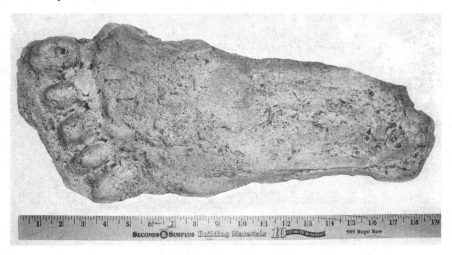

Footprint found at Elkins Creek
(From the collection of Lyle Blackburn, original cast by James P. Akin)

221

creases were observed in Areas "A" or "B". In area "C" [located at the center edge of the cast] the ridges flow lengthwise along the side of the foot. This does not occur in the human or the known non-human primate. This ridge flow is also consistent with the 1967 Blue Creek Mountain Road [Bigfoot] cast and the 1984 Walla Walla, Table Spring [Bigfoot] cast.

Based on the conclusions reached after careful study of the Elkins Creek Cast I give the following opinion:

The Elkins Creek Cast is that of an unknown primate.[216]

RIPPLES THROUGH THE WATER

The tangibility of the Elkins Creek Cast not only lends credence to the possibility that massive, man-like apes roam the southern reaches of the United States, it further reinforces the theory that "they always follow the creeks." This early concept put forward in *The Legend of Boggy Creek* continues to apply across the Deep South as the movie's effect resonates in a variety of ways.

In 2005, *The Legend of Boggy Creek* was the very thing that prompted a lawman to come forward with an encounter he had 20 years earlier near the massive Piedmont National Wildlife Refuge in Central Georgia, just 60 miles from Elkins Creek. The man was interviewed by researcher Sam Rich, who assured the witness that his name would remain confidential. He was a teenager at the time of the encounter but is now a respected police investigator, family man, and churchgoer. He was willing to share the details but not willing to risk his reputation, as such things often lead to ridicule.

In an interview conducted on November 2, 2005, the witness told Rich he and a friend often rode bikes on a logging road near their home in Jasper County when they were young.[217] The road was cut through dense hardwoods and was surrounded by hills, bottoms, and a few hay fields. In 1986, the witness said he and his friend peddled about a mile down the road, through a clearing and back into the woodline where the road eventually sloped down a few hundred feet before it crossed a small body of water called Turkey Creek. Beyond Turkey Creek the road sloped upwards again.

On this occasion the witness, who was 14 at the time, and his friend, stopped at the crest of the hill above the creek and got off their bikes. There they sat for a time talking and watching for animals as they often did. About 30 minutes before sunset, they were watching two does feed and sip water from the creek below when the deer suddenly raised their heads in alert. At first the boys thought the animals had detected them but soon realized they hadn't when the does turned their bodies towards the opposite slope.

After a few moments one of the deer snorted. The boys then noticed something moving on the opposite slope to their right. It appeared to be a darkly clothed man running at an angle down the hill. "As it made its way down the hill, we noticed that it was walking, by the leg movement, but it covered ground like it was running," the witness said.

The boys were frightened by the strange sight but remained steadfast. As the figure got closer, they realized it was not a man, nor a bear. It was covered in dark hair and appeared to be at least seven feet tall with long, swinging arms. It slumped slightly and had "shoulders that were broad but rolled forward, with its head cast down or slightly to the side." Its stride length was massive, which made it appear to be running while more or less walking down the slope.

By now the boys were overcome with fear. They jumped on their bikes and rode home as fast as they could, hoping the thing wouldn't follow. When they arrived home, they were each in tears but were met with the disapproval of their family for making up such stories. No one believed them, but it was something that both boys—now men—could not forget. They never ventured into those woods again.

As an adult, the witness is a veteran of the U.S. Army, having served in Iraq, Kosovo, and Bosnia, along with tours of Kuwait and Korea. He is also a successful investigator for a Georgia police department. When asked why he would report such a thing, especially since he was risking his reputation, the officer told Rich he had

Iconic poster for The Legend of Boggy Creek

just watched *The Legend of Boggy Creek* with his fiancée. Thinking back to his own experience all those years ago, he decided to do an internet search for more information. He ended up at the Georgia Bigfoot site where he submitted his report.

As irony would have it, there's a small Turkey Creek snaking its way through the bayou just a few miles from the infamous Boggy Creek. Both in a figurative and physical sense, the chilling encounters of the Deep South seem to connect through the waterways like veins in the body of a great mystery. The final convergence of which lies just ahead in the realm of the legendary Skunk Ape.

11. REALM OF THE SKUNK APE

On the night of January 3, 2016, my research partner Cindy Lee and I were hiking in Florida's Ocala National Forest. We had come to Florida to attend the International Cryptozoology Conference in St. Augustine but didn't want to miss an opportunity to explore the surrounding landscape while there. We were camped in one of the state parks, but on a Sunday in January it was eerily quiet. By the time we set out to hike into the woods at around 10:00 p.m. there was no one in sight.

We first crossed a series of boardwalks over some low, swampy areas and were now hiking along a dirt trail that wound its way into the darkness. The weather wasn't particularly cold, but a steady mist of rain rolled off the waxy foliage and dampened the ground below. Within the thick walls of evergreen oaks and sabal palmettos, it was like walking through a rain forest. I admired the prehistoric beauty of the surroundings. It was decidedly different than the forests we were used to elsewhere in the South.

As we navigated in the dim light of our headlamps, we began to hear a distinct "pinging" noise. It was hard to hear at first, amid the dripping rain and trudge of our boots, but when we stopped to listen, it was rather loud and close by. The sound was something like an empty soda can being hit with a stick.

I looked back at Cindy. She was also focused on the noise. Like me, she was trying to figure out what it was. It could have been rain drops hitting a can, but it sounded too loud given the misty nature of the rain. Without saying anything, I indicated I was going to move toward the sound, which originated from within the thick trees surrounding the path.

Cindy nodded as I turned and entered the treeline. Just as I did, something big moved in the brush. It was no more than 10 yards ahead, which caused us both to jump back in surprise. I quickly raised my handheld flashlight and shined it into the glistening trees. I couldn't see an animal, but whatever had been there was now running further into the woods with heavy footsteps. I immediately jumped into the brush and followed.

After about 10 yards, the footsteps stopped and so did I. I then moved forward more carefully, trying to make as little noise as possible as I scanned ahead with my beam. I had a good idea where the animal had stopped, so I concentrated on that area. The dense foliage was difficult to see through, but I was able to move forward easily enough. After another five yards, the animal started running again. I shined my beam directly at the movement but still could not a get a glimpse.

I continued to follow through the wet brush, but again the footsteps went silent as soon as I got close. When I progressed another seven or eight yards, the thing took off running yet again. I shined my light, but this time I could hear it moving further into the distance. At that point I realized there was no way I was going to get close enough to see it.

Heart pounding, I headed back to where Cindy was standing at the edge of the trail. She felt the same excitement, but without having seen it we could only venture to guess what it might have been. We both agreed that it was big, at least the size of a deer. However, I've come up on plenty of deer in the woods, and whatever this was sounded larger and moved with much more commotion. A feral hog was possible, but I found no telltale tracks or wallows indicative of pigs in the area. The Ocala Forest is also home to black bears. However, this animal's movements seemed more noisy than any I've encountered in the wild before.

While a bear still seemed most likely, there was one more possibility that had to be considered. It was, in fact, the reason we were tromping around in a Florida jungle in the first place: the Skunk Ape, a Bigfoot creature that has been reported by everyone from tourists, to hunters, police officers, fire fighters, teachers, and motorists in many parts of Florida, including the Ocala National Forest where we stood. As such, Cindy and I could not pass up an opportunity for a trip into its lair despite the soaked conditions.

And what about the "pinging" noise that stopped as soon as we heard the animal run? We did a search of the area and found an old tin can about 10 yards from the trail. Had the rain been hitting it, or was the animal hitting it? Had we been close to a legendary Skunk Ape? As the excitement of the event returned to the steady sound of mist on the palmettos, Cindy and I could only wonder.

WHAT'S THAT SMELL?

According to a tally at the BFRO database, Florida is third only to Washington and California when it comes to their highest number of "Bigfoot" reports. This statistic may be surprising to some, but it's one supported by an unusually large number of newspaper accounts and other documented reports, which suggest the state could be home to an unknown anthropoid species. These creatures, known as Skunk Apes due to their reputed foul odor, have been sighted in nearly every part of the state from swamps to woodlands to coastal ridges. Like other man-apes reported across the South, the Florida variety appear to be primarily bipedal with the usual variations in height, color, and degrees of anthropoid (apish) characteristics.

The origin of the term *Skunk Ape* has been debated among cryptozoological circles, but it's certain the term dates back to at least 1971 when news articles began using the name to describe the creature being seen more frequently in the Sunshine State. Since then, the term and the creature have become so well known that not only have there been hundreds of reports filed, but in 1977 a law was enacted to protect the cryptid. The bill, put forth by former State Representative Paul Nuckolls, made it a misdemeanor to "take, posses, harm or molest a Skunk Ape."[218]

With or without the bill, the alleged Skunk Ape seems to have little problem avoiding molestation or capture. Skeptics attribute

The author exploring the Ocala National Forest
(Photo by Cindy Lee)

this to the non-existence of the creature, while others question the feasibility for such an animal to even hide there. Florida is perhaps best known for beaches, nightclubs, and resorts, but there's no lack of wild country where large animals can and do roam.

As in much of the world, Florida's known wildlife has experienced habitat loss due to expanding urban development. But the native creatures seem resilient. Alligators, for example, have been threatened by both habitat loss and toxic contamination, yet their populations have increased in Florida wetlands since the 1970's.[219] Skunk Apes, who would conceivably have low populations to start with, also seem to be holding their ground as a steady stream of sightings continues to emerge.

According to Explore Southern History online, early Florida Indians told settlers of "a strange man-like creature that roamed remote swamps and woods. Covered with hair and much taller than normal humans, the monster was considered dangerous and most who encountered him would not approach him."[220] Later, as the European settlers began to displace the tribal natives, newspapers documented accounts of strange wild men and ape-like creatures. In the oldest account I could dig up, the *Apalachicola Gazette* stated that in June 1818 an "unknown animal" was discovered in the upper part of Apalachicola located in Florida's panhandle.[221] The animal managed to escape, but those who saw it said it resembled a "baboon." Judging from the size of its nest (made of loose cotton between several bales), the witnesses estimated the primate was five feet in height and carnivorous due to the "many bones [that] were found about the premises." This animal could very well have been a baboon, but at the time Florida's exotic animal population wasn't what it is today.

In 1884, a hair-covered "wild man" was actually captured in the vicinity of Jackson County north of Apalachicola. As the story goes, settlers living near Ocheesee Pond began to see a hairy, man-like creature with increasing frequency.[222] The thing was often seen eating berries or other edibles around the three mile pond or swimming in its waters as it moved between islands. At night, its eerie howl could be heard along the shores.

The more the sightings increased, the more the residents became concerned about their own safety. The creature seemed to shy away from human contact, yet its man-like appearance kept them awake at night, wondering what it might do. After a few meetings, they decided it would be best to organize a posse to drive out or capture the "monster."

In August of 1884, men equipped themselves with guns, boats, and horses (and presumably, pitchforks) and set their plan in motion. Not long after, *The New York Times* announced the following:

> Columbus, Ga., Aug.18 - News brought by the steamer Amos Hays from Lower River is to the effect that the wild man captured in Ocheesee Swamp, near Chattahoochee, and carried to Tallahassee, did not belong to a Florida asylum, and that all inquiry proved unavailing to identify him. He had been swimming in Ocheesee Lake, from island to island, and when taken

was entirely destitute of clothing, emaciated, and covered
with a phenomenal growth of hair. [223]

Judging from the text, the authorities believed the wild man
was truly a "man" and did their best to find out what asylum he had
escaped from, since he did not, or would not, speak. A week later,
the *Times* ran an update saying the man's identity was still a mystery, and authorities were unsure what to do with him. [224] As to his
ultimate fate, however, the reports never said.

On September 28, 1900, the *Davenport Daily Leader* announced that Kissimmee, Florida was being terrorized by a "shaggy
creature." According to the article, a Mrs. Arthur Shiver, who lived
a mile from town, saw a strange creature near her home. She described it as being about four feet in height with the "figure of a
man" and "covered in short, shaggy black hair." [225] The hair on its
head was also black and hung down below its shoulders. It had red
skin, long arms, and fingers that looked like claws as it "walked on
its feet in a crouching attitude," holding a stick between its legs.

Mrs. Shiver immediately called to neighbors who rushed out
and tried to catch the creature before it bounded into a ditch and
disappeared. They proceeded to track it to a swamp where it was
seen crawling into a patch of palmettos, but after that they could no
longer locate it.

The tracks it left were noted to be "about six inches long, with
a deep imprint of the ball of the foot and a claw mark showing that
the nail of the big toe was an inch long at least." The other toes likewise protruded and had claw-like marks at the end. Several bloodhounds were put on the trail, however, they "bristled up, showing
acute symptoms of fear." [226]

The overall opinion was that the "creature" was actually an old
Indian. This might explain the black hair atop its head and the red
skin but not so much the long arms and bodily fur. Or its "roar." In
another report, a gentlemen by the name of Bill Went said it "attacked" him at his house on Canoe Creek. When he shot at it, the
thing let out "a kind of roar" before escaping.

Aside from these older, ambiguous accounts, there is little on record until the 1940s when the modern era of the Skunk Ape begins. In one of these accounts, a woman claimed to have encountered such a creature at her home in Lakeland, Florida, east of Tampa in 1947. In a letter to author John Green, the woman stated that as a small child she saw it up close as it stood under an orange tree in her yard. She described it as "an upright animal with an almost human face."[227]

Cryptozoologist Loren Coleman documented another incident in which several men saw a huge, man-like creature while hunting in the Big Cypress Swamp near the Everglades in 1957. Coleman said the men were sleeping in hammocks one night "when they were awakened by heavy footfalls and splashing and breaking branches."[228] Alarmed, they quickly unzipped their hammocks, grabbed their firearms, and crouched with their backs to the fire. As the footsteps approached, the hunters could see a dark silhouette in the shape of a large man between the trees about 30 feet away. Their first thought was that it was a Seminole Indian, but upon studying it, they felt it was too big to be a human. After lingering among the cypress for approximately two minutes, the thing simply turned and walked away. As it did, the hunters could see that its "head had a different shape, sort of a slump with what also seemed like a heavy chin." One of the men also noted eyeshine, which would indicate an animal since humans don't possess the required *tapetum lucidum* layer behind the retina. Although most known primates don't exhibit eyeshine either, this trait has frequently been attributed to Bigfoot creatures, with witnesses reporting various colors of reflective illumination from red to amber.

In the 1960s, an ape-like creature was reported in the vicinity of Holopaw southeast of Orlando. According to paranormal investigator John Keel, it was first observed by several people as it ran across an open field.[229] The group, which included a local cattle rancher and citrus farmer, said they got within a few feet of the animal, and "it was definitely an ape of some kind."

The Holopaw Gorilla, as it came to be known, was also reported in 1966 and 1967. Witnesses described it as being five feet tall, broad, covered in hair, and definitely bipedal when it walked. In one incident the creature allegedly attacked two hunters at a place called Desert Ranch. They claimed to have shot the creature, but it escaped into the darkness, screaming as it ran. An unoccupied house on the ranch was later ransacked by what appeared to be a bleeding animal. The culprit, however, was never caught.

In the same timeframe we have what appears to be one of the first documented sources describing the famous rancid odor of Florida's mystery ape. In 1966, a man named Ralph "Bud" Chambers claimed he was walking in the woods along the Anclote River north of Tampa when he saw "a giant hairy thing standing in the trees."[230] He stated that: "The thing had a rancid, putrid odor like stale urine."

Alarmed but curious, Chambers quickly retrieved a friend and his dog. They were able to track the creature into a swamp, but at some point the dog refused to go any further. Chambers said he saw the creature again the following year when it came into his back-yard. His dog dutifully attacked, but the creature simply walked off in the direction of the swamp never to be seen again.

The reasons for creature's rancid body odor has been attributed to everything from bad hygiene to a territory marker to a defense mechanism. Several known animals—including the Tasmanian devil, lesser anteater, wolverine, and of course, skunks—emit pungent odors for the purpose of warning and defense, so it stands to reason the alleged Skunk Ape may use it for the same purpose. However, the need to protect themselves from superior predators doesn't seem likely, so perhaps it's simply the result of a large hairy animal living in a hot, humid, and often fetid swamp environment.

Regardless of the reason, in January 1967, four teenagers were confronted with a repugnant smell near the town of Elfers just west of the Anclote River. They were parked at a local lover's lane hang-out when one of the group noticed a foul stench wafting through the night air.[231] Suddenly, "an animal about the size of a large chim-panzee" leaped onto the car's hood. The girls panicked as the driver quickly turned the key and started the car. When she did, the ani-mal jumped to the ground and bolted into the woods.

Even though they were not supposed to be at the location,

Skunk Ape by D.W. Frydendall

the girls decided to report the bizarre incident to the police. They described the creature in detail, noting that it "looked like a big chimp, but it was greenish in color, with glowing green eyes." Police converged on the scene where they found a "sticky green substance" that could never be identified.

Several other encounters in the 1960s occurred near Brooksville, a mere 20 miles north of the Anclote River. In the first one, a Mrs. Eula Lewis told John Green she was watering a tree in her front yard when she looked up to see "a thing about six feet tall and covered with dark hair" gazing at her.[232] It was huge with broad shoulders and no visible neck. Mrs. Lewis immediately ran for the front door as the beast started toward her. She was able to make it inside the house and slam the door before it could catch her. Green noted that: "During the night she and her husband heard noises outside as if two creatures were calling to each other." The next day, big tracks were found around the home. These events occurred in March 1966.

On November 30, 1966, another woman said she encountered an even stranger beast while changing a tire. The woman said she was driving on a lonely stretch of road near Brooksville when she experienced a blowout.[233] As she was changing the tire, she became aware of some noise in the bushes followed by a horrible odor. When she turned to look, a "huge thing with large green eyes and an eerie greenish glow on one side of its hairy torso" stepped from the trees and looked at her. After a few terrifying moments, a passing car began to pull over. As it did, the creature walked back into the woods.

In 1967, a truck driver claimed to have been asleep in the cab of his truck near Brooksville when a "hairy, gorilla like creature" opened the door and grabbed his feet.[234] He reached up and hit the horn causing the creature to flee.

Aside from the occasional green glow, a profile of the Skunk Ape seemed to be solidifying for the modern era. The creature was notably ape-like, horribly odorous, and sometimes aggressive. Thus far the creature had been reported in a few scattered incidents, but the number of sightings and areas involved would dramatically increase in the coming decade.

MONSTERS IN THE MARSHLANDS

On a cool night in February 1971, five members of the Peninsular Archeological Society were camped in the Big Cypress Swamp of southern Florida when a huge, man-like creature emerged from the darkness. According to the group's president, H.C. "Buz" Osbon, as reported in the August 16, 1971, edition of the *National Observer*:

> There were five of us camped on top of this big shell mound—three in a large tent, two in a pup tent. About 2:30 a.m. one of the two heard a sound like an elephant walking on this shell mound.
>
> He looked out the tent flap and saw what appeared to be a big man, standing about eight feet away in the moonlight. He thought it was one of the party. He lay back down, then heard what sounded like a number of people all talking at once.
>
> So the two of them in the pup tent got up and woke us up—told what he'd seen. We looked around but saw nothing. But in the morning, we found these huge tracks. Footprints just like a man's, three different sizes. The largest 17.5 inches long, 11 inches across.[235]

Osbon's story was covered by a host of newspapers. He said they didn't see the creature again but did make plaster casts of the tracks.

As both an archeologist and board member of the Miami Museum of Science, Osbon added credibility to a creature the press now called the "Skunk Ape." As members of the Peninsular Archeological Society, Osbon and his colleagues had initially gone into the swamp to investigate strange pyramid structures, which they believed were created by an ancient race that once inhabited Florida. Now that they'd encountered a strange being, their subsequent trips focused on gathering more evidence or perhaps a photo of the creature, which the group profiled as being "a huge, hairy man-ape seven to eight feet tall."[236]

Many were skeptical of the claim, but those familiar with Skunk Ape history recognized its similarity to the earlier Big Cypress Swamp report from 1957. The Big Cypress Swamp—made up of pine flatwoods, prairie grasslands, and extensive marshes—is but one part of a vast wetlands ecosystem that dominates the southern portion of the state. This area includes the Everglades, which also offers miles of moisture-rich habitat with saw-grass marshes, tree-islands, and marsh prairies where sustenance and seclusion is abundant.[237] Combine that with nearby mangrove forests, tropical hardwood hammocks, and pine rocklands, and we have a region not only suitable for cryptid life but one where Skunk Ape sightings are prolific.

Not long after the Big Cypress incident, authorities responded to a call from residents living 16 miles west of Fort Lauderdale on the eastern border of the Everglades. According to news reports, a boy and girl allegedly spotted two ape-like creatures near their home at King's Manor Estate Trailer Court along the North New River Canal. The animals were described as having "monkey's faces, long arms, small eyes, gray splotches all over, and being 'taller than daddy,' or more than six feet tall."[238] Local residents quickly formed a posse to track down the creatures but had no luck.

In response to the hubbub, the Florida Highway Patrol asked Henry Ring, a county animal control officer, to conduct a search for the animals. During his investigation, Ring reportedly found "a bunch of strange tracks, like someone was walking around on his knuckles."[239] Later, in August 1971 while driving 10 miles west of Fort Lauderdale, he apparently had a first-hand sighting. "I saw this thing around midnight," he told a reporter from the *National News*.[240] "It walked like an ape, with long arms dangling nearly to the ground—but somehow stood straighter than an ape."

There were other area sightings which suggested the mystery apes could be dangerous. According to Bob Carr, a former Miami-Dade County Official Archaeologist and area historian, residents in the Davies area (east of the Everglades) had a real reason to be alarmed. "I talked to one gentleman who was a security guard [in the early 1970s], working at a trailer park next to an orange grove," Carr told a reporter from the *Miami News* in 1998. "He saw a large gorilla-type creature pulling a dead cow into a ditch at night while he was doing a patrol in his car."[241]

The incidents would only get stranger. At 3:30 a.m. on January 9, 1974, the Florida Highway Patrol received a call from a motorist who said he saw a tall, hairy creature limping along U.S. Route 27 near the Dade-Broward County border in the eastern portion of the Everglades. According to a *Miami News* article, the call came from a truck stop where troopers and sheriff's deputies converged a short time later.[242]

In the process of checking out the first claim, a second call came in from 35-year-old Richard Lee Smith, who claimed he had "struck a two-legged creature" with his Cadillac on the same road. Troopers were skeptical of Smith's claim since his car only had "a kind of brush mark" on one fender, but the calls were enough to warrant a search using personnel on the ground and two helicopters with powerful searchlights. This had some very interesting results. During the search, Hialeah Gardens Patrolman Robert Holmeyer said "he had arrived at the scene while it was still dark, and saw a 'shadowy, dark, 8-foot tall creature thrashing off into the underbrush.' He said he wasn't sure what it was, but it made a lot of noise thrashing about, and he didn't feel he should go in after it in the dark."[243]

By daylight, the search—which now included Bigfoot researcher Robert Morgan—hadn't yielded the two-legged creature, but authorities did find a large area of brush that looked as though it had been trampled by a sizable animal, along with a freshly uprooted holly tree. They also came across a mongrel dog "whimpering with four fresh puncture wounds, as if from teeth, in its throat."

The canine had been seen loitering in the area for a week and was thought to be a hunting dog from a local camp. One of the camp operators, Danny Fernandez, said "the bites looked as if they had been made by a large-jawed human rather than some wild animal."[244]

Another collision with a mystery ape can be found in the extensive files of Ramona Clark Hibner, whose early research into the Skunk Ape phenomenon has become a crucial part of its history. Hibner reported that on March 6, 1975, a Mrs. Humphrey was driving near Lake Okeechobee in Martin County when "they evidently collided with a 7-8 foot tall skunk ape/bigfoot that was running fast across the road."[245] The car was damaged, but the creature escaped.

Around the same time as the police hunt in Dade County, dozens of huge footprints were discovered at a catfish farm near the Everglades National Park. The prints, which measured "twelve inches long and seven and a half inches across, with a stride length of five feet," were examined by several experts, all of whom could not explain what kind of animal had left them. "It's beyond my comprehension that something could make a footprint that big," Everglades National Park Superintendent Jack Stark told the South Dade News-Leader. "I personally tend to disbelieve in the Skunk Ape or yeti, [but] I wouldn't say it's not the Skunk Ape — the discovery remains an unsolved mystery of the Everglades."[246]

A few months later, one of the most bizarre Skunk Ape incidents of all time was recorded by the Dade County Public Safety Department. Report #72168-1, filed on March 24, 1975, states that Ronald Bennett, his son Michael, and their friend Lawrence Groom were driving down a dirt road toward Black Point around midnight when "they observed what appeared to be a giant ape-like man approximately eight (8) to nine (9) feet tall and very heavy set, black in color with no clothes standing next to a blue Chevy and rocking the car back and forth with great force."

As they approached, a man got out of the Chevy and started yelling hysterically for help. Seconds later, the ape-like man turned and ran into the mangroves (small trees that grow in brackish, coastal waters). The witnesses continued down the road and eventually turned around. As they passed the Chevy again, they could hear movement in the mangroves but could no longer see the owner of the Chevy.

Ronald Bennett finally called police at 2:26 a.m. at which time a patrol officer was dispatched to the location. He searched the area but found no trace of the Chevy or the ape-man. (The exact location was given as the eastern end of 248th Street SW, 87th Avenue SW and Biscayne Bay and Snapper Point.)

The report doesn't explain why the Bennetts didn't stop to help or at least talk to the hysterical man, so it can only be assumed either they were too frightened or the man walked away from the road. The incident is truly bizarre, but presumably the men truly saw something unusual. Ronald Bennett probably would not have called the police otherwise.

The year 1976 registered another windfall of sightings. According to the files of Ramona Clark Hibner, she interviewed Lee County Florida Deputy Sheriff Tom Williams who said he spotlighted a strange animal drinking from a pond in June. "It loped off into the underbrush on two legs, was built large but was short, maybe four to five feet in height and short hair covered all over its body," he said.[247] A month later, resident Tom Drinkwater claimed to see an ape-like beast run across the road in the same area. It was "tall, hairy and smelled like it had tangled with skunks."[248]

On June 6, Hibner reported that John Holley, his brother Bill, and friend John Kersey were driving along a dirt road in the same county when all three saw an upright ape in a clump of pines 10 yards from the road.[249] It was approximately six feet tall and had black hair. They reported the incident to the local sheriff's office who dispatched a deputy to investigate. He reportedly found tracks and a clump of hair caught in a barbed wire fence. The hair was submitted for study, but the outcome is unknown.

In the same time frame, another flap of sightings occurred near the Skunk Ape's old stomping grounds of Brooksville in central Florida. Hibner reported that an ape-like animal was initially spotted by several children as it moved along a drainage ditch.[250] A woman saw a similar creature at Lake Lindsay, eight miles north of Brooksville, in April. The creature was walking across an open pasture at dawn. "It had long hair on its head down to its shoulders: was dark brown and walked fast like big, heavy men do when in a hurry," the report states.[251]

On June 25, several campers at the Croom Wildlife Reserve told Hibner they saw an "8-foot tall, black-haired, upright walking creature that smelled like a dead animal" near the Withlacoochee River.[252] It was wet and appeared to be coming from the river. When it saw the campers, the creature reportedly growled and ran back to the woods. A young man claimed he saw a similarly described brown hairy, upright creature "jump up a bank on Croom Road and run into an orange grove."[253]

The focus returned to the southern mangroves in 1977 when a man in southern Florida saw a strange figure lurking in a thicket near Key Largo. Charles Stoeckman, a Vietnam veteran and former policeman, told Monroe County Sheriff's Sergeant Rondall Chinn that he first encountered the dark, hairy creature on July 14 while he and his son were walking in a three-acre patch of mangroves. "It sort of stayed there, like a deer does when the wind shifts and it catches your scent," Stoeckman said in a news report.[254] He could also smell a foul odor which seemed to emanate from the animal.

A week later, Stoeckman's wife was awakened at 3:00 a.m. by the sound of something thrashing through a brush pile in their yard.

Marshlands of Florida
(Photo by Tracy Robinson)

241

When she looked out the window, she saw the silhouette of something with a large head and huge shoulders standing 30 feet away. It's "bright, colorless eyes" reflected in the backyard light, she said.

Stoeckman himself never claimed it was a Skunk Ape, but it seemed to be a possibility given the creature's profile and stench. Either way, the animal's presence had frightened the family so bad, Stoeckman considering moving them from the area. Sergeant Chinn told reporters: "There is definitely a problem there. These people are truly scared to death."

MYAKKA MYSTERIES

As reports continued, the aromatic ape became one of the South's most well-known cryptids. The catchy regional name tended to set the Skunk Ape apart from the general slew of Bigfoot reports, along with a profile that suggested it was somewhat shorter, more ape-like, and more likely to move on all fours than its Sasquatch counterpart. These characteristics, which have been noted in other reports across the South, led some researchers to theorize the creatures were not so-called Bigfoot at all, but a different species of unknown primate.

One of the early cases that contributed to this theory came from Sarasota County near the Myakka River. Like the Everglades, Sarasota has a history of dramatic ape sightings linked to the enormous Myakka State Park, which envelopes much of the county's central region. According to *The Sun Coast Times*, on Saturday July 7, 1975, around 10:00 p.m., 12-year-old Venice resident Ronnie Steves was asleep in his bedroom when he was awakened by the sound of his pet ducks thrashing and quacking in their pen outside. The boy looked out the window and saw "a vague, misty gray figure moving about in the cage, which was surrounded by a six-foot-high heavy chain-link fence."[255] Ronnie immediately woke his parents, who got up and turned on the outside lights. They were preparing to go out and check on the ducks when young Ronnie dashed ahead to the pen about 200 feet from the house.

"Next thing we knew, Ronnie was in the house like a shot yelling there was an ape out there," his father Ed Steves recalled.[256]

Ronnie said when he got to the pen he saw "an ape as tall as his father (about six feet) standing over the ducks." Ronnie spun around and ran for the house as the ape bounded off in the opposite direction toward Lazy T Ranch. "I looked around, there he was, and I took off screaming," Ronnie told a reporter from the *Herald-Tribune,* one of the many news outlets that ran a story about the event.[257]

Ed was convinced his son had indeed seen an unusual animal so he notified both the Saratoga County Sheriff's Department and the Florida Monkey Sanctuary (FMS). When officials arrived a short time later, they joined neighbors in a search of the area by flashlight. There was no sign of the animal, but officials found several fresh tracks near Lazy T Ranch where the animal had apparently crossed a ditch. FMS Executive Director Michael Corradino stated that "the prints resembled those of a chimpanzee but did not have the chimp's characteristic thumb-like big toe."[258]

Deputy Dennis Bosze and Corporal William Gordon, who responded from the sheriff's office, agreed that some kind of intruder had been present. An examination of the duck pen revealed that whatever it was, it was extremely powerful. "At one place the heavy-gauge metal chain-link was bowed out, and two other small areas were bent out of alignment as if from the pressure of a strong hand-grasp," investigators noted. It appeared that the creature had climbed in and then climbed back out, bending the fence in the process.

As strange as this incident was, it was only one of several involving local police and wildlife officials in the Myakka River area. Shortly after the duck pen incident, a family living on Venice Farms Road found three of their rabbits torn apart and their cages mangled. The owner, Mrs. Donald Madison, explained that chicken wire enclosed the rabbit cages. "On one cage, it looked like someone had put his hands through the chicken wire and then ripped it apart," she told reporters.[259] South County deputies went to the scene but found no signs of shoeprints or animal tracks around the pen.

Prior to investigating these incidents and others in Sarasota, FMS Director Michael Corradino didn't believe there could be an unknown species of ape present in Florida. As founder of the Monkey Sanctuary, he had been in the business of capturing escaped primates—primarily monkeys—so he knew those existed in the wilds of Florida. However, after another year of investigating the matter, his opinion shifted and he became convinced of the Skunk Ape's reality as well. "At first I scoffed, too, and said impossible," Corradino stated, "but the physical evidence could not be ignored."[260]

When Corradino made this statement, he had no idea Myakka would eventually produce two of the most controversial items in Skunk Ape history. This came in the form of two striking photos taken in late 2000 after a rather lengthy drought of Sarasota sightings. The photos, which have become known as the "Myakka Ape Photos," first came into the hands of the Sarasota Sheriff's Office on December 29, 2000, when they received an envelope addressed to their "Animal Services Department." Inside was an anonymous letter and two snapshots that appeared to show a live, ape-like animal standing behind a palmetto tree.

The writer—who only identified herself as a "senior citizen"— said she had taken the photos in late September or early October at her home near I-75.[261] (This location in Sarasota is near the Myakka River, hence the association.) Her husband thought it might be an escaped orangutan, so she refers to it as such in the letter. She explained that for two nights the "orangutan" had been taking apples from the back porch of their home. On the third night, she heard it making noise so she grabbed her camera and went to the backyard. According to her letter:

> It froze as soon as the flash went off. I didn't even see [the animal] as I took the first picture because it was so dark. As soon as the flash went off for the second time it stood up and started to move. I then heard the orangutan walk off into the bushes. From where I was standing, I judge it as being about six and a half to seven

feet tall in a kneeling position. As soon as I realized how close it was I got back to the house. It had an awful smell that lasted well after it had left my yard. The orangutan was making deep "woomp" noises. It sounded much farther away then [sic] it turned out to be. ... I was about ten foot away from it when it stood up.

The woman said they intentionally left out four apples (two whole and two cut in half) on the following night so they could entice the "orangutan" back for a better view. But they eventually went bed before it showed up. The next morning the two whole apples were missing. Shortly thereafter they got a dog and never saw the animal again.

The woman claimed she was concerned about the animal because her grandchildren often played in her backyard. She urged police to look into matter, suggesting perhaps an orangutan had escaped and was running loose in the area. "I don't want my backyard to turn into someone else's circus," she concluded. It was signed: "God Bless, I prefer to remain anonymous."

Even though the photos did appear to show some kind of ape, the Sheriff's Office reportedly laughed off the matter. According to cryptozoologist Loren Coleman, no case file was ever created or any immediate investigation launched.[262] The matter might have ended there and the photographs lost, if not for a call received by David Barkasy, owner of the Silver City Serpentarium in Sarasota. According to Coleman, a member of the animal control division called Barkasy to discuss a possible "orangutan problem," which "local authorities were matter-of-factly discussing."[263] During the call he was informed of the photos.

Barkasy was familiar with Skunk Ape reports, and if nothing else, thought the photos might be of interest in that matter. He was only given access to black and white copies at first, but it was enough to prompt a call to Coleman, who Barkasy felt could assist in determining if it was indeed a cryptid.

After a series of red tape dances and bureaucratic nonsense, Barkasy was finally able to get high-quality copies of both snapshots, which he shared with Coleman. The excitement was heightened by Barkasy's communication with several department officers who told him about "rumors of an animal bothering neighborhoods in east Sarasota County."[264] This prompted Barkasy to search several Myakka neighborhoods in hopes of spotting something himself. He also made sure no exotic pets of that nature had been reported lost.

Following his analysis, Coleman posted an initial report about the Myakka Ape Photos on February 5, 2001. This resulted in the usual array of public opinion, from a person in a costume to Photoshop manipulation to the real thing. Some of the debate centered around visible artifacts that had been introduced by the color copy method and subsequent scanning to a computer raster file. This process can introduce elements that are not part of the original print, and worse, introduce "color field flattening" that makes the figure look "flat" or like a cardboard cutout, as some skeptics noted.[265]

The scans were eventually examined by David Bittner, a photographic and film analyst and partner of Pixel Workshop, Inc., who told Colman: "I'm pretty impressed with it so far, at least in terms of it being a real photograph, and not a compositing job or a cardboard cutout." [266]

One of the interesting aspects of the photos was the resemblance to an actual orangutan. This led to speculation that the creature might indeed be an orangutan, or perhaps, the Skunk Ape was closely related to orangutans, which would support the notion that the creatures were more ape-like than traditional Bigfoot. The animal in the photo appears to have a white beard and lighter brow ridges, which is indicative of a masked chimpanzee (*Pan troglodytes verus*). This trait prompted theories that it might be another sort of feral primate, if not an unknown one.

All theories, however, are contingent on whether the photos actually show a real animal. To that end, Jay O' Sullivan, a University of Florida Department of Zoology Ph.D. student, pointed out that eyeshine can be useful in determining the authenticity of the subject. According to Coleman: "The expectation is that the pupils will contract in response to exposure to the first flash. The eyes would be wide open for the first photo, but smaller in the second." Measurements conducted by both parties indicated that eyeshine was

Myakka Skunk Ape photo (cropped and zoomed)

40 percent larger in Photo 1 verses Photo 2, which suggested it was indeed a real animal.[267]

Other experts disagreed, citing a probable hoax. In a May 2006 letter to the late Bigfoot researcher Bobbie Short, Mitsuko Choden—a primate specialist from Japan—stated "the Myakka ape is a costume familiar to them in assorted colors, with plastic teeth molded in the fashion of the great apes." Furthermore, Choden felt "the subject in the Myakka photograph expressed no body, arm or leg definition that would lend itself to the great apes."[268]

Given the varied opinions, it becomes crucial to interview the photographer and examine the site where the photos were taken. Unfortunately, as of this writing, no one has come forward to claim responsibility for the photos... real, hoax, or otherwise.

Amok in Ochopee

The Myakka photos are memorable due to the unusually clear image of the subject, but this isn't the only case of an alleged Skunk Ape caught on film. On the morning of July 21, 1997, Ochopee Fire District Chief Vince Doerr was driving to work through the Big Cypress National Preserve when a "tall, hairy, reddish-brown thing" crossed the road some distance in front of him.[269]

"It came from the left, which is the east, and then went across the road," Doerr told *Miami News* reporter Jim Kelly. "When it crossed the road, it looked like it was taking kind of long steps."

Doerr could rule out a bear—he'd seen plenty of those and they don't walk upright for such extended periods. When he got closer, he stopped his truck and grabbed the camera sitting beside him in the cab. He always carried it in case he had to document a fire or an accident scene. He jumped out and looked through the viewfinder. The animal was approximately 400 feet away at this point.

"I seen [sic] it walking in the woods, and I yelled," Doerr explained. "It kind of stopped, turned a little bit, and then it started north, parallel to the road. I had to turn my light meter on, then I adjusted and I snapped one picture. I looked at [the creature again], and it was kind of a small brown spot."

Realizing it would be pointless to take more shots, Doerr got back in his truck and continued driving. He wasn't convinced he had seen a so-called Skunk Ape—and in fact didn't develop the film for 10 days—but did discuss the incident in a joking manner with several co-workers.

As word got out, however, Doerr received a call from a reporter with the local *Everglades Echo* newspaper. After he told her what he'd seen, the reporter told him about two other incidents that had come to her attention. First, Jan Brock, one of Doerr's neighbors, said she saw the same sort of creature on the same road several minutes before the fire chief estimated his sighting had taken place. According to Brock, who worked as a county realtor, she was driving to work at 7:45 a.m. when an upright creature crossed approximately 1,000 feet in front of her car.[270] She said it was about seven feet tall and covered in thick, dark brown hair with what appeared to be a lighter colored patch on its chest. She had often seen wildlife in the area and was sure this was not a bear, noting that its legs were too long and it walked for a long distance as it crossed the road and headed for the trees.

Less than two hours later, 20 tourists in a van driven by Naples Trolley Tour guide John Vickers spotted it two miles away. As they were driving parallel to the Turner River Canal, they saw the thing run from east to west across Turner River Road. A short time later, Vickers was escorting most of the passengers on a "gator walk" along the canal, when the creature emerged from some bushes about 30 yards from the parked van and frightened three people—two woman and a young girl—who had stayed behind. Vickers ran back to the van when the girl began screaming but was too late to see the thing himself. He could, however, see the fear and panic on the little girl's face, so he cut the tour short and drove to the local ranger station to report what they'd seen.

Like many alleged Bigfoot photos, Doerr's image essentially shows a brownish-red spot that resembles an animal, but is by no means conclusive or compelling to most scientists. In this case, it's the circumstances supported by additional sightings that give it credibility. Those people either saw a person in a costume or an unusual animal. It cannot simply be written off as mistaken identity or mass hallucination.

The area where Doerr and the others had their encounter is also a short distance from where prominent Skunk Ape hunter Dave Shealy said he and his brother first saw one of the elusive creatures in 1973. Only 10 years old at the time, Shealy was hunting with his brother when they spotted a tall, upright subject entering the Turner River Swamp. As a child, he had heard stories of the creature circulating as far back as he can remember, but it was that moment which signaled the beginning of a lifelong relationship with the smelly anthropoid.

Shealy, whose family roots in the Everglades date back to 1891, has since dedicated much of his life to the pursuit and research of the Skunk Ape, which he claims to have laid eyes on two more times.[271] Nowadays Shealy is head of the Trail Lake Campground located in Ochopee where he operates a small museum and gift shop known as the Skunk Ape Headquarters. Here visitors can book a guided tour of the surrounding marshlands and view an array of alleged evidence, including footprint casts.

One of the footprints was found just after the flap of sightings in 1997 when a crew from WBBH-TV (Fort Myers) showed up at the museum asking if Shealy would show them around. While exploring the area of Turner Road where the creature was sighted, Shealy and reporter Grant Stinchfield came across several large tracks in the mud. The impressions measured approximately 13.5 inches in length by 6 inches wide and appeared to be missing one toe, or perhaps the toe didn't register in the cakey mud. Just beyond the tracks, Shealy also noticed some brown, three-inch-long hairs stuck to some brush. The hair was collected but never analyzed because, according to Shealy, it was confiscated four days later by two "men dressed in, like, suits, and long-type black coats" who showed up at his home unannounced.[272] Needless to say, it was the last anyone saw of the hair.

Whether this represents a bizarre conspiracy to cover up the existence of an unknown species or something deceitful on the part of Shealy, it has not phased his enthusiasm for the hunt. He continues to operate the Skunk Ape Headquarters, which draws a horde of curious visitors each year.

Meanwhile in Myakka, things remained relatively quiet for a number of years until a new set of photos roused the public's interest in 2013. The photos, along with an accompanying video, were the result of an alleged multiple-witness sighting that occurred on March 2 in the Myakka River State Park of Sarasota County. That afternoon, 45-year-old Mike Falconer and his son Justin were driving in the park when they spotted a large, dark figure moving across a savannah.[273] Quickly pulling over, he and his son jumped out of the car and started shooting video with their iPhones.

As they were filming, other drivers began to pull over and get out of their cars. It was quickly becoming a scene. Realizing they were too far away for a quality shot, Falconer and his son started walking through the high grass towards the figure. At this point they turned off the video feature and began shooting a series of still photos.

The resulting images—which were posted along with the video on YouTube—appear to show a hairy, upright figure, although it is still too far away and too grainy to make any definite identification[274] Park rangers acknowledged the presence of bears, which may provide a possible explanation, although the animal appears to be standing upright, at least when the shots were taken. A person in a suit cannot be ruled out either, but it seems unlikely that a person would remain visible for so long considering the risk of a bullet.

One way to clear up the matter would be to examine the photos taken by the other witnesses. The Falconer video briefly shows a woman taking photographs with a telephoto lens, which would likely result in a much clearer image despite being taken at a greater distance. But as things go in the pursuit of mystery animals, these photographs have yet to surface.

LASTING IMAGES

Sightings in other parts of Florida have added to the statewide mystery. One of these areas is the Green Swamp Wilderness located between Tampa and Orlando. This 560,000-acre expanse consists of wetlands, flatlands, and low ridges whose drainage creates the headwaters for four major rivers: the Withlacoochee, the Ocklawaha, the Hillsborough, and the Peace.[275] As with other murky woodlands, stories of strange, hairy inhabitants bubble to the surface on a regular basis.

In 2004, Jennifer Ward said she was driving through the Green Swamp in northern Polk County when she caught sight of a haunting, human-like figure in a drainage ditch. It was covered in "dark hair or fur and had whitish rings around its eyes," she told reporters.[276] It raised its head as she approached.

"It looked like it was doing something," Ward said. "Whenever it saw me, it probably took on the facial expression I had on because I was dumbfounded. It just watched me as I drove by."

As with other Florida witnesses, Ward was certain it wasn't a bear. She had never placed much stock in the reality of the Skunk Ape, but now she was forced to rethink her position. "I didn't really think it existed, but I'm convinced now," she admitted.

Ward didn't stop since her two daughters were sleeping in the back seat at the time, and she feared the creature might become spooked and "attack" the vehicle. However, she did return later to look for evidence such as footprints. Most of her friends and family were skeptical of the her story and laughed it off as hallucination or mistaken identity. But Ward was confident she saw something that can't be easily explained.

That same year, Bill Arnold was on a lonely stretch of road in northwest Florida when he caught sight of a similar upright figure. At about 6:30 p.m., the 52-year-old bike shop owner was driving through Tate's Hell Forest on his way to St. George Island when a

Road through the Green Swamp
(Photo by Tracy Robinson)

large, dark animal ran across the road on two legs.

"When I first saw it, I thought it must be a bear," Arnold told reporters.[277] "As I got closer and closer, I thought it might be a hunter. A big, hairy hunter."

But as he watched it run toward the trees on the other side of the road, he realized it was much too large to be a human. And much too "hairy." He estimated the creature's height to be upwards of eight feet tall with hair covering its entire body.

Before disappearing into the woods, it briefly glanced back at Arnold's approaching truck. When it turned, its torso turned too. The animal had virtually no neck. It looked strong and powerful. The thought gave him chills as he continued down the lonely road surrounded by miles of trees.

The impressive forestry of Tate's Hell is just east of the winding Apalachicola River, which extends from northern Georgia all the way through Florida's panhandle. As one of the most significant basins in the southeast, it's not surprising that a number of alleged Skunk Ape incidents have been reported along its curves. One such incident stands out from the rest, however, as it yielded not only an intriguing image but represents an advance in consumer technology that may eventually shed light, so to speak, on the mystery.

On the night of May 8, 2012, Stacy Brown and Stacy Brown Jr. were camped alone in Torreya State Park just east of the Apalachicola. They were there for the specific purpose of Bigfoot research. In a conversation with Stacy Brown Jr. he told me he was hoping to lure in one of the creatures by sitting in camp and playing loud rock music—particularly White Zombie—while he and his dad occasionally walked the perimeter and scanned the area with a thermal vision imager. The device works by detecting infrared radiation, typically emitted from a heat source, to render a picture for video output. It would allow them to see—and video—any warm-blooded creatures in the darkness, even if they couldn't be seen by the naked eye.

Sometime after midnight, the Browns were startled by a distinct knocking sound not far from the camp. It was loud enough to be heard over the music. The park was deserted except for the two of them, so they felt sure it wasn't another camper.

Brown grabbed the thermal imager as the two men headed out in the direction of the knocks. As they walked, the knocks continued periodically just ahead, as if whatever was making the sound was moving deeper into the forest. The elder Brown didn't believe in the Skunk Ape and was merely there to spend time with his son, but he couldn't deny the fact something was making deliberate sounds.

As Brown scanned the area ahead with the imager, he finally saw something with a "heat signature" behind a tree. The setting on the device was such that anything emitting heat would register as black against a contrasting white background. The tree trunk registered as white, while the heat source behind it was black. Brown immediately hit the record button.

As he watched and recorded, the black figure stepped from behind the tree and walked to the right. It was only visible for a few seconds before it disappeared again behind some brush, but it was long enough to clearly see a huge, human-like figure walking on two legs. The sight was unnerving. Brown immediately turned to his son and told him they needed to get out of the area. Brown Jr. was undaunted but nonetheless complied with his father's wishes. They broke camp and left shortly thereafter.

The resulting video sequence is quite intriguing. Unlike many blurry, blobby, or shadowy "Bigfoot" photos, there's no doubt this is either a Sasquatch or a human. In order to discern which, the Browns returned to the site several times to take measurements and to create a video comparison with a known-human form using the same imager. The trail where they recorded the footage was familiar to Brown Jr., so he was able to locate the exact spot where the encounter occurred.

As a result of numerous calculations to estimate the height, shoulder width, and step stride—conducted by multiple individuals including Cliff Barackman, cast member of *Finding Bigfoot*—the figure appears to be significantly larger than typical human proportions.[278] Though this conclusion must allow for a margin of error, when combined with the low probability of a tall, bulky human sneaking around in the dark woods, and the credibility of the

Brown's story, it's hard to completely dismiss the possibility of a brief glimpse at a legendary creature that, by all accounts, would have been invisible in the darkness.

The scene draws me back to the night Cindy and I were walking on a similar trail in the nearby Ocala National Forest. Whatever was out there—Skunk Ape or otherwise—managed to stay just ahead of my flashlight beam. It was a perfect microcosm of a mystery that continually lures us into the shadows with the promise of one astonishing moment of clarity. Perhaps soon, the answers will finally come into focus.

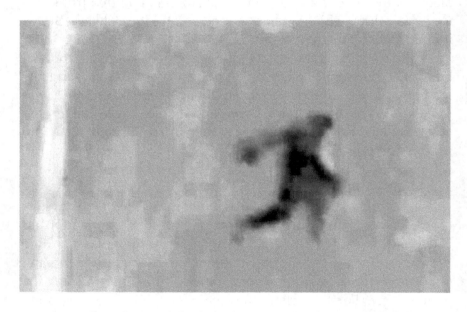

Figure from the Brown thermal video (cropped and contrast adjusted)
(Courtesy of Stacy Brown Jr.)

CONCLUSION

The Deep South is home to many great mysteries and perhaps none is more intriguing or perplexing than the man-ape reports we've encountered on our journey. The sightings are often fleeting and the evidence is hard to come by, yet in so many cases credible people have encountered something truly unexplainable.

The notion that ape-like creatures are inhabiting so many pockets of the American landscape is undoubtedly second only to the notion that these creatures could exist at all in our modern world. With the ever expanding urban centers, massive deforestation, and advances in technology it would seem as though we have uncovered every stone, or at least aimed a satellite at them. However, as we've seen in these example cases, people are still reporting encounters with mysterious, hair-covered anthropoids as they have for centuries.

This fact can be interpreted as either support for the existence of these creatures or as reason to doubt. On one hand, since they appear to have always been present and are reported by so many individuals, it suggests a viable entity is truly at large. On the other hand, the fact that people have always reported encounters without a single known specimen to show for it lends support to skeptics who says it's simply a phenomenon of the mind, perhaps harkening back to a primal shadow of our past. These creatures, they argue, couldn't possibly exist. Or could they?

Human presence may be expanding, but it has yet to erase all of the wild lands where such a creature could exist, especially if it is intelligent, exceedingly reclusive, and few in number. Yes, they have been seen on many occasions, but even those instances are brief as the creatures quickly move back into the shadows. For as many encounters as there are, there are surely countless other situations where the creatures simply stepped into the trees or darted away before they were noticed.

By archeological standards, apes have never been known to exist on the North American continent, but that doesn't mean there aren't suitable candidates that could account for their presence. One example is *Gigantopithecus*, a "giant ape" first identified in 1935 by a handful of fossilized teeth discovered in China.[279] As more teeth and mandible remains were discovered in subsequent years, scientists theorized the animal could have stood in excess of nine feet and may have developed the ability to walk bipedally. According to anatomy and anthropology professor Jeffrey Meldrum: "[If] the foraging strategies that convergently shaped the jaws and teeth of both *Gigantopithecus* and early hominids produced bipedalism in the one lineage, the possibility of the convergent evolution of bipedalism in *Gigantopithecus* under similar environmental conditions should at least be entertained."[280]

The creature, which is neither typical ape nor human, unquestionably aligns with the profile of Bigfoot and its counterpart in the Himalayas, the Yeti. Based on current evidence, *Gigantopithecus* is thought to have gone extinct some 100,000 years ago,[281] yet "There is no reason that such a beast could not persist today," notes Dr. David Begun, a paleo-primatologist at the University of Toronto. "After all, we know from the subfossil record that gorilla-sized lemurs lived on the island of Madagascar until they were driven to extinction by humans only 1,000 years ago."[282]

Asia is a long way from North America, but it's not out of the question that, if they survived, these giant pongids could have crossed the Bering Strait Land Bridge along with many other species during the continent's formative years. Once present in the New World, the apes could have spread into the various mountains, forests, and lowlands where they would presumably adapt as changes to environment and climate occurred.

The fact that fossilized remains have not been discovered in North America should not in and of itself rule out the possibility that *Gigantopithecus* or a similar anomalous anthropoid exists or has existed here. We know chimpanzees are real, yet not a single shred of fossil evidence was found until 2005 when researchers uncovered three teeth in the Rift Valley of Kenya, Africa.[283]

Bodies and bones have likewise been elusive in the quest for Bigfoot evidence but, like the absence of fossils, should not be used to dismiss the case out of hand. Discarded bones of other large animals such as bears are rare, and in the case of a creature with an extremely low population, even harder to find, especially considering the areas where they are most often reported. Mountainous environments, forests, swamps, and areas of high rainfall are not conducive for lengthy preservation of carcasses, nor do they offer the permanent sediment necessary to form fossils.[284] Combine that with the possibility Sasquatch creatures bury or dispose of their dead, and the chances of coming across a pile of their bones is decidedly remote.

Advances in technology make it hard for these creatures to hide, but again this shouldn't be used as a basis to completely rule out the possibility. Most people are now armed with a smartphone camera, however, chance encounters with these creatures typically last only a few moments, making it hard to pull out a phone, open the camera app, aim, and take a photo. It has been done, of course, but this results in fuzzy images that are no more conclusive than those that merely show a shadow in the forest.

Game cameras are more likely to capture a photo of one of these creatures, but these have inherent problems as well. First, they need to be in the right place at the right time. Even getting a mountain lion on film, for example, is not easy, and presumably there are more mountain lions than Bigfoot. In places where bears are present, cameras are often torn down and rendered useless. Bears are attracted to the smell of petroleum products used in the construction of many game cameras, and if bears can smell them, so could other animals. Perhaps the most eye-opening caveat is the fact that alpha coyotes are known to avoid cameras altogether.[285] If they can do it, then why not Bigfoot? All of these factors combined creates the proverbial needle-in-the-haystack effect on a grand scale.

Admittedly, each of these considerations could be viewed as excuses or long-grasping straws in order to explain why these creatures have yet to be proven—whether they're giant apes, relic subhumans, extant Neanderthals, or something else altogether. But the point here is simply to remind us that just because we don't yet have proof, doesn't mean they don't exist. The thought of man-like apes living among us may seem rather chilling and improbable, but it's not impossible. If these creatures are intelligent, agile, resourceful, and expertly elusive, then they may yet offer us a lesson in the true sense of being "green." By all accounts they are at one with a nature we're slowly leaving behind as we rely more on our electronic gadgets and modernized comforts. Perhaps we've lost the ability to recognize what is there before us in the fading shadows of our forests, swamps, and mountains. Or perhaps we are unwilling to concede that we haven't truly solved all of the scientific mysteries in our amazing world.

For me, it's that open-mindedness that acknowledges the unexplainable aspects of the Southern Sasquatch phenomenon without closing the door on the unexpected. Time and time again, I've come across level-headed, credible individuals who have undoubtedly seen something that doesn't fit our current understanding of what may be lurking on the fringes of our own reality. If even one of these witnesses saw an undocumented creature, then it not only implores us to listen carefully to the others, but opens the door for possibilities beyond our modern scope. Each time I set foot in these vast landscapes of Boggy Creek and beyond, I keep my eyes open and my ears tuned to the heartbeat of the woods. Perhaps it will not only bring me closer to the nature we're at risk of losing, but to the ultimate solution to the mystery of the Southern Sasquatch.

ACKNOWLEDGEMENTS

Special thanks to the following colleagues, friends, and family members who assisted with this book. Without them, it would not have been possible.

Eric Altman, John Attaway, David Bakara, Cliff Barackman, Sandy Blackburn, Ron Boles, Tal Branco, Brian Brown, Stacy Brown, Chris Buntenbah, Cole Carter, Loren Coleman, Daryl Colyer, Smokey Crabtree (RIP), M.K. Davis, Charles DeVore (RIP), Marc DeWerth, Danny DuPont, Michelle Fason, Joshua Foster, Ken Gerhard, John Green (RIP), Bobby Hamilton, James Hendrix, Jerry Hestand, Alton Higgins, Dana Holyfield, Bryan Impey, Sybilla Irwin, Jessica James, Scott Kessler, Jim Lansdale, Cindy Lee, Marvin Leeper, Donald McDonald, Frank McFerrin, Matt Moneymaker, Chester Moore, Larry Parks, Daniel Perez, Mary Martha Pike-Straw, Matt Pruit, Thom Powell, Charlie Raymond, Nick Redfern, Sam Rich, Mike Richberg, Rob Riggs (RIP), Denny Roberts, Rob Robinson, Tracy Robinson, Dale Ryan (RIP), Tom Shirley, Brian Sons, Jeff Stewart, Kathy Strain, Mark Swiatek, Jim Whitehead, Sean Whitley, Jason "JC" Williams, and Craig Woolheater.

And all the witnesses and organizations who graciously shared their experiences.

APPENDIX

MAPS

The following maps are included for reference.

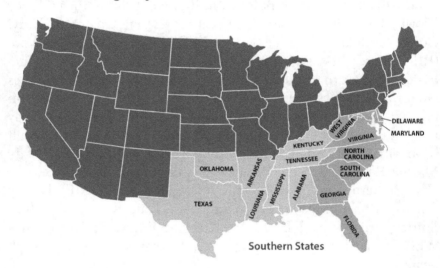

Southern States

West South Central States:
Arkansas, Louisiana, Oklahoma, Texas

East South Central States:
Alabama, Kentucky, Mississippi, Tennessee

South Atlantic States:
Florida, Georgia, Maryland, North Carolina,
South Carolina, Virginia, West Virginia, Delaware

Traditional "Deep South" States

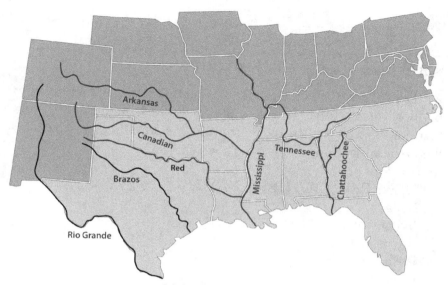

Major Southern Rivers

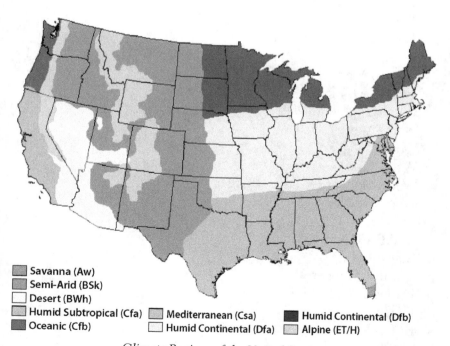

Savanna (Aw)
Semi-Arid (BSk)
Desert (BWh)
Humid Subtropical (Cfa)   Mediterranean (Csa)   Humid Continental (Dfb)
Oceanic (Cfb)   Humid Continental (Dfa)   Alpine (ET/H)

Climate Regions of the United States

SOUTHERN NAMES FOR BIGFOOT

The following is a list of localized and regional names given to Bigfoot-like creatures sighted in the Southern United States. (Note that if a name has been used in multiple states, then it appears in the General section.)

GENERAL SOUTHERN NAMES
Booger
Booger Bear
Brush Ape
Bush Ape
Devil Monkey
Hairy Booger
Monkey Man
Skunk Ape
Swamp Ape
Swamp Devil
Swamp Man
Swamp Monkey
Wildman / Wild Man
Wood Ape
Wood Booger
Wood Devil
Wooly Booger / Wooley Booger
Wood Howler

ALABAMA
Black Thing
Clanton Booger
Dallas County Monster
Downey Booger
Elijah Mae's Booger
Guntersville Terror
Monster of Marmotte Street

Shiny Gorilla
Tannehill Monster
White Thing / White Thang

ARKANSAS
Fouke Monster / Boggy Creek Monster
Caddo Gap Creature
Gun Flats Booger
Lake Conway Monster

FLORIDA
Abominable Sandman
Bardin Booger
Bardin Goomer
Bug-Eye Boogie
Everglades Ape
Fairvilla Gorilla
Green Chimp
Holopaw Gorilla
Myakka Ape
Ol' Orange Eyes
Sandman
Skunk Ape
Squattam's Growler
Swamp Ape

GEORGIA
Belt Road Booger
Billy Holler Bugger
Happy Valley Horror
Man Mountain
Pigman
White Man

KENTUCKY
Big Mo
Cave Yeller

Geneva Giant
Hairy People
Hebbardsville Hillbilly
Spottsville Monster
Beast of the Land Between the Lakes (LBL)
The Varmint
Wild Man of Abbott Mountain
Trimble County Beast
Possum Ridge Beast
Big D
Waddy Werewolf
Mr. Howdy
Matilda
Yahoo
Spookum
Screaming Jacks (also in Tennessee)

LOUISIANA
Creek Walker
Honey Island Swamp Monster
Wookie
Rougarou / Rugaru

MISSISSIPPI
Beaumont Booger
Booger Bear
Gorilla of Sharp's Bottom / Sharp's Bottom Monster
Monster Beast
Morpheus
Stratton Booger
Wootis

NORTH CAROLINA
Boojum
Chickly Cudly (Kecleh Kudleh)
Knobby
Mill Swamp Booger Man

Pine Tree Charlie
Yahoo

OKLAHOMA
Abominable Chicken Man
Big Ed
Bridge Creek Werewolf
Burstchi Beast
Cache Nature Man
Criner Creature
Dibble Demon
Dougherty Werewolf
El Reno Monster
Green Hill Monster
Hair Hulk
Hill Monkey
Lawton Wolfman
Manimal
Mud Creek Monster
Noxie Monster
Stands Back
Twin Lakes Red Eyes
Walaruckus
Wheatian

SOUTH CAROLINA
African Udilacus
Cold Point Creature
Fort Motte Devil
Hidebehind
Lizard Man / Lizardman
Monster of Joe's Island
Wateree Walking Bear

TENNESSEE
Arp Ape
Flintville Monster

Screaming Jacks (also in Kentucky)
Tennessee Wildman

TEXAS
Big Cypress Swamp Monster
Big Thicket Wildman
Boggy Bill / Hairy Bill / Skunky Bill
Caddo Critter
Chambers Creek Monster / Emhouse Goatman
Cuthand Critter
Dayton Monkey Man
Hawley Him
Horizon City Monster
Lake Worth Monster / Lake Worth Goatman
Marion County Monster
Moss Man
Mudcrest Mudman
Night Screamer
Ol' Mossyback
Ottine Swamp Monster
Route Monster
Sabine Thing
Tree Man
Turkey Creek Monster

VIRGINIA
White Thing

W. VIRGINIA
Grassman (also in Ohio)
Holla Yella

ENDNOTES

1   Powell, Jim. "Fouke family terrorized by hairy 'monster.'" *Texarkana Gazette* 03 May 1971.

2   Crabtree, J.E. Smokey. *Smokey and the Fouke Monster*. Fouke: Days Creek Production Corporation, 1974.

3   Montgomery, Dennis. "Farmers Hunt Chicken Man." *The Spokesman-Review* 01 Mar 1971.

4   Montgomery, Dennis. "Farmers Hunt Chicken Man." *The Spokesman-Review* 01 Mar 1971.

5   Berryman, Jane. "Hen House Terror Just Monkey Stuff." *The Oklahoma Journal* Vol. 7 No. 198, Feb 28, 1971.

6   "Coon hunter reports late night visual encounter on Canadian River in Central Oklahoma." North American Wood Ape Conservancy (http://woodape.org/reports/report/detail/1475)

7   "Coon hunter reports late night visual encounter on Canadian River in Central Oklahoma." North American Wood Ape Conservancy (http://woodape.org/reports/report/detail/1475)

8   http://www.state.sc.us/forest/refmgt.htm#us

9   http://www.southernforests.org/about/forest-service-partnerships

10   http://www.britannica.com/EBchecked/topic/555542/the-South

11   http://geography.about.com/od/politicalgeography/a/masondixon.htm.

12   "1950 Bigfoot Howling by the Moonlight." Sasquatch Chronicles (https://sasquatchchronicles.com/1950-bigfoot-howling-by-the-moonlight)

13   Jones, Mark and Teresa Ann Smith. "Has Bigfoot Moved To Texas?" *Fate* July 1979: 30-36.

14   Jones, Mark and Teresa Ann Smith. "Has Bigfoot Moved To Texas?" *Fate* July 1979: 30-36.

15   "Woman taking a walk has startling encounter near the Sulphur River." North American Wood Ape Conservancy (http://woodape.org/reports/report/detail/294)

16 "Direct Has Critter Too." *The Paris News* (day/month unknown) 1965.

17 Holley, David. "The Cuthand Critter." Scary Sasquatch Stories (www. network54.com/Forum)

18 "While searching for their uncle, two boys have visual encounter." North American Wood Ape Conservancy (http://woodape.org/reports/report/detail/127)

19 "While searching for their uncle, two boys have visual encounter." North American Wood Ape Conservancy (http://woodape.org/reports/report/detail/127)

20 Sicking, Jennifer. "'Haunted bridge' moves to Callisburg Wednesday." *Gainesville Daily Register* 3 June 2004.

21 "Youth reports sighting near bridge." North American Wood Ape Conservancy (http://woodape.org/reports/report/detail/263)

22 Owen, Penny. "Bigfoot, ominous tales swirl around cemetery." *The Oklahoman* 31 Oct. 1999.

23 Cockerell, Penny. "Sighting of creature terrifies Caney woman." *The Oklahoman* 30 July 2006.

24 "Two children have encounter while playing on creek not far from home." North American Wood Ape Conservancy (http://woodape.org/reports/report/detail/462)

25 Power, Irvin. "Boy Says For Real Sighting of Monster Renews Marion Legend." *Marshall News Messenger* 01 Sept. 1965.

26 "Town Fed Up With Monster Hunters." *United Press International* 20 Sept. 1965.

27 "Concerning the Longview, Texas, Reports." *Bigfoot Bulletin* 31 Oct. 1970: p. 3.

28 "Lurking Bigfoot Trick or Treat?" *Sentinel Star* 05 Oct. 1977. Print and web via John Green Database (www.sasquatchdatabase.com).

29 "Family reports visual encounter while target shooting near an open pasture." North American Wood Ape Conservancy (http://woodape.org/reports/report/detail/136)

30 "The Okefenokee Swamp." Our Georgia History (www.ourgeorgiahistory.com/places/okefenokee.html)

31 "A Gigantic Story." *Milledgeville (Georgia) Statesman* June 1929.

32 "The Wild Man Again." *Hornellsville Tribune* 08 May 1856.

33   "The 'Siege' at Honobia." Bigfoot Field Research Organization (http://www.bfro.net/avevid/ouachita/siege-at-honobia.asp)

34   "Caddo Indians." Texas State Historical Association (https://tshaonline.org/handbook/online/articles/bmcaj)

35   Howard, James and Willie Lena. *Oklahoma Seminoles–Medicine, Magic, and Religion*. Norman: University of Oklahoma Press, 1984. p. 211-212.

36   http://www.theamericanindiancenter.org/oklahoma-tribal-history

37   Love, Chad. "Who Believes In Bigfoot?" *Oklahoma Today* Sept-Oct. 2005.

38   Jackson, Ron. "Constant Sasquatch Watch Held in Honobia." *The Oklahoman* 07 Aug. 2005.

39   "Bigfoot – Human Oklahoma War 1855." Sasquatch and Bigfoot: Facts and History (https://sasquatchhistory.wordpress.com/2013/11/10/bigfoot-human-oklahoma-war-1855)

40   Dawes Final Roles. Oklahoma Historical Society (http://www.okhistory.org/research/dawes)

41   http://www.nramuseum.org/guns/the-galleries/the-american-west-1850-to-1900/case-18-hunting-and-military-arms-on-the-western-frontier/sharps-big-50-buffalo-rifle.aspx

42   Cottle, Sherry. "Giant man unearthed in Spiro Mound, Oklahoma!" *Mound Builder Children* blog. 25 Nov 2013. (http://sherrycottlegraham.com/2013/11/25/giant-man-unearthed-in-spiro-mound-oklahoma)

43   Jackson, Ron. "Constant Sasquatch Watch Held in Honobia." *The Oklahoman* 07 Aug. 2005.

44   "McCurtain County Has A 'Manbeast.'" *McCurtain Sunday Gazette* 09 July 1978.

45   Hudson, Cullan. *Strange State: Mysteries and Legends of Oklahoma*. Rochester, WA: Gorham Printing, 2006. p. 184.

46   "Monster Search Launched." *Coshocton Tribune* 05 Sept. 1975.

47   Hewes, Hayden C. "The Creature Takes a Holiday." *Probe the Unknown* Mar 1976.

48   Hewes, Hayden C. "The Creature Takes a Holiday." *Probe the Unknown* Mar 1976.

49   Hewes, Hayden C. "The Creature Takes a Holiday." *Probe the Unknown* Mar 1976.

50   Bigfoot Encounters (http://www.bigfootencounters.com/sbs/canadian.htm)

51   Brown, Brian. "Episode 4: Sasquatch on the Oklahoma Prairie." Bigfoot Information Project (audio). http://www.bigfootproject.org/index.html

52   Brown, Brian. "Episode 4: Sasquatch on the Oklahoma Prairie." Bigfoot Information Project (audio). https://www.acast.com/ bigfootinformationprojectpodcast/bipcast-4-sasquatch-on-the-oklahoma-prairie

53   Higgins, Alton. "Possible Wood Ape Photos From Central Oklahoma." 06 May 2012. (http://woodape.org/index.php/about-bigfoot/articles/220-oklahoma-prairie-photos)

54   Bord, Janet and Colin. *Bigfoot Casebook Updated: Sightings and Encounters from 1818 to 2004*. Pine Winds Press, an imprint of Idyll Arbor, 2006 (first published in 1982).

55   "Turkey hunter has close encounter near Carver Mountain." North American Wood Ape Conservancy (http://woodape.org/reports/report/detail/382)

56   "Turkey hunter has close encounter near Carver Mountain." North American Wood Ape Conservancy (http://woodape.org/reports/report/detail/382)

57   "Local family reports large tracks near Big Cedar." North American Wood Ape Conservancy (http://woodape.org/reports/report/detail/385)

58   Colyer, Daryl G., Alton Higgins, Brian Brown, Kathy Strain, Michael C. Mayes, and Brad McAndrews. The Ouachita Project, self-published, 2015. (http://media.texasbigfoot.com/OP_paper_media/OuachitaProjectMonograph_Version1.1_03112015.pdf)

59   Colyer, Daryl G., Alton Higgins, Brian Brown, Kathy Strain, Michael C. Mayes, and Brad McAndrews. The Ouachita Project, self-published, 2015. (http://media.texasbigfoot.com/OP_paper_media/OuachitaProjectMonograph_Version1.1_03112015.pdf)

60   Branco, Tal H. "Paron, Saline County, Arkansas 1990." 26 Nov. 2005. (http://www.bigfootencounters.com/stories/paron.htm.)

61   Branco, Tal H. "Paron, Saline County, Arkansas 1990." 26 Nov. 2005. (http://www.bigfootencounters.com/stories/paron.htm.)

62   Branco, Tal H. "Mt. Ida, Montgomery County, Arkansas 2002." (http://www.bigfootencounters.com/stories/mt-idaAR.htm)

63   Branco, Tal H. "Mt. Ida, Montgomery County, Arkansas 2002." (http://www.bigfootencounters.com/stories/mt-idaAR.htm)

64   Report 14 "Woman driving spots large creature." Sasquatch Research

Initiative, Nov. 2005.

65 Report 14 "Woman driving spots large creature." Sasquatch Research Initiative, Nov. 2005.

66 Hahn, Joyce. "Conway lake monster: believable or not believable?" 23 May 2001. (http://www.bentoncourier.com/content/hahn-conway-lake-monster-believable-or-not-believable)

67 Woods A.J., Foti, T.L., Chapman, S.S., Omernik, J.M., Wise, J.A., Murray, E.O., Prior, W.L., Pagan, J.B., Jr., Comstock, J.A., and Radford, M., 2004, Ecoregions of Arkansas (poster map): Reston, Virginia, U.S. Geological Survey.

68 Arment, Chad. *The Historical Bigfoot: Early Reports of Wild Men, Hairy Giants, and Wandering Gorillas in North America.* Landisville: Coachwhip Publications, 2006.

69 Arment, Chad. *The Historical Bigfoot: Early Reports of Wild Men, Hairy Giants, and Wandering Gorillas in North America.* Landisville: Coachwhip Publications, 2006.

70 Steele, Phillip W. *Ozark Tales and Superstitions.* Pelican Publishing Company, 1983.

71 "Seven Foot Prowler." *Northwest Arkansas Times* 08 Sept. 1969.

72 Barnes, Guy. "Bigfoot Has Long, Lively Local History." *The Morning News/NWAonline.net* 13 Oct. 2003.

73 Coleman, Loren and Patrick Huyghe. *The Field Guide to Bigfoot and Other Mystery Primates.* San Antonio. Anomalist Books, 2006. p. 56.

74 "Man has a close daytime encounter with a probable Bigfoot family outside Hardy." Bigfoot Field Research Organization (http://www.bfro.net/GDB/show_report.asp?id=40020)

75 http://tfsweb.tamu.edu/main/popup.aspx?id=7002

76 "A Texan Orang Outang." *Argus* (Michigan) 01 Sept. 1871.

77 "A Wild Boy Caught." *The Statesman* (Austin) 21 July 1875.

78 Rife, Phillip. *Bigfoot Across America.* New York: Writers Club Press, 2000. p. 109.

79 Marrs, Jim. "Fishy Man-Goat Terrifies Couples Parked at Lake Worth." *Fort Worth Star Telegram* 10 July 1969.

80 Marrs, Jim. "Police, Residents Observe But Can't Identify 'Monster.'" *Fort Worth Star Telegram* 11 July 1969.

81   Bills, E.R. "Lake Worth Monster revealed? Goatman? *Fort Worth Magazine* (Texas) 04 Jul 2009.

82   "'Monster' Bobcat? *Fort Worth Star Telegram* 14 July 1969.

83   Kennedy, Bud. "1969 Lake Worth Monster, was the 'Goat-Man' Hulk or Hoax? *Fort Worth Star Telegram* 08 June 2006.

84   Clarke, Sallie Ann. *The Lake Worth Monster*. Benbrook: self-published, 1969.

85   Clarke, Sallie Ann. *The Lake Worth Monster*. Fort Worth: self-published, 1969.

86   Clarke, Sallie Ann. *The Lake Worth Monster*. Fort Worth: self-published, 1969.

87   Whitley, Sean. Interview with Sallie Ann Clarke. Unpublished transcript: 2003.

88   Kennedy, Bud. "Thirty-Seven Years After Snapping Photo, Bigfoot Talk Gets Man's Goat." *Fort Worth Star Telegram* 08 June 2006.

89   Vaughn, Chris. "Is there a Lake Worth Monster?" *Victoria Advocate* 09 Aug. 2009.

90   Vaughn, Chris. "Is there a Lake Worth Monster?" *Victoria Advocate* 09 Aug. 2009.

91   Bills, E.R. "Lake Worth Monster revealed? Goatman? *Fort Worth Magazine* (Texas) 04 Jul 2009.

92   http://domainofhorrornewsmedia.blogspot.com/2016/03/north-texas-cryptid-lake-worth-goatman.html

93   Clarke, Sallie Ann. *The Lake Worth Monster*. Fort Worth: self-published, 1969.

94   "'Hairy Monster' Stomping Around." *Denton Record-Chronicle* 23 July 1963.

95   "Tall creature seen by witness." Bigfoot Field Research Organization (http://www.bfro.net/GDB/show_report.asp?id=2396)

96   Downing, Roger. "Youths Report Attack By the 'Hawley Him.'" *Abilene Reporter News* 07 July 1977.

97   "'Big Foot' Terrorizes Kelly Area." *The San Antonio Light* 01 Sept 1976.

98   Gerhard, Ken and Nick Redfern. *Monsters of Texas*. North Devon, England: CFZ Press, 2010. pp. 54-55.

99   http://www.bigfootlunchclub.com/2009/12/911-audio-and-full-transcript-of-san.html

100 Riggs, Rob. *In the Big Thicket: On the Trail of the Wild Man.* New York: Paraview Press, 2001. pp. 78-82.

101 Riggs, Rob. *In the Big Thicket: On the Trail of the Wild Man.* New York: Paraview Press, 2001. p. 89.

102 "Predawn encounter on east side of FM 1375 bridge over Lake Conroe." North American Wood Ape Conservancy (http://woodape.org/reports/report/detail/225)

103 "Predawn encounter on east side of FM 1375 bridge over Lake Conroe." North American Wood Ape Conservancy (http://woodape.org/reports/report/detail/225)

104 "Husband and wife observe massive upright animal in Sam Houston National Forest." North American Wood Ape Conservancy (http://woodape.org/reports/report/detail/26894)

105 http://gcbro.com/Txsanj002.htm

106 http://www.sasquatchdatabase.com

107 "Worker has early morning visual encounter while working on construction of Fox Sports Facility." North American Wood Ape Conservancy (http://woodape.org/reports/report/detail/1493)

108 "On duty security officer has early morning encounter at construction facility." North American Wood Ape Conservancy (http://woodape.org/reports/report/detail/439)

109 "Woman reports sighting from highway while riding as passenger." North American Wood Ape Conservancy (http://woodape.org/reports/report/detail/432)

110 "Deer hunter encounters bigfoot at Caddo Lake near Karnack." Bigfoot Field Research Organization (http://www.bfro.net/GDB/show_report.asp?id=8067)

111 "Bowfishermen have early afternoon encounter while on Sabine River." North American Wood Ape Conservancy (http://woodape.org/reports/report/detail/446)

112 http://gcbro.com/Txnew001.htm

113 Lansdale, Jim. "How I got interested in Bigfoot." *The Monster Hunter Newsletter* (date unknown).

114 Kane, James. "Compilation of Multiple Field Reports." *The Monster Hunter Newsletter* (date unknown).

115 Kane, James. "Compilation of Multiple Field Reports." *The Monster Hunter Newsletter* (date unknown).

116 Kane, James. "Compilation of Multiple Field Reports." *The Monster Hunter Newsletter* (date unknown).

117 Burdeau, Cain. "Bayou Bigfoot no laughing matter." *Daily News* 15 Sept 2000.

118 Griffin, Andrew. "Have you seen Bigfoot?" *Alexandria Daily Town Talk* 26 Aug 2000.

119 "Logger has two encounters over a three day period." North American Wood Ape Conservancy (http://woodape.org/reports/report/detail/421)

120 Griffin, Andrew. "Have you seen Bigfoot?" *Alexandria Daily Town Talk* 26 Aug 2000.

121 "Logger has two encounters over a three day period." North American Wood Ape Conservancy (http://woodape.org/reports/report/detail/421)

122 http://www.gcbro.com/LAstmartin0001.html

123 "While checking log book, truck driver has unnerving close encounter." North American Wood Ape Conservancy (http://woodape.org/reports/report/detail/410)

124 "While checking log book, truck driver has unnerving close encounter." North American Wood Ape Conservancy (http://woodape.org/reports/report/detail/410)

125 https://en.wikipedia.org/wiki/Honey_Island_Swamp

126 "Honey Island Swamp Monster: Fact or Fiction?" Cajun Encounters Tour Co. (http://www.cajunencounters.com/tag/letiche)

127 Newsom, Michael. "Sasquatch, rare woodpecker among strange Stennis tales." *Sun Herald* 26 Oct 2011.

128 Holyfield, Dana. *Honey Island Swamp Monster Documentations: Harlan Ford's Story & More Recent Encounters*. Slidell: Honey Island Swamp Books, 2012.

129 Conroy, Steve. "Honey Island Swamp Monster Busted! A long-time legend laid to rest" (interview with MK Davis and Jay Michaels). *The Monster Hunter Newsletter*, Sept-Oct 2003.

130 Baumann, Elwood D. *Monsters of North America*. Xerox Education

Publications (Franklin Watts), 1978. p. 69.

131 Chapman, S.S, Griffith, G.E., Omernik, J.M., Comstock, J.A., Beiser, M.C., and Johnson, D., 2004, Ecoregions of Mississippi, (color poster with map, descriptive text, summary tables, and photographs): Reston, Virginia, U.S. Geological Survey (map scale 1:1,000,000).

132 "A 'What Is It?' Seen in Mississippi." *Dubuque Daily Herald* (Iowa) 27 Jun 1868.

133 "A 'What Is It?' Seen in Mississippi." *Dubuque Daily Herald* (Iowa) 27 Jun 1868.

134 "A 'What Is It?' Seen in Mississippi." *Dubuque Daily Herald* (Iowa) 27 Jun 1868.

135 François-Xavier de Charlevoix, Pierre, *Charlevoix's Louisiana: Selections from the History and the Journal.* Louisiana State University Press, 1977. (Published for the Louisiana American Revolution Bicentennial Commission.)

136 http://www.native-languages.org/morelegends/lofa.htm

137 Green, John. *Sasquatch: The Apes Among Us.* Washington/Vancouver: Hancock House, 1978.

138 Neblett, Sallie Anne. "'Monster' reported in Greenville." *Delta Democrat Times* 22 Jun 1971.

139 http://www.gcbro.com/MShinds0002.html

140 "I think I saw a skunk ape - please help." *YouTube* 28 Oct 2013. (https://youtu.be/xb9YcIlkl_c)

141 "I think I saw a skunk ape - please help." *YouTube* 28 Oct 2013. (https://youtu.be/xb9YcIlkl_c)

142 "'Big Foot' is reported now in Mississippi." *The Valley Independent* 25 Mar 1976.

143 http://www.gcbro.com/MSalcorntish001.html

144 http://www.gcbro.com/MSalcorntish001.html

145 http://www.bigfootencounters.com/sbs/lauderdaleMS75.htm

146 http://www.bigfootencounters.com/sbs/lauderdaleMS75.htm

147 Keel, John A., *Strange Creatures From Time and Space.* Connecticut. Fawcett Publications, Inc, 1970. p. 110

148 Short, Bobbie. "Remembering Ramona Clark Hibner and the Bigfoot issues in the State of Florida that beset her…" 2009. (http://www.bigfootencounters.com/articles/ramona.htm)

149 Short, Bobbie. "Remembering Ramona Clark Hibner and the Bigfoot issues in the State of Florida that beset her…" 2009. (http://www.bigfootencounters.com/articles/ramona.htm)

150 http://sasquatchbioacoustic.blogspot.com/2011/11/examining-2004-mississippi-howl.html

151 http://sasquatchbioacoustic.blogspot.com/2011/11/examining-2004-mississippi-howl.html

152 Collum, Fred. Title unknown. *The Red Bay News* 06 May 1976.

153 Whitehead, Vera. "The Downey Booger." Winston County, Alabama: An Historical Online Database (http://www.freestateofwinston.org/downeybooger.htm). Date unknown.

154 "Multiple encounters at a home near Haleyville." Bigfoot Field Research Organization (http://www.bfro.net/GDB/show_report.asp?id=43120)

155 "Hairy Wild Man Sought In Swamp." *Oshkosh Northwestern* 15 Apr 1938.

156 Matthews, Rupert. *Sasquatch: True-Life Encounters with Legendary Ape-Men.* London: Arcturus Publishing Limited, 2006. p. 45.

157 Keel, John A., *Strange Creatures From Time and Space.* Connecticut: Fawcett Publications, Inc., 1970. pp. 98-99.

158 Keel, John A., *Strange Creatures From Time and Space.* Connecticut: Fawcett Publications, Inc., 1970. p. 99.

159 Green, John. *Sasquatch: The Apes Among Us.* Washington/Vancouver: Hancock House, 1978. p. 214.

160 "Evening sighting by family driving by Guntersville Lake." Bigfoot Field Research Organization (http://bfro.net/GDB/show_report.asp?id=18043)

161 Smith, Jim. "Two Deer Hunters Held In Deer Stand By Angry Bigfoot Near Lake Guntersville, Alabama." Alabama Bigfoot Society (http://www.alabamabigfootsociety.com/RecentSightings.html)

162 http://www.britannica.com/place/Appalachian-Mountains

163 "The Tennessee Wildman." *The Hagerstown Mail* 05 May 1871.

164 "The Wild Man of Tennessee." *The New York Times* 08 Feb 1889.

165 "A Wild Man." *Courier Journal* (Louisville) 24 Oct 1878.

166 Green, John. *Sasquatch: The Apes Among Us*. Washington/Vancouver: Hancock House, 1978. p. 221.

167 Green, John. *Sasquatch: The Apes Among Us*. Washington/Vancouver: Hancock House, 1978. p. 221.

168 Raynes, Brent. "Odds and Ends." *Wayne County News* (Tennessee) 02 Feb 1984.

169 Dougherty, Paul. "Mountain monster tried to snatch my boy, says mom." *The Star* 18 May 1976.

170 Cobb, Charles. "Hairy 'Bigfoot' Monster Terrorizes Tennessee Town." *National Enquirer* 29 June 1976.

171 Balloch, Jim. "Search in Smokies for lost boy, Dennis Martin, produces lessons for future searches." *Knoxville News Sentinel* 28 June 2009.

172 Paulides, David. *Missing 411: Eastern United States*. North Charleston: CreateSpace, 2011. pp. 125-126.

173 Palmer, Jennie. "Bear of Bigfoot: Knobby's Got 'Em Buzzin'." *Gastonia Gazette* 17 Jan 1979.

174 Palmer, Jennie. "Knobby: Where is He? What is He?" *Gastonia Gazette* 21 Jan 1979.

175 Palmer, Jennie. "Knobby: Where is He? What is He?" *Gastonia Gazette* 21 Jan 1979.

176 Palmer, Jennie. "Knobby: Where is He? What is He?" *Gastonia Gazette* 21 Jan 1979.

177 Palmer, Jennie. "Knobby: Where is He? What is He?" *Gastonia Gazette* 21 Jan 1979.

178 Lyttle, Steve. "Cleveland County man reports encounter with Bigfoot." *Charlotte Observer* 15 June 2010.

179 Sheridan, Ann. "North Carolina man says he saw Sasquatch." WCNC Channel 36 News (television) 23 Sept 2010.

180 "Charleston, S.C. May 17, 1793." *Boston Gazette* 01 July 1793.

181 "Charleston, S.C. May 17, 1793." *Boston Gazette* 01 July 1793.

182 "A Wild Man of the Mountains." *McKean County Miner* 03 Jan 1878.

183 "A Wild Man of the Mountains." *McKean County Miner* 03 Jan 1878.

184 "'Thing' Roaming North Carolina." *Latrobe Bulletin* 16 Sept 1976.

185 Griffith, G.E., Omernik, J.M., Comstock, J.A., Lawrence, S., Martin, G., Goddard, A., Hulcher, V.J., and Foster, T., 2001, Ecoregions of Alabama and Georgia, (color poster with map, descriptive text, summary tables, and photographs): Reston, Virginia, U.S. Geological Survey (map scale 1:1,700,000).

186 Wells, Jeffery. *Bigfoot in Georgia*. Washington: Pine Winds Press, an imprint of Idyll Arbor, 2010. p. 40.

187 "A Wild Man in Walker." *Atlanta Constitution* 04 Feb 1889.

188 "Oregon 'Apemen' Roam Again: 10-foot Monsters Seen In Cascade Wilderness." *Nevada State Journal* 14 Aug 1964.

189 Green, John. *Sasquatch: The Apes Among Us*. Washington/Vancouver: Hancock House, 1978. p. 217.

190 Pruit, Matt. "Daylight sighting by artifact hunter northwest of Cleveland." Bigfoot Field Research Organization (http://www.bfro.net/GDB/show_report.asp?id=21402)

191 Bord, Janet and Colin. *Bigfoot Casebook Updated: Sightings and Encounters from 1818 to 2004*. Pine Winds Press, an imprint of Idyll Arbor, 2006 (first published in 1982). pp. 182-183.

192 Collins, Morris. "Campers see animal observing campsite in Cohutta Wilderness." Bigfoot Field Research Organization (http://www.bfro.net/GDB/show_report.asp?id=25043)

193 Collins, Morris. "Campers see animal observing campsite in Cohutta Wilderness." Bigfoot Field Research Organization (http://www.bfro.net/GDB/show_report.asp?id=25043)

194 From the files of J.C. Williams. Southeastern Bigfoot Research Group, 14 Nov 2013.

195 https://en.wikipedia.org/wiki/Appalachian_Trail

196 "Shambling Beast Terrorizes Town: Hairy Animal Reported In South Carolina Village." *The Daily Gleaner* 09 Feb 1938.

197 "Distant Relative Of Mobile's Monster Reported." *Delta Star* (Mississippi) 06 Feb 1938.

198 C.L. Murphy. *Sasquatch/Bigfoot Chronicle*. Unpublished, 2013. Obtained from Sasquatch Canada website (http://www.sasquatchcanada.com). pp 6-7.

199 Marston, Red. "In S.C., Bigfoot is making tracks." *St. Petersburg Times* (Florida) 08 July 1974.

200 Marston, Red. "In S.C., Bigfoot is making tracks." *St. Petersburg Times* (Florida) 08 July 1974.

201 Green, John. *Sasquatch: The Apes Among Us.* Washington/Vancouver: Hancock House, 1978. p. 219.

202 "Monster: '89 Creature Sightings Increase." *Spartanburg Herald*, 01 Aug 1989.

203 "Monster: '89 Creature Sightings Increase." *Spartanburg Herald*, 01 Aug 1989.

204 Statement of Bertha Mae Blythers. Lee County Sheriff Official Documentation, 02 Aug 1990.

205 Statement of Johnny Blythers. Lee County Sheriff Official Documentation, 31 July 1990.

206 "Strange Creature Seen Here." *The Newnan Times-Herald* 09 Aug 1979.

207 "Belt Road Booger Is Seen Again." *The Newnan Times-Herald* 16 Aug 1979.

208 McRae, Alex. "Could Bigfoot Be in Coweta?" *The Newnan Times-Herald* 24 Apr 2005.

209 Wells, Jeffery. *Bigfoot in Georgia.* Pine Winds Press, an imprint of Idyll Arbor, 2010. p. 68.

210 Casebook: Paranormal. 02 Aug 2015. (https://www.facebook.com/permalink.php?id=595133427180792&story_fbid=1109553279072135)

211 Tuten, Jan. "Florence man says he wounded 'Lizard Man.'" *The State* 06 Aug 1988.

212 From the files of Mike Richberg. Carolina Cryptids, 08 Aug 1997.

213 McRae, Alex. "Could Bigfoot Be in Coweta?" *The Newnan Times-Herald* 24 Apr 2005.

214 Bishop, Jeff. "Do You Have Memories of the 'Belt Road Booger?'" *The Newnan Times-Herald* 14 Oct 2009.

215 Bishop, Jeff. "Do You Have Memories of the 'Belt Road Booger?'" *The Newnan Times-Herald* 14 Oct 2009.

216 Chilcutt, J.H. "Dermal Ridge Examination Report: Georgia Casting." Bigfoot Encounters (http://www.bigfootencounters.com/sbs/elkins.html)

217 From the files of Sam Rich. Georgia Bigfoot / Sasquatch Research Initiative, 02 Nov 2005.

218 "Bill Protects Florida's Skunk Ape." *Indiana Evening Gazette* 21 May 1977.

219 Griffith, Glenn (US EPA), Daniel Canfield, Jr. (University of Florida), Christine Horsburgh (University of Florida), James Omernik (US EPA), and Sandra Azevedo (OAO Corp.), 2003. Lake Regions of Florida (color poster with map, descriptive text, summary tables, and photographs).

220 Cox, Dale. "The Wild Man of Ocheesee Pond – Jackson, County, Florida." Explore Southern History (http://www.exploresouthernhistory. com/ocheeseewildman.html), 10 Mar 2014.

221 C.L. Murphy. *Sasquatch/Bigfoot Chronicle*. Unpublished, 2013. Obtained from Sasquatch Canada website (http://www.sasquatchcanada.com). p 7.

222 Cox, Dale. "The Wild Man of Ocheesee Pond – Jackson, County, Florida." Explore Southern History (http://www.exploresouthernhistory. com/ocheeseewildman.html), 10 Mar 2014.

223 "The Wild man of Ocheecee Swamp." *The New York Times* 19 Aug 1884.

224 Cox, Dale. "Update on the Wild Man of Ocheesee Pond." *Two Egg Blogspot* (http://twoegg.blogspot.com/2012/07/update-on-wild-man-of-ocheesee-pond.html), 20 July 2012.

225 "Bloodhounds Fear. Part of Florida Terrorized By Shaggy Creature." *The Davenport Daily Leader* 28 Sept 1900.

226 "Bloodhounds Fear. Part of Florida Terrorized By Shaggy Creature." *The Davenport Daily Leader* 28 Sept 1900.

227 Green, John. *Sasquatch: The Apes Among Us*. Washington/Vancouver: Hancock House, 1978. p. 271.

228 Green, John. *Sasquatch: The Apes Among Us*. Washington/Vancouver: Hancock House, 1978. pp. 271-272.

229 Keel, John A., *Strange Creatures From Time and Space*. Connecticut. Fawcett Publications, Inc., 1970. p. 102.

230 Keel, John A., *Strange Creatures From Time and Space*. Connecticut. Fawcett Publications, Inc., 1970. p. 102-103.

231 Keel, John A., *Strange Creatures From Time and Space*. Connecticut. Fawcett Publications, Inc., 1970. p. 104.

232 Green, John. *Sasquatch: The Apes Among Us*. Washington/Vancouver: Hancock House, 1978. p. 272.

233 Keel, John A., *Strange Creatures From Time and Space*. Connecticut. Fawcett Publications, Inc., 1970. p. 103-104.

234 Newton, Michael. *When Bigfoot Attacks: A Global Survey of Alleged Sasquatch/Yeti Predation.* Great Britain: CFZ Press, 2009. p. 57.

235 Bothwell, Dick. "'Skunk Ape' in the Everglades – A Hairy Giant That Smells Bad." *National Observer* 16 Aug 1971.

236 Bothwell, Dick. "'Skunk Ape' in the Everglades – A Hairy Giant That Smells Bad." *National Observer* 16 Aug 1971.

237 Griffith, Glenn (US EPA), Daniel Canfield, Jr. (University of Florida), Christine Horsburgh (University of Florida), James Omernik (US EPA), and Sandra Azevedo (OAO Corp.), 2003. Lake Regions of Florida (color poster with map, descriptive text, summary tables, and photographs).

238 Bothwell, Dick. "'Skunk Ape' in the Everglades – A Hairy Giant That Smells Bad." *National Observer* 16 Aug 1971.

239 Coleman, Loren. "Mysterious World: The Myakka Skunk Ape Photographs." *FATE Magazine*, May 2001: 8-11.

240 "Big-Footed Monsters Invade Earth." *National News Explorer* 13 August 1972.

241 Kelly, Jim. "Creature Feature." *Miami News* 19 Feb 1998.

242 Glass, Ian and Jon Hall. "'Skunk Ape" on Prowl? Glades Creature Sought." *Miami News* 09 Jan 1974.

243 Glass, Ian and Jon Hall. "'Skunk Ape" on Prowl? Glades Creature Sought." *Miami News* 09 Jan 1974.

244 Glass, Ian and Jon Hall. "'Skunk Ape" on Prowl? Glades Creature Sought." *Miami News* 09 Jan 1974.

245 Short, Bobbie. "Remembering Ramona Clark Hibner and the Bigfoot issues in the State of Florida that beset her…" 2009. (http://www.bigfootencounters.com/articles/ramona.htm)

246 Kelly, Jim. "Creature Feature." *Miami News* 19 Feb 1998.

247 Short, Bobbie. "Remembering Ramona Clark Hibner and the Bigfoot issues in the State of Florida that beset her…" 2009. (http://www.bigfootencounters.com/articles/ramona.htm)

248 Short, Bobbie. "Remembering Ramona Clark Hibner and the Bigfoot issues in the State of Florida that beset her…" 2009. (http://www.bigfootencounters.com/articles/ramona.htm)

249 Short, Bobbie. "Remembering Ramona Clark Hibner and the Bigfoot issues in the State of Florida that beset her…" 2009. (http://www.bigfootencounters.com/articles/ramona.htm)

250 Short, Bobbie. "Remembering Ramona Clark Hibner and the Bigfoot issues in the State of Florida that beset her…" 2009. (http://www.bigfootencounters.com/articles/ramona.htm)

251 Short, Bobbie. "Remembering Ramona Clark Hibner and the Bigfoot issues in the State of Florida that beset her…" 2009. (http://www.bigfootencounters.com/articles/ramona.htm)

252 Short, Bobbie. "Remembering Ramona Clark Hibner and the Bigfoot issues in the State of Florida that beset her…" 2009. (http://www.bigfootencounters.com/articles/ramona.htm)

253 Short, Bobbie. "Remembering Ramona Clark Hibner and the Bigfoot issues in the State of Florida that beset her…" 2009. (http://www.bigfootencounters.com/articles/ramona.htm)

254 "Legendary Skunk: Florida reports mystery animal like Bigfoot, Yeti." *Valley News* (California) 28 July 1977.

255 "Will the Skunk Ape Strike This Year?" *The Sun Coast Times* 17 Jan 1976.

256 "South County's mystery ape man strikes again." *The Gondolier* 12 June 1975.

257 "12-Year-Old Reports Sighting of Strange Apelike Creature." *Sarasota Herald-Tribune* 1975.

258 "Will the Skunk Ape Strike This Year?" *The Sun Coast Times* 17 Jan 1976.

259 "3 Rabbits, Cages Found Mangled." *Sarasota Herald-Tribune* 1975.

260 Mulligan, Hugh A. "The Skunk Ape: Florida's Monkey Catcher Says It's Really 'Bigfoot.'" *The Evening Independent* 27 Feb 1978.

261 Anonymous letter sent to the Sarasota Sheriff's Office, postmarked December 22, 2000. (http://www.lorencoleman.com/letter.html)

262 Coleman, Loren. "Mysterious World: The Myakka Skunk Ape Photographs." *FATE Magazine*, May 2001: 8-11.

263 Coleman, Loren. "Mysterious World: The Myakka Skunk Ape Photographs." *FATE Magazine*, May 2001: 8-11.

264 Coleman, Loren. "Mysterious World: The Myakka Skunk Ape Photographs." *FATE Magazine*, May 2001: 8-11.

265 Coleman, Loren. "Mysterious World: The Myakka Skunk Ape Photographs." *FATE Magazine*, May 2001: 8-11.

266 Coleman, Loren. "Mysterious World: The Myakka Skunk Ape Photographs." *FATE Magazine*, May 2001: 8-11.

267 Coleman, Loren. "Mysterious World: The Myakka Skunk Ape Photographs." *FATE Magazine*, May 2001: 8-11.

268 Short, Bobbie. Personal notation. Bigfoot Encounters (http://www. bigfootencounters.com/articles/myakka2002.htm)

269 Kelly, Jim. "Creature Feature." *Miami News* 19 Feb 1998.

270 "Series of reports (6) concerning the Skunk Ape. Bigfoot Field Research Organization (http://www.bfro.net/gdb/show_report.asp?id=721)

271 http://www.skunkape.biz/dave-shealy

272 Kelly, Jim. "Creature Feature." *Miami News* 19 Feb 1998.

273 Farberov, Snejana. "Is this 'Big Foot's smelly cousin'? Competitive truck puller claims he has found Florida's 'Skunk Ape.'" *Daily Mail* 14 Jun 2013.

274 "Myakka Skunk Ape." *YouTube* 13 Mar 2013. (https://youtu.be/MWPw_ D5vpuw)

275 https://en.wikipedia.org/wiki/Green_Swamp_(Florida)

276 White, Gary. "Woman's Sighting of Ape-Like Green Swamp Creature Among the Theories Studied by Cryptozoologists." *The Ledger* 13 Nov 2004.

277 Laufenberg, Kathleen. "Florida's Monster." *Tallahassee Democrat* 14 Aug 2005.

278 Barackman, Cliff. "The Brown Footage." (http://cliffbarackman.com/ research/field-investigations/the-brown-footage)

279 Napier, John. *Bigfoot: The Yeti and Sasquatch in Myth and Reality.* New York: E.P. Dutton & Co., Inc. 1973. pp. 176-177.

280 Meldrum, Jeff. *Sasquatch: Legend Meets Science.* New York: Tom Doherty Associates, LLC. 2006. p. 90.

281 Strauss, Mark. "The Largest Ape That Ever Lived Was Doomed By Its Size." *National Geographic News* 05 Jan 2016. (http://news. nationalgeographic.com/2016/01/160106-science-evolution-apes-giant)

282 Meldrum, Jeff. *Sasquatch: Legend Meets Science.* New York: Tom Doherty Associates, LLC. 2006. p. 91.

283 Walker, Cameron. "First Chimp Fossils Found; Humans Were Neighbors." *National Geographic News* 31 Aug 2005. (http://news.nationalgeographic. com/news/2005/08/0831_050831_chimp_teeth.html)

284 Fortey, Richard A. *Fossils.* New York: Sterling Publishing. 1982. p. 46.

285 Sequin, E.S., Jaeger, M.M., Brussard, P.F., & Barrett, R.H. (2003). *Wariness of coyotes to camera traps relative to social status and territory boundaries.* USDA National Wildlife Research Center, Staff Publications. University of Nebraska, Lincoln. Can. J. Zool. 81: 2015-2025.

INDEX

ORGANIZATIONS

PLACES

TRIBES

ABOUT THE AUTHOR

Lyle Blackburn is a full-time author, musician, and cryptid re-searcher from Texas. His investigative cryptozoology books, *The Beast of Boggy Creek* and *Lizard Man*, reflect his life-long fascina-tion with legendary creatures. Lyle has been heard on numerous radio programs, including Coast To Coast AM, and has been fea-tured on television shows such as *Monsters and Mysteries in Ameri-ca* and *Finding Bigfoot*. Lyle is also a writer for the monthly horror magazine, *Rue Morgue*, frontman for the band Ghoultown, and co-producer of the documentary film, *Boggy Creek Monster*.

For more information, visit the following websites:

www.lyleblackburn.com
www.foukemonster.net
www.ghoultown.com

CPSIA information can be obtained
at www.ICGtesting.com
Printed in the USA
BVHW061600100719
553094BV00011B/178/P